Without God or Reason

Without God or Reason

The Plays of Thomas Shadwell and Secular Ethics in the Restoration

Christopher J. Wheatley

Lewisburg
Bucknell University Press
London and Toronto: Associated University Presses

Associated University Presses
440 Forsgate Drive
Cranbury, NJ 08512

Associated University Presses
25 Sicilian Avenue
London WC1A 2QH, England

Associated University Presses
P.O. Box 338, Port Credit
Mississauga, Ontario
Canada L5G 4L8

The paper used in this publication meets the requirements
of the American National Standard for Permanence of Paper
for Printed Library Materials Z39.48-1984.

Some material in chapter three appeared in an altered form in "The Defense of the Status Quo and Thomas Otway's *The Atheist*," *Restoration and Eighteenth-Century Theater Research*, s. s. 4, no. 2 (1989): 14–30, and is used by permission of the journal.

Library of Congress Cataloging-in-Publication Data

Wheatley, Christopher J., 1955–
    Without God or reason : the plays of Thomas Shadwell and secular
ethics in the Restoration / Christopher J. Wheatley.
        p.   cm.
    Includes bibliographical references and index.
    ISBN 0-8387-5243-8 (alk. paper)
    1. Shadwell, Thomas, 1642?–1692—Ethics.   2. Ethics, Modern—17th
century.   3. Ethics in literature.   4. Ethics—England.   I. Title.
PR3671.S8Z94   1993
822′.4—dc20   92-54622
                                                                                        CIP

For My Mother and Father

Contents

A Note on Citations

All references to Shadwell's works are to Montague Summers's edition *The Works of Thomas Shadwell* (London: 1927), by volume number, act number, and page numbers. I have included act numbers despite the absence of running act headers in Summers's edition because I think it useful for the reader to know when dialog occurs in a play; in consideration of the memory curve alone, dialog from the first and last acts is more likely to be remembered by an audience than dialog from the middle of a play. Dates for the premieres of Shadwell's plays are listed below and are drawn from Robert Hume's *The Development of English Drama in the Late Seventeenth Century* (Oxford: The Clarendon Press, 1976).

The Sullen Lovers (1668)
The Royal Shepherdesse (1669)
The Humorists (1670)
The Miser (1672)
Epsom Wells (1672)
The Tempest (1674)
Psyche (1675)
The Libertine (1675)
The Virtuoso (1676)
The History of Timon of Athens (1678)
A True Widow (1678)
The Woman-Captain (1679)
The Lancashire Witches (1681)
The Squire of Alsatia (1688)
Bury-Fair (1689)
The Amorous Bigotte (1690)
The Scowrers (1690)
The Volunteers (1692)

Acknowledgments

This book began life as a dissertation at the University of Wisconsin-Madison, where, as director, Eric Rothstein patiently read and wisely rejected a number of early versions. On every level, I owe a great deal to his thoughtful criticisms. As readers, Phillip Harth and Keith Yandell also saved me from myself with diagnoses of weaknesses in my argument and evidence. My father, John Wheatley, as a non-English literature type, also read several drafts and forced me to be more clear than I might otherwise have been by insisting on the elimination of a great deal of techno-philosophico-litero babble—not to mention the fact that my father and mother have always been a soft touch for crucial loans when money was short. Andrew Weiner was frequently my link with sanity in grad school. Howard Weinbrot also read a section of the dissertation and made helpful observations. Alan Fisher pointed me in the direction of some useful sources, Thomas Lockwood provided helpful advice, and Alan Fausel brought the paintings of Genari to my attention in a London pub.

Thanks are also due to the Graduate School at Wisconsin for a Fellowship while I was researching the dissertation and to the Vilas Foundation for a travel grant that enabled me to read in the British Library. I would also like to thank the libraries of the University of Wisconsin-Madison, the University of Washington, the University of Tennessee, The Catholic University of America and the Folger Shakespeare library for their help.

Since the dissertation stage, individual chapters have been read by Kirk Combe, Allen Dunn, Judith Kalitski, and Robert Stillman. Douglas Canfield also made helpful suggestions in an extended commentary on the entire manuscript.

Above all, I am thankful to the friends who over many beers at many times listened politely while I pontificated about ethics and literature: I must single out Kirk Combe, William Demastes, S. J. Larsen, Bruce Peterson, Ernest Suarez, and Michael Vanden Heuvel, who remained pleasant despite repeated provocation.

Any idiocies that remain are undoubtedly a consequence of an occasional, stubborn refusal to accept good advice.

Without God or Reason

Introduction: The Complexity of Restoration Ethics

Even aside from Restoration comedy, many works from the period seem ethically confused. John Garfield's periodical *The Wandering Whore* went through six numbers in 1660. Exactly what kind of periodical one would want to call it is unclear. The following passage from the beginning of number three offers several possibilities:

> *Julietta.* I will show thee a pure pair of naked breasts, smooth Buttucks, Lovely and ivory Thighes whiter than untrod Snow, with the best red-lip'd C— in Christendom, such as *Europa* never showed *Jupiter, Orithya Boreas,* nor *Helena Theseus,* when the[y] cornuted their husbands, not at the Wrastling amongst the naked *Roman* virgins.
> *Francion.* . . . therefore lye down dear heart and make my P— rise, disclose thy curled silver colour'd turnpikes and Perfumed Cabinet lyes in the Valley sweeter than Violets; then lead me with my ivory fingers to it's fancy, where I will enter it's Port with a full spring tide between thy bum's riding safe at Anchor within thy harbor.

The purpose here may be pornographic, and the dramatic form allies it with most sixteenth- and seventeenth-century pornography as these works too were written in dialogue.[1] But if this is pornographic, it is pornography softened by classical allusions and extended metaphors. The periodical also published a directory of all the active whores and pimps in London indicating where they could be found. Once the reader is excited, he knows where to seek relief. The periodical may be a kind of Restoration entertainment guide.

But simple classification of *The Wandering Whore* as pornography is undercut by Garfield's claims that his periodical is published for the public good as a warning against malefactors. He says at the end of the second issue that he is in danger because of his investigative reporting:

> Whereas several of the persons concerned in the following Dialogues, have threatened the publisher hereof, and offered large Sums for his Apprehension, fearing the discovery of their bold and impudent practices and Cheatings; Let all persons know the design and intent hereof is to rout those Caterpillars, and give the Magistrates notice of the vileness and wickedness of their Actions, hoping a severe and strict Observance will be taken for their Suppression.

If we believe this passage, Garfield's intentions are rigorously ethical, but, if so, one wonders why he does not limit the dialogues to the discussion of the cons by which fools are gulled, as is the case in the anonymous *The Crafty Whore: or, the mistery and iniquity of bawdy houses* (1658).[2]

In the latter work, the author's design is avowedly to convert the reader from hedonism to stoicism:

> I have been heretofore so far from opposing that generally beloved thesis of injoying pleasure, as that I rather studied how I might be an affector and promoter of that doctrine; but now experience hath reformed my judgment; so that I can now look on a handsome woman, with as little ardour as upon a well proportioned statue, which that you may do so, shall be the continuall prayer of him: who is
>
> > Your Countryman

The dialogue between Thais and Antonia is admirably contrived to promote distrust of women and boredom with venery. The book is a lengthy catalog of examples of the hypocrisy of whores and women in general, ending with a list of remedies to avoid being entangled and a few horror stories of the consequences of illicit sex. Unlike Garfield's periodical, at no point is there a sense that sex can be fun.

Yet Garfield, as we have seen, although he could have been straightforwardly "moral" in his treatment of the flesh trade, instead wants both to present sex as attractive and to claim his journal promotes the public well-being by exposing the reality of prostitution. These are not incompatible goals per se; the problem occurs when the sex remains attractive even with a prostitute. If, despite all the tricks, Julietta remains an appealing object of fanciful desire, then why should anyone wish to avoid the models for her behavior? In other words, if the benefit that Julietta provides to society remains more attractive than the possibility of poverty and disease, then the magistrates are unlikely to take an active role in suppressing her.

An obvious objection would be that the problem I have in determining the ethical framework of *The Wandering Whore* is the consequence of a faulty assumption that there is any kind of ethical system informing Garfield's choices about what to include and exclude from the work. In the latter view, the salacious elements could be explained as being included because that will help the work to sell, whereas the claims that the periodical is intended to provide social benefit are included to deflect criticism and possible prosecution. Rhetorical concerns provide the principles of inclusion and exclusion. But if one is interested in ethics as an expression of social relations it is not clear that we need to be able to tell the difference. Whether I act as a libertine because I believe that ethics are arbitrary, or because I think the role is likely to help me achieve some nonethical ends, my actions remain the same. The distinction between rhetorical choices and ethical choices is not meaningful.

There is in ethics invariably a dialectic between external standard and personal interpretation. Religion and society provide a framework in which the individual finds meaningful terms to consider his actions and to justify them. After an individual has acted, both he and society must judge the action, and there are three distinct possibilities of judgment: society and the individual agree that his activity was right or wrong; society and the individual disagree, with the individual claiming that his action was justified within the terms of society, and the society claiming that it was not; society and the individual disagree, with the individual claiming either a knowledge of moral law or a right that transcends society's right to judge him. Even in the latter case, where the individual claims an ethical standard transcending society's, his position may remain unclear, but society's does not, as the words martyr and enthusiast indicate the existence of a standard by which the solitary is judged. And since writing and painting are by their nature social activities, our proper concern when considering the ethics in such works is the social attitudes, if any, that they embody.

Thus, when *The Wandering Whore* pairs erotic dialogue and moralistic commentary, it is because Garfield must believe that his audience will find the pairing plausible, whether he does it because he thinks it will make the periodical sell or because he genuinely sees no incongruity. Even if Garfield's choice is rhetorical (rather than ethical) the strategy can only make sense if he believes that an audience will not perceive incompatibility in the elements of *The Wandering Whore*. Conceivably Garfield simply wants honest whores, ones who supply their services in a sanitary way without attempting to extort more money than is their just due. Such a reading would be possible if we did not assume a priori that a person in the Restoration must think sex for money is immoral. Sex could be seen as a commodity, amusing and entertaining but not very important. Such a proposition could be validated, although not proved, by finding historical evidence that such a view was possible in the period, and seriously undercut, although not refuted, if no such confirmational evidence were found.

Garfield is not alone in pairing the erotic and the moral. Consider, for instance, the fascinating case of painter Benedetto Gennari, a Bolognese artist in England from 1672 to 1688, who received a yearly stipend of five hundred pounds from Charles II and in his autobiography claimed to be court painter to James II.[3] Gennari has much in common with his contemporaries in England, portraitists like Lely, Kneller, and Dobson, and allegorical painters like Verrio, Thornhill, and Cheron. He did more than one portrait of Catherine of Braganza, all with some religious symbolism, and had a predictable quantity of religious paintings.

What separates him from his contemporaries, at least in England, is the quantity and kinkiness of the eroticism in his paintings. A drawing of Susanna and the Elders shows two old men leering around a wall at a naked girl. A contemplative Mary Magdalen is, for no discernable reason, practically naked. A painting drawn from Tasso's *Jerusalem Delivered* (16.17–23) of Rinaldo bewitched by love for Amida is a careful subversion of pastoral romance. In a country setting, a beautiful girl, partially undressed of course, holds a mirror while a handsome man leans on her shoulder, two men look on from the bushes, and two cupids cavort around them. The fact that the man is looking at himself in the mirror exemplifies the uxoriousness and narcissism of Rinaldo in a powerful and compact way. But Gennari's depiction of Carlo and Ubaldo is odd: one looks on in concern while the other smiles complacently and motions for silence. The voyeurism is not in Tasso: nor is the cupid urinating in Rinaldo's helmet.

For the queen Gennari painted portraits and religious works. For Charles II he painted scenes from Ovid's *Metamorphoses* and the *Sleeping Shepherd*, which hung on the king's bedroom wall; in it, an apparently innocent young shepherdess takes a flute from the sleeping shepherd's hand, while an older woman looks at the shepherdess and points at the shepherd's crotch suggestively. The painting was a hit. Gennari did copies of it for the duchess of Devonshire and the earl of Pembroke. Gennari may have been the artist as rhetorician: he painted what his audience wanted, and if he troubled himself over distinctions between sacred and profane art, there is no record of it. But it is at least possible that Gennari may not have seen any incongruity between religious devotion and frank eroticism.

The artistocratic artist like Gennari found himself with one segment of his audience, the queen, that required "moral" art. Was Garfield, writing popular literature, faced with a similar situation—that is to say, at least a segment of his market that was interested in moral or ethical issues? The answer seems to be yes. Popular broadsheet ballads frequently are explicitly concerned with the ethical basis of events. For instance in 1668, presumably after the London apprentices had burned a brothel as was their wont occasionally, a series of ballads argued over the moral standing of the actors and the act from a variety of different ethical perspectives.

"The Whore's Petition to the London Prentices" asks for quarter on the grounds that the apprentices are in no position to make moral judgments:

> We do not justify ourselves yet must
> Account that *Theft's* a sin as well as *Lust*,
> We know our crimes are bad, and tis a curse,
> To punisht be, by them which commit worse.

I think the echo here is of Christ's injunction that only he who is without sin should cast the first stone (John 8:7), and the whores are therefore taking the religious high ground. "The Prentices Answer to the Whores Petition" merely asserts the criminality of the whores and threatens that if they do not mind their place worse will come to them. The apprentices are justified by the immorality of the whores and, implicitly, by the whores' inability to do anything to stop them—might makes right, and what is, is right. In the "Citizens reply to the Whores Petition and Prentices Answer," the apprentices are criticized because their usurpation of justice will have disastrous social consequences:

> You raile on Whores, tis true, they bad do live,
> And yet yourselves as bad example give,
> Will you in such contempt and rudeness stand

> To seek to wrest the sword from justice hand?
> What can be thought of such a bold intrusion
> But that it will bring all unto confusion.

The apprentices are wrong within an ethical framework that judges from consequences and relies on predictive capacity for support. What I wish to emphasize is that all three ballads consider the morality of the event and from three different ethical perspectives. For instance, no Christian framework is necessary for the prentices' and citizens' positions to make sense, whereas the whores' petition requires one.

There is nothing unusual about the "whore" series—any number of other ballads could be cited arguing over the ethical import of other events. Popular literature in the seventeenth-century made at least a stab at dealing with ethical issues because either the authors or the audiences or both were interested in them, or felt that they had to appear to be interested in them. And although any given ballad, periodical, or painting may be simplistic—or simpleminded—there are a great many possible, complex ethical systems available that the authors could regard as justification for their own position. Attitudes toward the nature and foundation of ethical systems differ along religious lines, not merely between Catholic and Protestant dogma, but between various Protestant sects, modified still further by individual conscience and interpretation. Changing scientific and philosophical conceptions about human nature, and the consequent changes in theories of human behavior inevitably affected ethical beliefs. Moreover, the rise of capitalism and the movement toward individual economic freedom was beginning to undermine not only traditional social hierarchies but the entire foundation of ethical systems that imposed ethical restraints from outside the individual.

Perhaps this diversity accounts for the wide variety of claims that historians and critics have made about what was the dominant paradigm for the age. Harold Love calls the Restoration "an age of builders," and believes that most were quite certain of what the social order was and should be:

Insofar as the poet was involved in politics—and at times it was impossible for him not to be—he would naturally be a party writer, but he would take good care, however fierce the controversies in which he was engaged, not to disturb the gentlemen's agreements which had been reached about the big, intractable questions that had set the previous generation to apostolic blows and knocks. Those who, like Milton, insisted on keeping these questions open did so at the risk of neglect and ridicule.[4]

Susan Staves, on the other hand, argues that although there were "attempts to bury the embarrassing realities of the interregnum past" in the early years of the Restoration, the issues that were raised by the civil war never went away: "The 1670s and 1680s saw a revival of many of the issues raised but not resolved in the civil wars and franker acknowledgment of the confusion of values left in the wake of the fighting."[5]

Incompatible claims about the amount of political agreement, or lack thereof, are mirrored by contradictory claims about religious beliefs. Norman N. Holland argues that the playwrights of the Restoration believed in only a very limited version of providence, one that no longer involved "the continuous participation of God in the ordinary affairs of the world." Instead God becomes another element in the widening schism between "fact" and "value":

> A version of Providence, however, could be salvaged, because man's science could be said to be inadequate to fathom the total plan, the "Ends of Providence," the "universal Good." But the sense of God's workings becomes a sense only of a final end. God drops out of the space and time of the real world. He ceases to be immanent and becomes transcendent.[6]

On the other hand, Aubrey L. Williams starts from the assumption of "a still commonly shared, and fundamentally Christian, vision of human existence," and suggests that the Restoration theater would have regarded the happy accidents that move the comedies as examples of a constructed Providence that mimics the real action of Providence in the world:

> Today we may dismiss or smile over Dryden's words when he says he could "easily demonstrate" that "no Heroick Poem can be writ on the *Epicurean Principle*," because the English people, "better taught" by their "Religion" than the Romans were by theirs, "own every wonderful Accident which befalls us for the best, to be brought to pass by some special Providence of Almighty God; and by the care of guardian Angels." Yet Dryden's words are perfectly consonant with those of Stillingfleet when he rebukes Epicurean notions of a fortuitously created universe by asking if we can "imagine" that a Being of "*Infinite power should stand by* and leave things to *chance and fortune?*"[7]

Of course one could argue that these two conceptions are not really that far apart, in that both allow that what appear to be chance happenings in the plays are actually a product of providence. But there is an immense gap between Holland's general providence and Williams's specific providence, which imply entirely different views of God's role in the events of the world: in Holland's case, God has set up natural laws that will move the world to the end that he has foreseen for it, and in Williams's model, God directly intervenes in the moment-to-moment affairs of the world.

It would be a mistake to claim that any of these critics are wrong, for all can adduce an impressive body of evidence. The problem is that each (with the exception of Staves) assumes a dominant paradigm, a single set of ideas that sets the tone for the age. We would think it simplistic if someone claimed that the population of any major city today could be characterized by a uniform set of beliefs; it seems equally unlikely that the Restoration theater world can be categorized in so simple a fashion. What Staves and Love, Holland and Williams can claim is that their reading of various texts is internally consistent and rendered plausible by a wide variety of other texts that share the same characteristics. The fact that all their seemingly inconsistent claims are so plausible is evidence of the complexity of the context, the wide variety of positions that a writer could meaningfully adopt and oppose. And the apparent unanimity of opinion on a particular end or means should not hide complete disagreement on the related means or end. Discussing the goal of national unity, for instance, Michael McKeon says that "the conventional language of national interest and unity in the 1660s expresses a sustained consciousness of how commonly held national aims may entail preferences for widely differing policies, preferences which depend on the group perspective from which the aims are examined."[8] Most people agree that the national deficit of the United States is not such a good thing, but substantial disagreement is possible as to why, or what the solution is.

What I would like to argue in this book is that not merely are the presentations of ethical systems by Restoration writers problematic, but determining what ethical system is being presented in any given work is problematic. In other words, critics of Restoration comedy in particular assume ethical systems are not numerous, nor in themselves complex; only the form of the drama itself is complex. Thus a twentieth-century critic might well assume that there is something incongruous about the works of Gennari and Garfield because of the common belief that the seventeenth century saw sexuality as dangerous to social order. Dale Underwood, for instance, sees a historical opposition between what he loosely calls the "epicure" and the "stoic":

> The epicure represents the beast in man, the stoic, man's convention-ally alleged moral possibilities. While the epicure glorifies the senses, the stoic glorifies reason; while the epicure follows "plea-sure," the stoic follows "virtue." Consequently, to the epicure's "free-dom," the stoic opposes restraint; to his individualism, conformity; to his self-interest, obligation and duty; and so on through a list which will by now be largely self-evident.[9]

In other words, the stoic's ethical system is deontological, social, and ascetic, whereas the epicure's is teleological, personal, and hedonistic.

The problem with this group of distinctions is that it is far from being universally held. Underwood is aware that the position he ascribes to Epicureanism is not really Epicurean,[10] but he does suppose that this was the popular conception of Epicure-anism, and that Christianity was allied with the stoics: "At the same time they present, on the one hand, that blend of Academic, Peripatetic, Stoic and Christian thought which from the Middle Ages had constituted the accepted moral code, and, opposing it on the other, the combination of Epicurean, skeptical, and natu-ralistic ideas with which we have been concerned."[11] By no means did everyone view Epicurean philosophy in this fashion, which should indicate there was no monolithic "accepted moral code." Eric Rothstein argues that on some important issues, such as the belief that ideally the individual should be self-sufficient, many thought that the Stoic and Epicurean positions were iden-tical, and he cites Temple as an example.[12] The notably pious John Evelyn translated all six books of Lucretius, although he was so disappointed with the publisher's sloppy production of the text that he allowed only the first to be released.[13] Jeremy Taylor, even though he thought there was some danger to the ignorant from Evelyn's translation, did not attempt to convince Evelyn not to do it: "I will not say to you that your Lucretius is as far distant from the severity of a Christian as the faire Ethio-pian was from the duty of the Bishop Heliodorus; for indeed it is nothing but what may become the labours of a Christian Gentleman."[14] Epicurus was, of course, primarily being rehabili-tated for his utility to the new science. But Joseph Glanvil, in the course of an attack on Aristotelian science, also states his preference for Epicurus as less objectionable on religious grounds:

> So that the Great and most Learned *Origen*, was not unjust in prefer-
> ring *Epicurus* before the adored *Stagyrite*. And possibly there have
> been few men in the world have deserv'd less of *Religion*, and those
> that profess it. How it is come about then, that the assertour of such
> *impieties*, should be such an Oracle among *Divines* and *Christians*;
> is I confess to me, matter of some astonishment. And how *Epicurus*
> became so infamous, when *Aristotle* who spake as *ill*, and did *worse*,
> hath been so *sacred*, may well be wondred at.[15]

Another example of the respectability of Epicurean philosophy is Dr. Walter Charleton's *Epicurus's Morals* published in 1656 and reprinted in 1670. Charleton's work is an adaptation rather than a translation; Epicurus's writings are fragmented and Charleton has both expanded and imposed an order to create a coherent system. Charleton was not an obscure figure. An acquaintance of Gassendi's and Hobbes's, he was also a member of the Royal Society and became president of the College of Physicians in 1689. Nor was he interested in arguing for agnosticism. Charleton's defense of Epicurus's errors is that the truth of the immortality of the soul and the illegality of suicide is difficult to discover without revelation, and that Epicurus did not have this advantage. Indeed, Epicurus's claim that we owe the gods no reverence becomes a sign of the glimmerings of true religion when we consider the gods he rejects. Epicurus is "Temperate, Good, *and* Pious," and is regarded by Charleton as being perfectly compatible with Christianity.[16] Moreover, for Robert Boyle and other scientists, a Christianized Epicureanism proved valuable for both scientific and social applications.[17] I am not arguing that there was widespread acceptance of Epicurean philosophy; there was, however, widespread interest in it.

But even more important is Underwood's agreement with the common and erroneous notion that Christianity was universally opposed to self-interest and pleasure (and, as a subset, sexual pleasure). That some versions of Christianity were is unquestionable. The basic Catholic notion of asceticism is clearly shown in Malebranche's *De la Rècherche de la vérité* (first published in 1674–75). For Malebranche, sins of the flesh are inevitable consequences of the Fall and the improper connection between body and spirit it entailed. The connection between body and mind is merely that the body offers unreliable data to the mind and consequently misleads us in our search for truth. Malebranche is a hard-line rationalist, and the only use of sense is to capture our wandering attention.[18] It is immoral for us to enjoy physical pleasure:

> Parce que le plaisir étant une récompense, c'est faire une injustice que de produire dans son corps des mouvements qui obligent Dieu, en conséquence des lois générales qu'il a établies, à nous faire sentir du plaisir, lorsque nous n'en meritons pas. . . . L'homme avant son péché pouvait avec justice goûter les plaisirs sensibles dans ses réglées: mais depuis le péché il n'y a plus de plaisirs sensibles entierement innocents, ou qui ne soient capables de nous blesser lorsque nous les goûtons, car souvent il suffit de le goûter pour en devenir esclave.[19]

Malebranche does not become an important figure in England until the 1690s, nor was he always popular with the Catholic hierarchy; but the idea that although pleasure is by its nature a good we have no right to enjoy it places Malebranche in the mainstream of seventeenth-century Catholic thought. Berulle's exaltation of the priesthood in the face of Protestant attacks upon it, and his and De Sales's insistence on self-abnegation as a necessity for everyone, are all of a piece—the resurgence of Catholic asceticism in response to the Reformation.[20] Moreover, Malebranche was a philosopher conversant with the new science and is an example of how it could be made compatible with asceticism, a very old strain in Christianity.[21]

The problem occurs when people assume that this is what the Protestants thought. Roy Porter, for instance, would presumably agree with Underwood: "Within popular religion, and seventeenth-century Puritanism in particular, sensuality was associated with the Fall and with sin."[22] And this is a gross oversimplification. Marital sexuality is an example of a kind of sensuality leading to pleasure that few Protestants would have regarded as sinful. It was not justified merely for the sake of procreation, or as a defense against fornication, but was regarded as the physical bond on a spiritual union, and many Protestants were careful to disassociate themselves from the Catholic notion that celibacy was a virtue per se; as Edmund Leites says, "From the 1620s to the 1660s, in the great age of their writing on marriage, all the Puritan preachers and theologians urged spouses to maintain a steady and reliable delight in their mates, a pleasure both sensuous and spiritual."[23] This attitude toward sex begins early.

Calvin, for instance, interprets Paul's famous dictum, "I say therefore to the unmarried and the widows, it is good for them if they abide even as I. But if they cannot contain, let them marry: for it is better to marry than to burn" (1 Corinthians 7:8, 9), as meaning no more than that it is likely to save trouble for a man who has naturally the gift of celibacy: "Therefore Paul's words can be made to yield no more than this, that it is indeed advantageous and suitable for a man not to be bound to a wife, so long as he is able to do without one." And if you don't have that special gift, marital sexuality is not merely legitimate, but sanctified: "The intercourse of husband and wife is a pure thing, it is proper and holy; for it is the institution of God. The uncontrolled passion with which men are aflame is a vice springing from the corruption of human nature; but for believers *marriage is a veil that covers over that fault,* so that God sees it no longer."[24] There is, here, an association of the Fall and sex, but the association is meaningless in marriage.

At the extreme, radical Christianity could allow any kind of sensuality, which at least undercuts claims that the libertinism of Restoration comedy was a kind of unwelcome import, along with the duchess of Portsmouth, from France. As Christopher Hill observes, "Restoration comedy does not merely pick up the old Inns of Court naughtiness: it also learnt something from the Ranters, whom Samuel Sheppard depicted as *The Jovial Crew.*"[25] But less radical Protestants such as John Milton, and mainline High Church clergy like Jeremy Taylor, also argue that marital sex carries no stigma and, in effect, deemphasize even adultery and fornication on the hierarchy of sins.

Jean Hagstrum has already discussed at length Milton's celebration of marital sexuality in *Paradise Lost.* Milton does not condemn sexuality because it is pleasurable, but only the abuse of it where sex becomes an exercise in lust and narcissism.[26] The antidotes are temperance, where reason maintains its dominance over sense, and mutuality. Moreover, the sins of sex (adultery, fornication) are minor in comparison with social sins. In *The Doctrine and Discipline of Divorce,* Milton lists the order of reasons for marriage common to Protestant ministers in the seventeenth-century: "Godly society, next civil, and thirdly, that of the marriage bed."[27] In consequence, adultery is a relatively minor offense, and there is an inconsistency in the divorce laws in that one can get a divorce for barrenness or adultery but not for violations of civility or marital peace:

For no wise man but would sooner pardon the act of adultery once and again committed by a person worth pitty and forgivnes, then to lead a wearisome life of unloving & unquiet conversation with one who neither affects nor is affected, much lesse with one who exercises in all bitterness, and would commit adultery too, but for envy lest the persecuted condition should thereby get the benefit of his freedom.[28]

James Turner has recently shown Milton's ambivalence toward sexuality, but at least a part of Milton regarded adultery as not a major sin, because sex was not that important a component in marriage: "(Far from being the gravest of disasters, Milton believes, adultery need not diminish and may even stimulate the love that preserves a marriage.) God did not create male and female for the sexual 'work of male and female,' but for spiritual companionship."[29]

Jeremy Taylor repeats Calvin's argument that there is no particular virtue in celibacy and that marriage is a mystical symbol for Christ's marriage to the church: "Single life makes men in one instance to be like Angels, but Marriage in very many things makes the chast pair to be like to Christ."[30] Fornication and adultery are unnecessary and contemptible in that marriage provides a legitimate place to satisfy desire. An unfaithful man "make[s] himself base as the mixtures of a harlot, by breaking the sweetest limits, and holy festivities of marriage." But the sins of pleasure are primarily associated with the young, and are an example of foolishness rather than man's corruption:

> For a man cannot take pleasure in *lusts of the flesh*, in *gluttony*, or *drunkenness*, unless he be helped forward with *inconsideration* and *folly*. For we see it evidently that grave and wise persons, men of experience and consideration are extremely less affected with lust and loves, than the hare-brained boys.[31]

Since they do not know any better, the young cannot be heavily blamed for this error; moreover, their tendency toward this error, as long as it does not become a habit—Taylor later in the same sermon says that custom is the greatest perpetuator of sins of the flesh—will eventually dissipate through time and experience.

By no means am I arguing with the claims of Lawrence Stone and William and Malleville Haller that the majority opinion on even marital sexuality was that it was a blessing best enjoyed in moderation.[32] The chief ends of marriage were mutual support

and procreation, and this was the view on both ends of the Protestant spectrum. Also, the Puritans were harder, at least in theory, than Catholics on sins of the flesh, because the Puritans
thought that marriage provided a blameless outlet for the sex
drive. Whether they were in practice is another question. Edmund Morgan argues that American Puritans, at least, were substantially more tolerant than commonly supposed, although it
may be, as Edward Shorter suggests, that this is not good evidence about European mores, because America was "born modern."[33] For the Catholics, married or unmarried, sex for pleasure
was wrong, although married it was permissible for the purpose
of procreation; you could copulate if you didn't enjoy it. But the
consequence of this is to diminish the moral impact of adultery
and fornication. One went to confession to be forgiven these sins,
but one also had to confess sex on a holy day, or an intemperate
lust for one's wife.[34]

But Protestant or Catholic, you could justify, or accept as un-
avoidable, pleasure—in this case, sex—without recourse to any
kind of libertinism, naturalism, or Epicureanism: in the former
group within wedlock, and in the latter group as an inevitable
consequence of man's corrupt nature forgiven and absolved in
confession. Once one includes the potential influence of Epicureanism, one can conceive of a Protestant audience shrugging off
youthful indiscretions; after all Taylor associates it with "hare-
brained boys." Attitudes toward sex, and pleasure in general, are
the red herring of Restoration comedy in that a fondness for
wine, women, and song need not make a character in a Restoration comedy a rake, at least in Underwood's sense of someone
who is in opposition to the religious and societal norms of his
day. A study of the ethical beliefs that underlie the plays must
concern itself with the reasons why a character is for or against
particular possibilities of pleasure. Both an Epicurean and a
Protestant are entirely in favor of taking pleasure in marital sexuality; the reasons they would advance for the position are entirely
distinct.

To examine the foundations of ethical beliefs, we have to disa-
sociate ourselves from the tendency to regard sexual behavior as
central to any discussion of ethical beliefs in Restoration literature in general, however much it may be applicable to particular
cases.[35] A contrast between Behn's *Love Letters Between a Nobleman and His Sister* and Crowne's *City Politicks* reveals two Tory
writers who interpolate sexual misbehavior into works concerned primarily with political misbehavior. In the first case sex-

ual misbehavior is linked to political sins, while in the second, despite the characters' tendency to make the parallel, it isn't really relevant.

In Behn's case the (legally) incestuous relationship is emblematic of political crimes. Philander seduces his sister-in-law Sylvia while at the same time being involved in a conspiracy to overthrow the crown. Sylvia herself makes Philander's dishonor explicit: "if *Sylvia* could command, *Philander* should be loyal as he's noble; and what generous maid would not suspect his vows to a mistress, who breaks 'em with his prince and master?"[36] Unfortunately, she doesn't listen to her own advice and Philander proves as false to her as he was to her sister. He remarks, "that cause is always good that is prosperous, that is ill which is unsuccessful" (39). This is a plausible ethical position: ethics are translatable without remainder into social approval. It cannot, however, justify Sylvia and Philander's incest and treason; they are remarkably unsuccessful in politics and love, although Philander is eventually pardoned while Sylvia becomes ever more degraded.

Further, it is hard to believe that Behn regards ethics as a compromise between self-interest and social judgment. Octavio is, perhaps, the one consistently admirable character in the novel, even when in love. According to the narrator, "all he spoke was honourable truth. He knew no guile, but uttered all his soul, and all that soul was honest, just and brave" (285). Before becoming a monk, he forgives Philander and Sylvia everything they have done to himself and his family. Ultimately he rejects both self-interest and social judgment and joins a monastery; the narrator says flatly,

> Had he died, there had not been half that lamentation; so foolish is the mistaken world to grieve at our happiest fortune; either when we go to heaven or retreat from this world, which has nothing in it that can really charm, without a thousand fatigues to attend it: and in this retreat, I am sure, he himself was the only person who was not infinitely concerned; who quitted the world with so modest a bravery, so entire a joy, as no young conqueror ever performed his triumphs with more.

(400)

Even if we question Behn's belief in heaven and self-abnegation as felicitous ends, Octavio at least escapes the moral decay of the rest of society. Self-interest may be served in achieving tranquility, but social judgment and prosperity defined in social terms are clearly wrongheaded. Philander's belief that ethics are no more than social approval cannot be justified if Octavio is a normative character.

For Crowne, cuckolding is an offense only when done by someone who is already politically damned. Throughout *City Politicks* the audience is provided with a series of morally bankrupt Whigs attempting to achieve a political control beyond what they are entitled to by their station. Further, we are invited to see this attack on political order as conducive to a disruption of the family structure. Craffy, the son of the podesta and a self-described "true Protestant," desires to cuckold his own father and regards any claim of morality founded in religion as nonsense:

> *Florio.* Then, 'tis a thing of reputation with thee to commit incest?
> *Craffy.* Incest? Prithee don't trouble me with hard names. I don't think it is any more incest to lye with the same woman my father does, than to drink in the same glass, or sit in the same pew at church.
> *Florio.* Is there no difference between your father's wife and his pew?
> *Craffy.* He makes none, for they only lay him asleep. I would make a difference, I confess, in the sweet use, not that I think his wife more sacred than his pew, for the locking of a man to a woman in marriage, or in a pew in a church, are only a couple of church tricks to get money, one for the priest, and t'other for the sexton; that's all.[37]

Presumably the audience is at liberty to see Craffy's contempt for the sanctity of marriage as compatible with his contempt for the sanctity of the king's office.

And presumably Florio is tarred with the same brush as Craffy since he, too, seeks to cuckold the podesta. He, as much as Craffy, pretends to being a true Protestant and Whig to gain access to Rosaura; the only difference between the two is Florio's success. When discovered by the podesta, he defends himself by asserting the relationship between political teleology and sexual teleology: "Our principles are, He is not to be regarded who has a right to govern, but he who can best serve the ends of government; I can better serve the ends of your lady than you can" (2:202).

The problem is that Artall, who cuckolds the lawyer Bartoline, is presented as an honorable gentleman. When discovered by Bartoline, Artall downplays his offense in comparison with Bartoline's crimes ("suppose she and I have sinn'd, hast thou got an estate in the Devil's service") with a statement of gentlemanly superiority to petty legalistic restrictions ("Better be ruled by the swords of gallant men than the mercenary tongues of such rascals as you" 2:188). Artall's cuckolding is a minor offense, if not justifiable, at least not terribly important. Florio's true crime is not his cuckolding of the podesta either; rather, it is his contribution to political disorder in his attempt to gain access to Rosaura. Artall's first scene with Florio emphasizes why Florio is a villain: "Where's this damn'd confounded hypocrite? This religious, factious, dying saint? I come to give you thanks for the legacy you leave the nation; a sweet rogue you have helped into power" (2:107). The hypocrisy doesn't bother Artall, nor the goal. Sexual adventures are amusing, but political turmoil is immoral: "Ha! Ha! Ha! the dissimulation of these fellows is pleasant; but a pox on't, we pay to dear for these jests, they cost us confusion and almost ruin" (2:109).

For Crowne, political authority is a consequence of social station, and any movement toward democracy is dangerous: "And so, gentlemen, henceforward be wise, leave off the new trade you have taken up of managing State affairs, and betake your selves to the callings you were bred to, and understand. Be honest! meddle not with other men's matters, especially with government; 'tis none of your right" (2:209). Government is a "right," and acting in accordance with one's station is what it means to be honest. The close relationship between sexual and political misbehavior in Behn is absent in Crowne. Craffy, Florio, and Artall are all interested in adultery, and the two latter are successful at it. But Florio is preferable to Craffy because he is a gentleman, and Artall is much superior to both because he acts in accordance with his political station. Sexuality shouldn't affect our moral judgments about these characters whatsoever.

I have argued that critics have failed to determine the substructure of ethical belief in Restoration literature because of a number of faulty assumptions: first, that there is a meaningful distinction between rhetorical stance and ethical belief; second, that there is a dominant, accepted moral code; third, that sexual behavior will serve as a key to determining ethical beliefs rather than being merely one factor. What I would like to suggest is a different approach to the problem that begins by discarding these assumptions.

If we cannot perceive an ethical system that can account for The Wandering Whore and Gennari's paintings, it does not follow that such a system does not or did not exist. Rather we should suspect that precisely because we do not know of one, there are grounds to believe in a historical change that has expelled such a system from the accepted field of ethical discourse.

My goal is very modest—not to delineate the full range of ethical beliefs possible in the Restoration, but to show how a complex system of beliefs is necessary to make sense out of an ordinary writer (Shadwell), whom nobody appears to have found overly complex during the late seventeenth century, and yet, as I shall argue in the next chapter, is a playwright who modern critics have argued was either a fool or a knave when he claimed he was writing morally instructive drama.

Shadwell is suitable where a greater playwright like Wycherley is not. The chaotic disagreement that surrounds studies of Wycherley has been described by Robert Hume more than once,[38] and Hume's explanation for the variety of plausible, yet contradictory, interpretations is accurate: "The plays possess no clear internal moral norms."[39] Moreover, there were debates about the morality of Wycherley's plays not merely in his own lifetime but in the plays themselves—witness Olivia and Eliza's discussion of *The Country Wife* in *The Plain Dealer*. The variety of plausible interpretations is, however, evidence of the variety of ethical beliefs available.

But arguments about the morality of Shadwell's plays begin only after his death. Even Dryden restricts himself to an attack on the dullness of Shadwell's plays; he never attacks their morality. Yet within a decade of Shadwell's death, despite his repeated claims that he was taking the moral high ground in relation to his competition, his wide popularity disintegrated. Some of this may be a consequence of *MacFleckno*, but some is not and as such shows Shadwell as a striking victim of the change in ethical beliefs that occurred in the late seventeenth and early eighteenth centuries. Shadwell's theatrical success over three decades shows public acceptance; his sudden rejection shows a change in theatrical taste that, in the case of Steele, for instance, is a consequence of changing ethical beliefs.

Shadwell's very ordinariness makes him an exemplary figure for an examination of seventeenth-century ethics.[40] If my explanation of Shadwell's ethical system is plausible, then it will be apparent that we need to be much more careful in our assumptions about ethical positions in seventeenth-century literature, since Shadwell prided himself on his judgment, yet modern critics have trouble understanding how he could have thought of himself as a didactic playwright. We need to reevaluate Restoration literature in terms of the complex interplay of competing systems, recognizing their interaction, rather than assuming their exclusivity.

1

Ethics and Drama

There was little debate in the Restoration that one of the functions of comedy was moral instruction. In 1673, in the preface to *The Dutch Lover*, Aphra Behn said flatly that no play was ever written with the purpose of providing moral instruction, but by 1686, her dedicatory epistle to *The Lucky Chance* now claims that plays are particularly suited for that task.[1] Dryden says that the poet must be ethical: "False reasonings and colours of speech are the certain marks of one who does not understand the stage; for moral truth is the mistress of the poet as much as of the philosopher; Poesy must resemble natural truth, but it must be ethical."[2] The prologue of *City Politicks* defends Crowne's satire by claiming that Crowne is following the fashionable practice:

> But some will say, A poet mend the age?
> In these high matters how dare they engage?
> Why, sirs, a poet's reformation scorn,
> Since the reformer now all poets turn?[3]

Maybe Behn's initial statement is more "sincere" than her later comment or than Dryden's or Crowne's, but to claim that is as much an act of mind reading as to deny it. An attempt to reconstruct the moral systems that inform Restoration comedy seems worthwhile simply because of the number of claims made by playwrights that their plays were morally pure and even, occasionally, morally instructive.

Ben Ross Schneider, Jr., says about the Collier controversy that "anyone who interprets this pamphlet as a debate about *whether* plays should be moral misses the real issue. It is a debate about *what* morality plays ought to propagate."[4] Just as in other popular literature, such as ballads, there seems to have been a general expectation that comedy should deal with moral issues, but exactly how comedies approach moral issues is another question. Robert D. Hume in *The Development of English Drama in the*

Late Seventeenth Century argues that there was "an immense variety of options open to the writers" and that in consequence, we have to be careful in applying generalizations to individual playwrights.[5]

This is, I think, where Schneider's book, the most ambitious attempt at dealing with ethics in Restoration comedy, goes wrong. Schneider's factorial analysis of the personality attributes of 1,127 characters in eighty-three comedies is couched in terms of a set of oppositions such as Liberality versus Avarice or Courage versus Cowardice and thus predetermines how the analysis will come out. If one starts from the assumption that courage is a good thing and cowardice is a bad thing, one is very likely to decide that a character who shows courage is a good character and one who shows cowardice is a bad one. For instance, Sparkish in Wycherley's *The Country Wife* is used as an example of how cowardice identifies a "Witwoud." What is interesting, however, is that, according to Schneider, Sparkish "takes comfort in the knowledge that Pinchwife is on hand, with a mind to be an ally."[6] The casual mention of Pinchwife illustrates the weaknesses in Schneider's approach. He is quite right that Pinchwife is perfectly willing to be anyone's ally in a duel; in fact, over the course of the play, he is willing to fight Harcourt and Horner. Pinchwife is clearly not a coward, and yet surely not a hero.

There are many brave villains in Restoration comedy and many characters whose courage or cowardice is probably irrelevant to understanding the ethical framework of the plays. Schneider does not make clear under what circumstance we should regard courage as a virtue, or, alternatively, why courage is a virtue regardless of the context. He seems throughout his book to operate from the assumption that why or whether something is a virtue is perfectly apparent; all he attempts to do is rank the relative importance of virtues. He is by no means alone in this assumption. John T. Harwood's careful examination of how critics have attempted to justify the claim that Restoration comedy is "moral" reveals that virtually without exception they "are vague about acknowledging the ethical values that shape their responses."[7]

The absence of a coherent statement of ethical standards has important consequences for critics. First, Harwood's primary interest concerns the slippery critical claims about whether Restoration comedy is moral: his solution is to call for research on the effects of art on audiences. While he says that it is possible to approach the morality of the plays on their own terms, his examination of the formal elements of four plays (*The London Cuck-olds, The Country Wife, The Squire of Alsatia,* and *The Souldiers Fortune*) implies a fair amount of doubt on his part that any such attempt can succeed. I shall concentrate on *The Squire of Alsatia* because Shadwell reiterated throughout his career that his plays were morally instructive, the play itself was successful, and un-like Harwood's other three examples, no one prior to Collier doubted that the play was moral.

Harwood's reading of *The Squire of Alsatia,* the most fre-quently written about of Shadwell's comedies, is typical of the difficulties most critics have had with the play and with Restora-tion comedy as a whole. After admitting that Shadwell's purpose is moral, he turns the plays into a rat's nest of apparent contradic-tions:

> What Shadwell claims to say and what the play "says" are quite different. The grim reality of Termagant's situation (in the final act, we learn that Belfond Junior has kidnapped her child to keep her at bay) and the obvious pathos of Lucia and her father make Belfond Junior's reform necessary but not necessarily convincing. Both char-acters are developed too attractively and too vividly for the audience to dismiss them as literary conventions. If Shadwell had wanted to produce a thoroughly convincing reform comedy, then he has failed. . . . Though it is tempting to see *The Squire of Alsatia* either as a comedy that endorses debauchery or proclaims moral reform, the comedy cannot be both nor convincingly be interpreted in either way.[8]

Harwood's chief difficulty with the play is Belfond Junior's se-duction of Lucia, complicated by his lie to Lucia's father and attempt to buy both father and daughter off: the lie is "gratui-tous," Lucia and father are genuinely hurt, and Belfond Junior's "pattern of deception-under-pressure surely works to his dis-credit":[9] in short, we find Belfond Junior's reformation unbe-lievable.

I think that Harwood's reading of the play suffers from the same weakness for which he criticizes other commentators on Restoration comedy: he is making a series of assumptions about what constitutes moral behavior, and in his failure to examine these assumptions or consider whether Shadwell and he have the same assumptions, he fails to make sense out of the play. Harwood assumes that lies are immoral, that young men should not seduce young women and then move on, and that if they engage in the first two activities, their future reliability is doubtful. Further, while Harwood implies that these moral imperatives may be conditional, no conditions apply in this play (Harwood is at pains to show that Belfond's lie about Lucia's innocence will not be believed by anyone). Granted these assumptions, *The Squire of Alsatia* is a very problematic play, and Shadwell has clearly failed in his attempt to write moral comedy.

Not everyone finds the morality of the play problematic. Paul E. Parnell, Donald Bruce, and Ronald Berman all regard Belfond Junior as acting as a rational calculating machine. Parnell says that "The younger Belfond's reformation does not, however, occur because of Sir Edward's rebuke, but because the youth's life of pleasure has reached the point of diminishing returns."[10] Bruce claims that Belfond Junior "wheadle[s] others when it suits his purpose, and . . . behave[s] with a hard selfishness when there is nothing to be gained."[11] The implication is that Belfond Junior's reform has nothing to do with ethics because ethics are not tainted by self-interest. Berman presents the play as an example of Shadwell's belief in the Lockean error of "the fallacy of rational calculation," which accounts for why we find the reformation hard to swallow. Shadwell presumably expects us to take Belfond Junior's repentance seriously and that is a mistake: "The error lies not in sympathy with vice but in the assumption that it automatically transmutes itself from youthful error to mature conscience."[12] From a completely different standpoint, J. H. Smith regards the reformation as equally straightforward. Belfond Junior is converted by his love for Isabella.[13]

But several have seen the same difficulties with the play that Harwood sees, although usually not with as much willingness to grant deliberate complexity. Alan S. Fisher, annoyed with Shadwell in general as the high priest of "Whiggery," writes in apparent outrage that Shadwell's ethics "are those of special privilege": "Shadwell allows a well-bred, witty man behavior he would censure in lesser mortals."[14] This insightful comment is not developed by Fisher; such an attitude is simply immoral because it seems to support a double standard. Robert D. Hume finds the play "ambiguous," not complex. Belfond's claim to Lucia that he "must marry" is simply a lie, and the superiority of liberal town education to conservative country education is something Shadwell expects us to buy without having constructed a play where we can do so. The reformation is "perfunctory": the morality of the play is "offensive bilge."[15] Even Don R. Kunz, who throughout most of his book is very sympathetic to Shadwell, finds it difficult to rehabilitate *The Squire of Alsatia*.

The play is transitional for Shadwell in his "straight-forward progress from neo-classical philosophy and aesthetics toward the romantic" and suffers from Shadwell's inability to reconcile the two. Shadwell, in the process of moving toward a drama of sentiment, cannot reconcile yet his distrust of "natural benevolence" with his new journey toward this "idealistic, inspiring thesis."[16]

A simple solution to the critical charge of unconvincing and unattractive reformation is to assert that we are supposed to have doubts about the harmony at play's end. Michael W. Alssid, in line with his tendency to find ethical complexity in most of Shadwell's plays, thinks "Ned's surrender to hymen is qualified."[17] Belfond Junior's energy and attractiveness cast doubt on the finality of the reformation and we are supposed to wonder whether his "new-found joy will be short-lived." This is an attractive alternative but not very helpful. Except for the prologue to *The Woman Captain,* where Shadwell sulks over the poor reception of *A True Widow* and says he is writing down to the audience's taste, Shadwell again and again insists that drama should be, and his is, morally instructive. An argument that we should have doubts about the reformation in *The Squire of Alsatia* needs to explain much more than Alssid attempts and leaves unanswered all the important questions. Is reformation or marriage or both unnecessary? Is Belfond Junior not a hero because we doubt his reformation? Is Belfond rendered contemptible by his treatment of Lucia? Most important, what is the foundation for ethical judgment in the play? If none of these questions is answerable, then some explanation is needed as to why that is the case.

Peter Holland has argued that *The Plain Dealer* is a play designed to confuse the audience,[18] but nobody has made the same claim about *The Squire of Alsatia*; such a claim would have to find a way around the prologue, which says that Shadwell "to correct, and to inform did write." (204) Another possibility is to dismiss the *Squire of Alsatia* as a bad play, which is what Allardyce Nicoll does; he regards the play as "hopelessly and permeatingly vulgar, brutal, and immoral," and thinks it strange that Shadwell thought he had a moral purpose.[19] This option also requires us to regard the Restoration theater audience as either hopelessly stupid or remarkably vicious since the play was phenomenally successful.[20]

The principle of charity in philosophy and hermeneutics in textual interpretation is that when one is confronted with an argument that appears very poor on the face of it, one attempts to find a context in which it does make sense. Shadwell said again and again that his plays were moral and prior to his death there is no evidence that anyone doubted the claim. In this case, the question is whether it is possible to construct an ethical system within which Shadwell's claim that he is providing moral instruction makes sense. Sheldon Sacks says that "even a direct statement of moral intention is crucial evidence only of moral intention and not of the form in which it is implemented."[21] I would add to this that Shadwell's statement of moral intention does not guarantee that Nicoll, for instance, will recognize Shadwell's conception of morality, for it either may be embodied in a way he does not expect, or it may entail ethical views that Nicoll would find immoral.

Robert Darnton argues, "When we cannot get a proverb, or a joke, or a ritual, or a poem, we know we are on to something. By picking at the document where it is most opaque, we may be able to unravel an alien system of meaning."[22] And there is good reason to believe that Shadwell's ethics are likely to be alien to us. Some of the most interesting work currently being done in ethical theory, in particular by Alasdair MacIntyre and Martha Nussbaum, argues that ethics changed over the course of the seventeenth and eighteenth centuries. The Kantian revolution created a view of ethics as clearly distinguishable from interest, class, and gender; in other words, our view of ethics as entailing general obligation irrespective of social role is a recent phenomenon. Of course, Kant did not single-handedly create that change and is partially providing only a new synthesis of various philosophical threads. As will become apparent, I regard Shadwell as attempting to reconcile one of the new threads, the individual's right to act freely, and the older view of virtue as dependent on role.

My practice then will be to attempt what Harwood denies can be done: find a potential ethical system that can account for the problems of The Squire of Alsatia. My assumption of ethical coherence in the play is fair, I think, on the grounds that while most of us live and act upon inconsistent ethical beliefs, those who purport to instruct us usually attempt consistency at least within their writings. Eric Rothstein and Frances Kavenik have recently argued that critics impose coherence on Restoration comedy rather than "discovering" it in the plays, which, in fact, are meant to speak to as many tastes as possible; perhaps this is true, though they do concede that The Virtuoso, the play of Shadwell's they examine in the most detail, "veers furthest from

our model in offering so narrow a range of possible appraisals."[23]
Still, I would suggest that an explicitly didactic playwright,
while under a necessity of entertaining, is likely to avoid ethical
inconsistency precisely beccause his initial claim of moral purpose invites attack on the grounds of ethical inconsistency;
again, there is no record of such attacks on *The Squire of Alsatia*
during Shadwell's life. My reading of the play is inherently pro-
visional, but it gives Shadwell the benefit of the doubt.

A hypothetical ethical system purporting to make the ethical
content of *The Squire of Alsatia* coherent would have to account
for the three things that most critics of the play have found incompatible with Shadwell's statement of moral intent: first, the
supposed superiority of the liberal town education to the conservative country education when, apparently, the product of the
town education has not learned such moral principles as honesty, chastity, and, failing that, fidelity (the list could be length-
ened to include sobriety and responsibility); second, the
dramatic fact that Belfond Junior is the hero of the play as center
of the action when his treatment of Lucia rather types him as a
contemptible cad; third, the doubts that his treatment of Lucia
and Termagant cast on his likely fidelity to Isabella.

The rudiments of such an account are already present in previous criticism of the play. Fisher's remark that Shadwell seems to
have an ethic of "special privilege" is similar to a statement that
Berman makes: "Terence does not make the elementary error of
confusing role and value," with the implication that Shadwell
does.[24] Unfortunately, neither critic develops these observations.
If one waives Berman's Platonic perception of true morality, the
confusion of role and value has an ancient and honorable history: Homer, Aristotle, and Aquinas all make the same error. In
by far the best article on Shadwell, Stephen D. Cox examines
Shadwell's entire corpus and notices that Shadwell "never
places steady emphasis on sexual purity." Unlike most critics of
Shadwell, Cox does not then make the assumptions that Shadwell is incompetent, hypocritical, or stupid:

> Yet if we do not confine our ideas of morality to sexual purity or the
> rigorous observance of traditional mores, we can still recognize a
> serious ethic underlying both Shadwell's critical statements and the
> action in his plays. . . . [Shadwell] emphasizes riotous injuries to
> public safety rather than the quiet immoralities of private life.

Cox demonstrates that all of Shadwell's heroes exhibit at least

one capacity, "the competent defense of civilized order."[25] Since
Cox is writing a corrective to superficial views of Shadwell's
plays, he deemphasizes the extent to which Shadwell also examines the nature of private morality, but he makes the crucial
point in stressing the social nature of virtue. If we postulate that
Shadwell believes what we call morality is largely a matter of
social custom tested by social consequences, then it should be
possible to make sense out of much of what critics regard as
immoral in *The Squire of Alsatia*.

Such a reading of the play is consistent with the moral debates
of Sir Edward and Sir William where they disagree over the character of Belfond Junior:

> *Sir William.* I find that Wealth alone will not make happy. Ah
> Brother, I must confess it was a kindness in you, when Heaven had
> blest you with a great Estate by Merchandize, to adopt my Younger
> Son, and take him and breed him from his Childhood: But you
> have been so gentle with him, he is run into all manner of Vice
> and Riot; no Laws and Customs can restrain him.
>
> *Sir Edward.* I am confident you are mistaken; He has as fair a Repu-
> tation as any Gentleman about London: 'Tis true, he's a good fel-
> low, but no Sot; he loves mirth and society, without Drunkeness:
> He is, as all young Fellows I believe are, given to Women, but it is
> in private; and he is particular: no Common Whore-master: in
> short, keeps as good Company as any man in England.
>
> (4.1.219)

The two brothers are talking past each other. Belfond Junior does
drink, but that is not a vice in Sir Edward's view because he is
not a drunk; he does whore around, but discreetly, as a gentleman should.

Sir William categorizes actions independently of the manner
in which they are carried out, while Sir Edward regards the manner of the action as crucial:

> *Sir Edward.* Infamy: Nay there you wrong him; he does no ungentle-
> menlike things: Prithee consider Youth a little: What if he does
> Wench a little; and now and then is extravagant in Wine? Where
> is the great Crime: All young fellows that have mettle in them will
> do the first; and if they have wit and good humour in them, in this
> drinking Country, they will sometimes be forc'd upon the latter;
> and he must be a very dull phlematick Lump, whom wine will
> not elevate to some Extravagance now and then.

Sir William. Will you distract me? What are Drinking and Whoring
no faults?

(4.1.220)

A desire for women is natural, a tendency to drink is a part of
the social climate of England, and Sir Edward regards these as
sufficient justifications for Belfond Junior's participation in these
activities. Sir William does not deny the claim that nature com-
pels and society requires; the activities remain, for him, immoral,
because morality is independent of such factors. For the sake of
convenience, Sir William's position can be called deontological
in that nonmoral factors are irrelevant to moral judgment,
whereas Sir Edward's position is teleological in that morality is
contingent upon nonmoral factors.[26]
Sir Edward is consistent in his view throughout the play. Even
Sir William's position is explained by nature and custom, and,
because they are men of similar age and social position, Sir Edward has some sympathy for it.

Sir Edward. One would think you had been Drinking and were
maudling; think what we our selves did when we were young
fellows; You were a Spark, would Drink, Scour and Wench with
the best o'th' Town.
Sir William. Ay, but I soon repented, married and settled.
Sir Edward. And turn'd as much to the other extreme; and now
perhaps I mislike these faults, caus'd by the heat of Youth. But how
do you know he may not be reclaimed suddenly[?]

(4.1.220)

Sir William's moral views are a consequence of his age, and Sir
Edward, as an old man, agrees with him. The difference is that
Sir Edward knows that age rather than some moral standard is
the root of his dislike for Belfond Junior's faults. Even Sir Edward's moral obligations to his adopted son are a product of
custom, as is clear from his response when Sir William persists
in thinking that he has some responsibility for Belfond Junior.

Sir Edward. Why should you be so concern'd? He is mine, is he not?
Sir William. Yes, by Adoption, but he is mine by Nature.
Sir Edward. 'Tis all but custom.

(4.1.221)

Social custom alone will not generate a very satisfactory explanation for the ethical problems of *The Squire of Alsatia.* The

customs of Alsatia encourage and legitimate violence, fraud, and theft, which Sir Edward is not prepared to tolerate; the play ends with his vow to "Rout this knot of most pernicious Knaves, for all the Priviledge of your Place" (4.5.280). To be able to criticize the customs of Alsatia there must be some sort of ethical primitive that allows the individual to judge between competing social customs—something that whatever its source (quite conceivably it too is originally the product of social custom) takes precedence of social custom and is the test of "good" social customs.

The individual's right to act freely provides such a principle for Sir Edward and informs his idea of education. Two possibilities are suggested as the foundation of individual rights in the play. The first is pragmatic; individuals will act freely and trying to stop them only creates problems. As Sir Edward tells his brother, "Too much streightness to the minds of Youths, like too much lacing to the Body, will make them grow Crooked" (4.1.220). Experience shows that boys will experiment with wine, women, and song; a strict education that seeks to bar children from what their parents regard as immoral is doomed to failure:

> Sir William.   He knows no Vice, poor Boy.
> Sir Edward.   He will have his turn to know it then; as sure as he will have the Small Pox; and then he'll be fond on't, when his brother has left it.
>
> (4.2.231)

The expectation that people will act freely extends to the women in the play, too. Scrapeall attempts to control Tiresia and Isabella through religion. Tiresia refers to it as "tyranny" (4.3.250), and Scrapeall is rewarded with the same lack of success as Sir William.

The second reason is basically tautological; individual men and women must be allowed to act freely because such action is appropriate to men and women. When Sir William argues that only through regimentation is control possible, Sir Edward responds that under those circumstances that which is controlled is not worth the controlling: "I must govern by Love. I had as lieve govern a Dog as a Man if it must be by fear; this I take to be the difference between a good Father to Children, and a harsh Master to Slaves" (4.1.221). Sir Edward does not explain his position by showing it as a deduction from some moral principle. His explanation emphasizes a contrast between roles, one of which is appropriate while the other is not.

At the core of the contrast of educational systems is the position that Sir William's strict governance is not merely impractical but immoral, because it treats men as if they were dogs or slaves. Sir William tells Belfond Senior that he has raised him with care, and his son responds that his care has been misdirected: "Yes, with care to keep your Money from me, and bred me up in the greatest Ignorance, fit for your Slave and not your Son" (4.4.263). Again the emphasis is on appropriateness of action in relationship to one's role, as is the case when Sir William rages and threatens to beat Belfond Junior after the latter has lied about not being with a woman. Sir Edward states that Sir William's behavior is more culpable than Belfond Junior's actions: "Shame of our Family; you behave yourself so like a Madman and a Fool, you will be begg'd: These fits are more extravagant than anything he can be guilty of. Do you give your Son the words of Command you use to Dogs?" (4.2.230). Sir Edward does not justify Belfond Junior's lie, but the lie is something one can expect from a young man under pressure. Sir William's intemperate wrath is inappropriate because of his social station as an elderly father in a respectable family.

The purpose of Sir Edward's educational system is not merely practical, nor does it have knowledge as an object. If knowledge were the object, Shadwell would presumably give Sir Edward some response when Sir William makes a telling criticism of the study of history: "How can there be a true History, when we see no man living is able to write truly the History of last week?" (4.2.231). Nor is it "practical" in Sir William's sense of the term. When Sir Edward says that some knowledge of mathematics and science "will use a man to reason closely," Sir William asks "Can he Reason himself into six Shillings by all this?" (4.2.232).

Berman points out that Sir Edward's educational plan is Lockean in that it attempts to teach the child how to tell the difference between long- and short-term interest.[27] That is partially true, but it is the less important half of the story—presumably other educational schemes attempt the same. Edmund Leites examining the same subject makes a more interesting point about Locke's educational program: "Young gentlemen require 'breeding'; that is, they must be taught the carriage and manners which will prepare them to act and feel in a manner suitable to their station."[28] Education creates the capacity to "feel" what is appropriate behavior; "breeding" provides an aesthetic sense of morality. This is what Sir Edward's educational plan is designed to teach Belfond Junior; it will make "him a Compleat Gentleman, fit to serve his Country in any capacity" (4.2.232). Belfond Junior does not need a practical education because he is going to be a rich man anyway. But Greek and Latin are necessary because they increase one's capacity to move in society: "To make a man fit for the Conversation of Learned Gentlemen is one noble end of Study" (4.2.231). Further, travel and history, law and the arts enable the individual to form comparative judgments on social behavior. And the ultimate goal of education is to prepare a gentleman to act like a gentleman, as Sir Edward explains to Belfond Junior:

> 'Tis time now to take up, and think of being something in the World: See then, my Son, tho thou shouldst not be over busie, to side with Parties and with Factions, that thou takest a care to make some figure in the World, and to sustain that part thy Fortune, Nature and Education fit thee for.
>
> (4.3.238)

Sir William's conception of the role of education, on the other hand, is solipsistic and antisocial. He does allow his son some indulgence in alcohol and women when there is a profit to be made from it:

> Sir William.   . . . he never Whores, nor Drinks hard, but upon design, as driving a Bargain, or so; and that I allow him.
> Sir Edward.   So: Knavish and Designing Drunkenness you allow; but not good fellowship for mirth and conversation.
>
> (4.2.231)

When Sir Edward claims that his educational scheme has made Belfond Junior fit to serve his country, Sir William responds, "Pox on his Country: 'Tis a Country of such Knaves, 'tis not worth the serving: All those who pretend to serve it, mean nothing but themselves" (4.2.231). Self-interest, according to Sir William, is the motivation of action. But even more than that, Belfond Senior has been raised to be unsocial—preying on others rather than being in fellowship with them. This happens to be the ethic of Alsatia as well; starved for society, Belfond Senior becomes the victim of the antisocial ethic.

If my argument is valid thus far, three points should be clear. For Shadwell, (1) moral standards are the product of society, and (2) the individual has the right to act freely and is probably going to in any case. A moral individual is (3) one who recognizes his role in society and acts in accordance with it. The first point is a theory of morality, the second is both an empirical observation and a moral principle, and the third is a normative claim. Of necessity, the relationship between the first and second must be dialectical, because, strictly speaking, they are contradictory; that is, I am ascribing to Shadwell the view that social roles would have no ethical content unless the individual were free to choose them, and that freedom without the limits of social roles would equally be ethically meaningless. However, if the individual is free to act, then the individual is also morally responsible for his actions, and this, I think, is why Shadwell may expect us not to be too hard on Belfond Junior for his treatment of Lucia.

Critics who lay stress on Belfond Junior's seduction of Lucia never mention what Lucia herself says in the fifth act when Belfond Junior tells her that he is going to marry Isabella:

> *Belfond Jr.* It is with some Convulsions I am torn from you; but I must marry I cannot help it.
> *Lucia.* And must I never see you more?
> *Belfond Jr.* As a Lover never; but your Friend I'le be while I have Breath.
> *Lucia.* Heart, do not swell so. This has awakened me, and made me see my Crime: O, that it had been sooner!
>
> (4.5.275)

Even if he had promised to marry her, as he has not, Lucia would still be "a Fool, to be catch'd in so common a snare" (4.4.261) as Isabella says about Termagant. Lucia calls her acceptance of Belfond Junior "my crime" because she has, in her limited moral freedom, acted in a way inappropriate to her role in society.

Gayle Rubin, in her important article "The Traffic in Women," accepts Lévi-Strauss's theory that women are the most important of "gift" transactions in the creation of social organizations "because the relationship thus established is not just one of reciprocity, but one of kinship." But she goes further and states that the constraint of female sexuality is a necessary consequence of such a sex/gender system since "from the standpoint of the system, the preferred female sexuality would be one which responded to the desire of others, rather than one which actively desired and sought a response."[29] This restriction on female sexuality is crucial to understanding why Lucia is in a sense more culpable than Belfond Junior.

Shadwell seems to present women as having the right to act as freely in love as men. Isabella and Teresia claim the right to marry where they choose:

Isabella. No: I can assure you, Sir, I would never have perform'd that bargain of my Unkles: We had determin'd to dispose of our selves before that; and are more resolv'd.

Teresia. We have broken prison, by the help of these Gentlemen, and I think we must e'en take the Authors of our Liberty.

(4.5.278)

And their Uncle Scrapeall does regard himself as having been cheated in his right of disposal:

Scrapeall. Oh Sir *William*, I am undone; ruin'd: The Birds are flown, Read the Note they left behind 'em.

Sir William. Peace, they are Dancing, they have dispos'd of themselves.

Scrapeall. Oh Seeds of Serpents! Am I cheated then? I'll try a Trick of Law, you Froggs of the bottomless Pit, I will and instantly— What Dancing too? then they are fallen indeed.

(4.5.280–81)

Isabella and Teresia can and do escape the right of disposal vested in their male kin, Scrapeall.

But their freedom is limited in that they must choose within their own class for financial security and social approval. Belfond Junior and Truman make that clear when initially approaching Teresia and Isabella:

Belfond Jr. Your Unkle has sold you for 5000 *l.* and for ought I know, you have not this night good for your deliverance.

Truman. Consider, Ladies, if you had not better trust a couple of honest Gentlemen, than an Old Man, that makes his market of you: For I can tell you, you tho his own Daughter, are to be sold too.

Teresia. But for all that, our consents are to be had.

Belfond Jr. You can look for nothing, but a more strict confinement, which must follow your Refusal.

(4.4.259)

If Isabella and Teresia are to escape, it can only be through marrying men with sufficient wealth and social standing to stand up to Scapeall's threats of legal action.

And Belfond Junior's choice is limited as well. Sir Edward assumes that there is an appropriate level at which Belfond Junior can marry: "But if you be valiant enough to venture, (which, I must confess, I never was) I'll leave it to your own choice: I know you have so much honour, you will do nothing below yourself" (4.3.238). In other words, free "choice" is fine, as long as the

choice is not "below" Belfond Junior's social level. When Sir
Edward is satisfied that that level is achieved in Isabella, he insures that their social status can be maintained:

> *Sir Edward.* Now Madam, if you please to accept him for a Husband,
> I will settle Fifteen Hundred Pound a Year on him in present,
> which shall be your Jointure. Besides that, your own money shall
> be laid out in Land and settled on you too. And at my Death the
> rest of my estate.
> *Isabella.* You do me too much Honour, you much out-bid my Value.
> (4.5.279)

Sir Edward's generosity is both a reward for appropriate behavior
and a guarantee of the wherewithall to pass it on to future genera-
tions of Belfonds. Isabella's response both comments on Sir Edward's generosity and acknowledges that she as a women can be
at least partially "valued" in monetary terms.

Thus Belfond Junior's claim that he "must" marry Isabella
need not refer to a contractual agreement, as Hume supposes,
and hence be a lie; alternately, Smith is not entirely wrong when
he claims that Belfond Junior is converted by his love for Isabella
(I shall argue in chapter 4 that love plays a crucial role in Shadwell's ethical system). But love has a social and economic function in preserving the existing social structure as members of a
social class can marry only within that social class. The compul-
sion upon Belfond Junior to marry is an internalized defense of
the status quo that insures he will love only one whom he can
marry with Sir Edward's approval.

Lucia has not acted appropriately in underestimating the restrictions of her class. As the daughter of a lawyer, Lucia has no
chance to marry Belfond Junior; her father does not even have a
name in the play, being merely "Attorney" in the cast list and
dialogue. Her father's response when Termagant accuses Lucia
of fornication is enlightening: "Have I bestow'd so much, and
taken so much care in thy Education, to have no other Fruit but
this?" (4.3.248). He expects a return on his care of Lucia, the
"Fruit" of respectable marriage, and she has damaged her value.
Women are in a double bind. Though objects of exchange, they
are obliged to remain responsible for their own actions by preserving their value as objects and hence are co-opted into being
accessories in their own constraint.

Yet to see Lucia as a victim, irrevocably ruined by Belfond
Junior, is to see the world in Sir William's deontological terms.

Sir Edward offers to help Lucia's father; Sir William sees no help possible:

> *Sir Edward.*   Sir, I am extreamly sorry for this, if it be so; but let me beg of you, play the part of a Wise man; blaze not this dishonor abroad, and you shall have all the Reparation the case is capable of.
>
> *Sir William.*   Reparation, for making his Daughter a Whore! What, a Pox, can he give her her Maiden-head again?
>
> *Sir Edward.*   Mony, which shall not be wanting, will stop the Witnesses Mouth; And I will give your Daughter such a Fortune, that were what you believe true and publicly known, she shou'd live above Contempt, as the World goes now.
>
> *Attorney.*   You speak like the worthy Gentleman the World thinks you; but there can be no Salve for this Sore.
>
> (4.4.255)

Notice again Sir Edward's injunction to "play the part of a wise man." Fornication may or may not be a vice in and of itself, although the whole thrust of the play is that it is natural to youth. But the real effect of fornication can be repaired "as the World goes now"; Sir William's and Sir Edward's memories of their own youth tend to undercut the notion that Sir Edward thinks the world was ever otherwise. Belfond's necessary lie at the end of the play may not fool her father, but it is likely to deceive the rest of the world, because only Termagant will contradict it and, as Sir Edward tells the attorney, she "can never have credit" (4.5.275). Once a problem has occurred, the wise man ameliorates the consequence as much as possible. Belfond Junior is culpable in that he has violated his correct role, as a well-educated young man, to preserve social order. He, too, is punished by almost losing Isabella. But to claim the Belfond Junior has some obligation to make an honest woman out of Lucia is to argue that the answer to Belfond Junior's question "if a man lies once with a Woman is he bound to do it forever?" (4.2.228) is yes. Nothing in the play supports such an answer. In Lucia's seduction there are two kinds of moral judgment: personal and social. Insofar as Belfond Junior and Lucia have violated their roles they are culpable—she more so than he. But consequences play a part in moral judgment as well, and, by that standard, they both escape lightly.

Nowhere is the importance of consequences as an ethical standard more apparent than in Shadwell's treatment of lies. At the end of the play, Belfond Junior promises Isabella that he is being truthful in assuring her of his future fidelity:

> I have been so sincere in my Confessions, you may trust me; but I call Heav'n to witness, I will hereafter be entirely yours. I look on Marriage as the most solemn Vow a Man can make; and 'tis by consequence, the basest Perjury to break it.
>
> (4.5.279)

Presumably, if we are to regard his reformation as convincing, we need to believe he is serious here despite his previous lies in the play. Belief is possible if we see that there are "necessary" lies where the negative consequences of truth outweigh any putative moral imperatives against lying.

Belfond Junior, while hiding Lucia and Termagant in his closet, tells Sir Edward and Sir William that he "scorn[s] a Lye, 'tis the basest thing a Gentleman can be guilty of" (4.2.229). When Termagant forces Lucia from the closest, he lies like a trooper and says "she brought me linen from the exchange" (4.2.230). Undoubtedly Shadwell is drawing attention here to the difficulties that wenching bring upon Belfond Junior, but even after his reformation, Belfond Junior repeats the lie to the attorney: "Sir, I beg a thousand pardons, that I should attempt to injure your Family, for it has gone no further yet: For any Fact, she's innocent; but 'twas no thanks to me, I am not so. (If a Lie be ever lawful, 'tis in this case)" (4.5.275). Without the lie, Lucia's value, and hence her happiness, cannot be salvaged, and that takes precedence over any divine command or rational principle that prohibits lying.

Further, Truman clearly accepts the idea that there are necessary lies when he "dissembles" love to Ruth to get close to Isabella and Teresia; he calls it "drudgery," but it is crucial to his and Belfond Junior's success with Isabella and Teresia (4.4.252). Even Isabella accepts the basic principle that lies are occasionally necessary: "'Tis such a pain to dissemble, that I am resolv'd I'll never do it, but when I must" (4.4.258). If Belfond were to break his vow of fidelity, it would be the basest form of perjury, not because of the breaking of the vow per se, but because the consequences would imperil the stability of marriage, which, as an institution, is essential to social order. He is likely to be faithful, because he recognizes the high stakes involved.

Belfond Junior and Sir Edward help Lucia because it is their role to solve social problems. In the same way, Belfond Junior rescues his father and brother from the sharpies of Alsatia, and Sir Edward vows to bring order to the rats' nest. Those who act to the detriment of social order have to be stopped because the social order both creates and allows the existence of morality. Not everything can be fixed however. The attorney says, "next to her [Lucia] being innocent, is the concealment of her shame" (4.5.275), but it is only second best; she has acted immorally, and both she and her father feel that. The attorney, while completely innocent, suffers for his daughter's acts, and yet we know that rigid parental control probably would not have helped. Are we to agree with Sir William who says at the end of the play that "all Human care is Vain" (4.5.278)? Some individuals will not act in a role beneficial to the maintenance of society, and purely by chance one may be caught by their actions.

Shadwell's response to this is, in a loose sense of the word, both Lucretian and Aristotelian. Belfond Junior is first introduced as an Epicurean:

> *Belfond Jr.* Honest Truman! All the pleasures and diversions we can invent are little enough to make the Farce of Life go down.
> *Truman.* And yet what a coil they keep: How busie and industrious are those who are reckon'd grave and wise, about this Life, as if there was something in it.
> *Belfond Jr.* Those Fools are in earnest, and very solid; they think there's something in't, while Wise men know there's nothing to be done here but to make the best of a bad Market.
>
> (4.2.225)

We cannot swallow this wholesale. Belfond and Truman have just fallen in love, something against which both Lucretius and Epicurus recommend. But that the world cannot be entirely controlled, that chance is a part of life, and that the wise man makes the best of it is affirmed throughout the play. When Sir William finds out the truth about Belfond Senior he rages impotently, and is rebuked by Sir Edward: "Brother, a Wise man is never disappointed. Mans life is like a Game at Tables; if at any time the Cast you most shall need does not come up, let that which comes instead of it be mended by your play" (4.5.271). There are no guarantees in this world, only efforts to make the best of it. In this sense, what we call morality is a kind of prudence. We make judgments based upon an expectation of consequences; depending on the consequences we revise our behavior, and we cannot separate whether an action was good or bad from the consequences.

As the play stands, most critics are quite right: we cannot be assured that Belfond Junior will be constant to Isabella. Despite his vow of fidelity to Isabella at the end of the play, there remains the fact of human nature that Belfond Junior explains to Truman when both characters are first introduced into the play: "we may talk of mighty matters; of our Honesty and Morality; but a young Fellow carries that about him that will make him a Knave now and then in spite of his Teeth" (4.2.226). His vow to Isabella, although partially a generic convention, is ethically an ideal that may or may not be realizable, and both he and she must make the best of it if it turns out not to be so. But that does not undercut the morality of the play, if we remember that morality exists in the individual's attempt to mediate between the social standards appropriate to his role and his natural drives through prudential judgments based on probable consequences.

The role of God in this play is purely as a perfunctory witness to Belfond's conversion when he calls on heaven to witness his vow of fidelity. But this has little regulatory impact; Termagant also calls fearlessly on heaven to witness the entirely fraudulent claim that she is contracted to Belfond Junior (4.4.261–62). And God must be separated from religion. Isabella and Teresia discuss the difference between their Uncle Scrapeall's religion and "true" religion:

> *Isabella.* I can never persuade my self, that Religion can consist in Scurvy out of fashion Cloaths, stiff constrained behaviour, and Sowre Countenances.
> *Teresia.* A trisful Aspect, looking always upon ones Nose, with a Face full of Spiritual Pride.
> *Isabella.* And when one walks abroad, not to turn ones Head to the right or left, but to hold it strait forward, like an Old blind Mare.
> *Teresia.* True Religion must make one chearful, and effect one with the most ravishing Joy which must appear in the Face too.
>
> (4.3.250)

True religion is recognized by its consequences, a visible "joy," just as appropriate ethical behavior is judged by its probable consequences. Moreover, the false religion of Uncle Scrapeall— again, apparently false because of its consequences—is the only religion presented in the play.

Religion is conspicuously absent in both Sir Edward's and Sir William's educational schemes, and appears in connection with Belfond Junior only when he seeks divine verification for his assertions. Other than in the preceding example, Isabella and

Teresia never invoke divine guidance, nor does Truman. The ethicality of any given action is dependent on consequences and custom, not any divine fiat; although it need not follow that custom and consequences are incompatible with divine morality, nothing in the text invites us to seek guides for ethical behavior above the mundane.

If my reading of *The Squire of Alsatia* is plausible, then we can see that it is possible for Shadwell to have had ethical beliefs such that he could indeed claim that he had written a morally instructive play. Belfond Junior has not reformed if by that is meant that we know he has come to recognize some immutable ethical standard and will act henceforth in accordance with it. He can be said to have reformed if we see him as recognizing, under pressure, that he has outgrown the role of gay rake and must assume the role of responsible pillar of the community. More is required, however, to determine whether we can reasonably believe that Shadwell had anything of the sort in mind.

We can examine other evidence that may tend either to confirm or deny claims about what Shadwell believed. For instance, the fact that this reading of the play has not occurred to other twentieth-century critics despite, I think, its superior explanatory force in terms of the problems of the play would seem to be a strong objection to accepting it. In other words, that which I claim to be the ethical framework that underlies the play has not been recognized by previous critics as having anything to do with ethics at all. If I am right about *The Squire of Alsatia*, different conditions must shape Shadwellian ethics and the ethics of modern critics.

Shadwell's ethics are contingent upon the society one lives in. Even the individual's right to act freely exists partly because society has decided it is a good thing, and when it goes too far, as do the sharpies of Alsatia, society can revoke the right. The individual can condemn Alsatia only because an alternative society exists alongside it that he can prefer, and that preference is an aesthetic judgment based on the sense of taste developed through an appropriate education. A devout Christian (or a Moslem or a Jew) is not going to see this as an ethical system. God is both the source and the guarantee of ethics—they are not society-specific. Also, changes in philosophy make it difficult to regard Shadwell's version of relativism as ethics. For instance, anyone who has read and been persuaded by Kant believes that ethical claims are deducible from universalizable principles. There are no universalizable principles in *The Squire of Alsatia* except for the right of the individual to act freely, only roles that are subject to change from social and natural forces. Further, Shadwell appears to be deriving moral values from social values. If there were no society, there would be no oughts. From the fact that society is the way it is comes the oughts, and the belief that we ought to uphold society is itself a consequence of the way society is. Some part of that which is, is right or there would not be a concept of right in the first place. Thus Shadwell conflates the source of ethics and the grounds of ethics.

Worse yet is an ethic of special privilege based on role, class, and gender, an idea offensive to twentieth-century humanists. Morality is different for Isabella and Lucia, and even more different for Belfond Junior and Lucia, who are not equally guilty of fornication. To a certain extent, objecting to such an ethic is a consequence of societal changes since the seventeenth century, but many orthodox Christians at that time would have regarded special privilege as reprehensible too. My argument requires that morality be partly contingent on, in Kenneth Burke's terms, a recognition that moral judgment requires a realization that moral action must be evaluated within the potential limits of an individual who acts within a scene.[30] Chance determines at birth what role in society you will play, and different roles require different virtues. Chance also determines what will constitute virtuous behavior at any given time. Sir Edward's comments on chance reflect a tradition that goes back to Aristotle; as Martha Nussbaum describes it, "Indeed, part of the 'art' of Aristotelian practical wisdom . . . seems to consist in being keenly responsive to the limits of one's 'material' and figuring out what is best given the possibilities, rather than rigidly aiming at some inflexible set of norms."[31] Previous critics of Shadwell and Restoration comedy have not recognized that morality in some of the plays is contingent on social context.

One way of approaching the question of what Shadwell must have believed to regard his play as moral is by way of what he could not have believed. For obvious reasons he presumably could not have believed that seventeenth-century Anglican Protestantism is the sole source of ethics. And although reason is a component in ethical judgment, it does not discover ethical standards such as a "natural law," but rather allows one to make prudential judgments based on the consequences of violating the ethical standards associated with one's station in society. Supporting evidence that Shadwell could have rejected religion and "natural law" as sources of ethical belief would be historical examples from the same period of others who doubted that these were satisfactory foundations for ethics.

Just as Shadwell conflates the grounds and the source of ethics, he conflates the grounds and the reasons for ethics. For a Christian, there is a distinction between the grounds of ethics and the reasons for ethical behavior. God's declaration that murder is wrong provides the grounds for the ethical standard, whether or not God wills the good because it is so, or the good is so because God wills it. The Christian's reason for acting ethically, however, may be his desire to reach heaven and avoid hell. Similarly, the same distinction can be made for the hard-line rationalist. The preservation of life may be taken as a basic principle—either intuited or inevitable as a condition of rationality—from which we can deduce that murder is a bad thing under any circumstances. One man's reason for not committing murder may be to avoid frying in the chair. What I have described as the positive content of Shadwell's ethics, however, works out from a dialectic between the individual's desires and socially sanctioned behavior. In effect, the grounding for ethical action becomes indistinguishable from the reason for ethical action. I regulate my desires, which are partly instinctive and partially formed by society, by my judgment of what society will allow, and that is conditional upon my role in society. Ethical problems occur when either I insufficiently understand my role (Belfond Junior and Belfond Senior to lesser and greater extents) or when I reject my role in society and refuse to regulate my desires (the individuals of Alsatia who form a society that is antisociety). This requires a notion that my desires are neither good nor bad in themselves, and that the individual is not wholly a product of society, as well as a belief that society is more than the sum of the competing individuals who make it up. Supporting evidence that Shadwell could have held such a view would be found in historical examples of people linking the grounds and reasons for ethical behavior or blurring the distinction between them.

Philosophy and theology, as well as practical examinations of ethical situations, seem to be plausible places to look for social precepts that may help us to understand the plays. This may need justification. To claim that the philosophical and theological works of a given period constitute an intellectual context for an entirely different kind of writing is to assume that there is some kind of overlap between the species; both a shared semantic universe and a willingness on the audience's part to assume that such a universe exists are implied in an attempt to use one to gloss the other. I think both are legitimate assumptions. Any utterance or written statement requires some shared knowledge between encoder and receiver to be meaningful. That is, if someone writes or performs something that is wholly outside the context of the receiver, the receiver will be unable to make any sense out of it at all—hence the use of analogy and the insistence on defining terms in philosophy; a part of the context of Restoration comedy is the discussion of philosophy, history, and religion that occurs in Restoration comedy. As to the latter claim, one may cite the persistent cross-referencing that occurs between discursive and nondiscursive writing. Sermons and philosophers refer to the works of poets and dramatists, and they return the compliment. Indeed, one of Shadwell's attacks on *The Duke of Guise* is that it is false to the histories of Henry III, something every educated man would recognize. I am not arguing here that the form and content of a play are in some way distinct. But the terms of discourse do not take their meaning solely from the play itself, and in fact could have no meaning if they did not overlap with a usage that is distinct from the theater.

My goal is not to claim direct influence by any of the writers cited in the following chapter, although I think it likely that Hobbes and Milton, among others, may have had some. Nor am I trying to show the existence of some dominant paradigm for the age, a goal rather less likely to be achieved than the search for the Holy Grail. Short of numerically tabulating various specified elements in every piece of writing produced in a given period of time, we can only have vague impressions of agreement among what appears to be a majority; even then, we have arbitrarily selected the years and are perforce limited to what people wrote, which may be different from what the "age" thought. Even if we were to accept that the majority of people in a given age agreed upon some principles, that would be not be conclusive evidence as to what any individual thought.

What I hope to show is that the ethical beliefs I have ascribed to Shadwell in order to make sense out of *The Squire of Alsatia* could plausibly be held by an individual in the Restoration who was not a member of the lunatic fringe and that they were sufficiently bruited about for an audience to recognize them and, more important, to respond to them, when they were embodied in a play. I attempt to show the variety of possible beliefs available, that doubts that God or rationality provided a sufficient foundation for ethics were present among writers who were explicitly dealing with ethical issues, and that the blurring of the distinction between the grounds of ethics and the reasons for ethics was not uncommon. As Eric Rothstein and Frances Kavenik point out, the Restoration audience, accustomed to a repertory theater, were perfectly capable of enjoying Shadwell's *The Libertine*, Etherege's *The Man of Mode*, and Tuke's *The Adventures of Five Hours*, embodying three incompatible moral universes, in the space of a month.[32] When I suggest that the audience would respond to the moral view I have ascribed to Shadwell, I require only the relatively tolerant audience that Rothstein and Kavenik propose: "the members of the audience might well have quite various notions of what was moral, but be willing to accept a substitute from among the consensual possibilities."[33] And that the Restoration audience would be willing to accept various notions of morality seems to me very likely: as Durkheim remarks,

> Let us not be surprised to see a single society riven, at a given moment, by divergent or even contradictory currents. Does it not happen constantly that the individual is divided against himself: that part of him is pulled in one direction, while all the rest is pulled in another direction? Now these divergencies, indeed, even these contradictions are perhaps more normal in society than in the individual.[34]

From a society in the grip of radical philosophical, social, and economic change, a Restoration tolerance for ethical "divergence" should be expected rather than being a source of surprise. Fredric Jameson has discussed the inevitable "structural coexistence of *several* modes of production all at once."[35] At any given time, more than one kind of cultural production is competing with older kinds, and thus society will evidence competing ideologies. In the case of Shadwell, this turns out to be a conflict between the older, aristocratic ethics of role (an expression of an ideology that justifies the wealthy by granting them an opportunity for a "higher" ethical achievement), and a rights-based ethics that asserts the freedom of the (upper-class) individual (an expression of the increasing economic pressure upon the aristocracy caused by the explosion of economic opportunities in the late seventeenth century and usually associated with the rise of capitalism).

As will become apparent, my interest is in the superstructure rather than in the base. While I attempt to point out the interdependence of economic change and ethical change, I am primarily interested in how ethics, as an aspect of ideology, allows the subject to "act." To explore how the ethical subject in Shadwell is constituted, I have had to accept one of the premises of bourgeois ideology. Rosalind Coward and John Ellis, in their analysis of Althusser's concept of hegemony, describe this product of ideology: "It puts in place the contradictory subject, puts him in positions of coherence and responsibility for his own actions so that he is able to act. This acting is the 'initiation' of acts: the subject appears to be the origin of his own activity, responsible for it and for its consequences." As they also point out, this is not a "false consciousness" because "any social system needs to represent itself through subjects in certain positions, thinking along certain lines." The job of the critic, social or literary, is to show that this is only "a specific organization of reality, i.e. a specific mode of production organized to the interests of one class, a mode that is in contradiction and necessitates these representations of freedom."[36] In chapter 5 I shall make apparent how Shadwell's assumption of a unified individual consciousness is necessarily incompatible with his ethics of role.

The cliché is that Restoration comedy avoids serious or complex issues, unlike, for instance, Jacobean comedy. I think this is nonsense. On the contrary, I am inclined to believe that when Jacobean comedy does deal with ethical issues, the result is usually an affirmation of the existing moral order (Shakespeare, Jonson, Dekker, Heywood) or a rather cheap cynicism (Middleton, Marston). Restoration playwrights, after the civil war, which made it apparent that the social order itself could unravel rapidly, were confronted much more immediately than their predecessors with a major philosophical problem: if it is necessary to establish ethics independently of God (if only because the valorization of the individual conscience makes disagreements about God's will extremely likely) and rationality is ineffectual, what is the foundation of ethics? Shadwell and others in the Restoration recognized the difficulty and attempted to find alternatives. If the audience at a modern production of *The Squire of Alsatia* finds Shadwell's alternative unattractive, they should try to construct their own to see how difficult the project is, for it is not clear that anybody since has come up with a very successful solution.

2

Ethical Possibilities

I have argued in the previous chapter that the facts of *The Squire of Alsatia* can be reconciled with Shadwell's claim that he is writing morally instructive drama if we assume the following beliefs inform the play:

1. Neither religion nor reason provides universalizable ethical principles.
2. The test of an action's ethicality is its probable consequences; that is, the grounds of ethics merge with the reasons for ethics.
3. Human drives are value neutral.
4. An individual's role in society determines the ethical obligations particular to that individual.

These beliefs are not modern creations; neither Aristotle nor Epicurus would find anything novel in them. In combination, these beliefs constitute a pragmatic, social ethics. I shall attempt to show that Shadwell could plausibly have had these beliefs in that they were, in one form or another, present in a variety of writers. Many have argued that late seventeenth century was a period of conceptual revolution; the beliefs I have just listed were among those under examination.

The positive form of the first belief (that religion and reason *can* provide universalizable ethical principles) is associated with deontological ethics, whereas the second belief is associated with teleological ethics. A deontological ethical system is one in which ethical claims exist independently from other claims. An action is moral or not in terms of ethical standards that are not translatable into some cash value of pleasure or utility or the common good. The other method of constructing ethical systems is teleological. An action is ethical when it leads to some end that does not itself have an ethical value. Hedonists offer teleological explanations of ethical decisions, but in other teleological systems the action could be measured, for instance, in terms of how it leads to knowledge, the common good, happiness, or perfection. "Utility" or "the common good" take on an ethical value only in the sense that the morality of an action is judged by how it aids or hinders the achievement of that end. The "ought" is derived from the "is" of probable consequences. Deontological systems can be further broken down into act-deontological and rule-deontological systems. The former (e.g., existentialism) argues that each ethical decision is independent of all other decisions, whereas the latter (e.g., Kantian ethics) claims that ethical decisions are deducible from rules that are universal in their application.[1]

Christian ethical systems can be either deontological or teleological. Actions are not right or wrong because of consequences in a Christian deontological ethical system, but because of their compatibility with ethical principles either universally or personally held. For a Calvin or Pascal there is no morality separate from God, the source of all correct judgment about morality. Now it may well be that nonmoral and yet valuable consequences result from morality—everlasting felicity comes to mind, as well as possible temporal happiness—but that is not the standard of judging morality, nor is it the reason for acting morally. If one is correctly in tune with the divine order, one will do things because they are correct and because they please God, rather than because the works will move God to reward you. Luther puts it succinctly:

> So a Christian who lives in this confidence toward God, knows all things, can do all things, undertakes all things that are to be done, and does everything cheerfully and freely; not that he may gather many merits and good works, but because it is a pleasure for him to please God thereby, and he serves God purely for nothing, content that his service pleases God. On the other hand, he who is not at one with God, or doubts, hunts and worries in what way he may do enough and with many works move God.[2]

Despite the pleasure involved in pleasing God, Luther's position here is not teleological. We have a duty to please God because God has assigned us that duty; the nonethical end of pleasing God is not the reason for the duty. It cannot but be pleasing to please God in the nature of things, but the work is done because God wills that it ought to be rather than for the value that accrues in the doing or some inherent virtue separate from God's assigned value. What ends the work accomplishes are in God's hands rather than ours and remain irrelevant to morality; consequences are therefore irrelevant.

In *After Virtue*, Alasdair MacIntyre argues that in the sixteenth and seventeenth century ethics lost the teleological character inherent in Aristotelian and Thomist ethics and began to become deontological under the influence of Protestantism and Jansenism, both of which embodied a conception of reason where reason could supply no genuine comprehension of man's true end. Although divine law could still in theory provide a substitute in its statement of what man is, what he should be, and the rules to get to the latter from the former, the new science's limitations on what constituted knowledge undercut the possibility of any meaningful discussion of man's essence or ultimate end. The ultimate consequence of this split between fact and value is that modern ethics maintain the old assumptions and language of ethics without the context that made them meaningful.[3] For my purposes, MacIntyre is relevant because he describes a situation where reason cannot be regarded as a reliable source for moral imperatives.

There is abundant evidence for MacIntyre's general claim that some members of the "reformed" religions viewed reason as having limited utility in ethics, although one disposed to quibble could argue that the pleasure that Luther talks about is very close to the good that MacIntyre perceives in "practices."[4] MacIntyre's claims about the influence of the new science on ethics may seem less obvious but are equally sound. Bacon says uncompromisingly that moral truth cannot be attained by reason but must be imprinted by God; conscience exists as an emblem of man's unfallen state, but is insufficient: "but how? sufficient to check the vice, but not to inform the duty. So then the doctrine of religion, as well moral as mystical, is not to be attained but by inspiration and revelation from God." Reason has a role for Bacon in "inferring and deriving of doctrine and direction thereupon," but is inadequate for "conception and apprehension." Moral philosophy too can only be "a wise servant and humble handmaid."[5] If felicity is an end of morality for Bacon, it is not in this world but the next and hence is not even something we can seriously consider. Moral principles are givens and not computed in their relation to some other value. Samuel Butler also argues that we have no notion of the "end" of man:

> It is very probable we do not understand (although we may believe) the Purpose for whch wee were created, for if wee are ignorant of

the immediate, and nearest Causes of our selves, much more must wee be so of the most remote, The End for which we are, which do's not seeme to bee for our own sakes, more than a Goldsmith make's a Cup for it self to drink in.[6]

This does not mean we necessarily do not serve some purpose of God's, but we can have no notion of what that purpose is.

Claims that morality is a product of "right reason" do not always mean that the principles of morality are a product of a rational faculty. Henry More is, I think, misinterpreting Aristotle when he ascribes to him a view that man possesses a "moral sense":

> The Philosopher, in another place, defines *Right Reason* thus, *That such Reason was right, as was Conformable to Prudence.* Now whereas *Prudence* it self is nothing but that natural *sagacity,* or well cultivated *Diligence* of the Mind; which he elsewhere calls, *The very Eye of the Soul:* This only brings back the same answer as before; resolving right Reason rather into an *inward Sense,* or an *inward faculty* of *Divination;* than into any certain and distinct Principles, by which a Man might judge of that which in every thing were best.[7]

Aristotle's view is teleological in that prudence judges from commonly received notions of what constitutes a good life. More, however, is arguing for what he elsewhere calls "The Boniform Faculty of the Soul"—that we have an innate notion of what good and evil are. The role of reason is to determine how we ought to act based on this innate notion, but the notion is itself is prerational. More's fellow Cambridge Platonist, John Smith, argues the same point:

> Divine truth is not to be discerned so much in a mans *Brain,* as in his *Heart.* . . . All the thin Speculations and subtilest Discourses of Philosophy cannot so well unfold or define any Sensible Object, nor tell any one so well what it is, as his own naked sense will doe. There is a Divine and Spiritual sense which only is able to converse internally with the life and soul of Divine Truth, as mixing and uniting itself with it.[8]

Like More, Smith is not arguing that there is no role for reason in morality, but the principles of morality are perceived directly in the same way we perceive the objects of the external world: "they are all so clear and perspicuous, that they need no Key of *Analytical* demonstration to unlock them." Of course, once we postulate a moral sense, there is no need to see God as the source of it. In the twentieth century, G. E. Moore claimed that we directly perceive "good" without any recourse to a deity. Moreover, there was a great deal of interest in the seventeenth century in the idea of natural law, and the axioms of natural law, according to people like Hooker and the Latitudinarians, are neither the product of reason nor revealed by God; they become obvious in the course of experience and are incapable of demonstration.[9] It is instructive to note that when Locke, the great popularizer of natural rights as a consequence of natural law, argues for individual rights in *The Second Treatise of Government* (sections 4–5), he cites Hooker. Individual rights are not justified as a means to an end, but are prior to ethics. Ethical systems are a consequence of a natural law that is universal. In such a system there will always be a clear distinction between the grounds of ethics and the reasons for ethics. A woman should not have sex prior to marriage because it is immoral, irrespective of the prudential consideration that if she does, some societies will make her wish she hadn't.[10]

If changing conceptions of knowledge made it difficult for some to see reason as the source of principles of ethical obligation, equally the same changing conceptions created doubt for some that God was a satisfactory source for ethics. While Newton believed in God, his postulation of universal laws (although championed by Clarke and others as proof of divine order) made it easier for others not to, or at least to doubt the Christian framework of the universe. Religious sources of knowledge, as Margaret C. Jacob remarks, were becoming problematic: "The psychological epicenter of that crisis lay predictably within Protestant culture, where the traditional responses of piety, prayer, and biblical prophecy came to be seen as increasingly inadequate."[11] And the dismantling of the temporal mechanisms of church control in seventeenth-century England is a clear example of the shift from religious to social definitions of law: from 1660 to 1688, king, Parliament, and common-law judges all asserted their supremacy over church law, and after Archbishop Sheldon under Clarendon, no clergymen held high political office in the Restoration.[12] And one need not have been an atheist to see a need to establish morality independent of divine sanction. Shaftesbury makes clear that to see God as virtuous, we must already possess the idea of virtue:

> For whoever thinks there is a God, and pretends formally to believe that he is just and good, must suppose that there is independently

such a thing as justice and injustice, truth and falsehood, right and wrong, according to which he pronounces that God is right, righteous, and true. If the mere will, decree, or law of God be said absolutely to constitute right and wrong, then are these latter words of no significancy at all.[13]

Shaftesbury is not denying the existence of God, but he is asserting the logical independence of morality from divine will. In the eighteenth century, God becomes increasingly irrelevant as a grounding for the social expression of morality: the law.[14]

Paralleling the diminution of the intellectual and temporal authority of religion was the decline of belief in the trump card of religious authority: hell. D. P. Walker does argue, however, that while there were increasing doubts about the existence of hell, many considered it dangerous to divulge these doubts to the vulgar for fear anarchy would result.[15] In the popular literature at least, this is less of a problem than Walker supposes: Oroonoko dismisses the idea that fear of divine punishment has any practical consequences:

But punishments hereafter are suffered by one's self; and the world takes no cognizance whether this God has revenged them or not, it is done so secretly and deferred so long; while the man of honor suffers every moment the scorn and contempt of the honester world, and dies every day ignominiously in his fame, which is more valuable than life. I speak not this to move belief [in Oroonoko's oath], but to show you how you mistake, when you imagine, that he who will violate his honor, will keep his word with his gods.[16]

If honor will not restrain a man, fear of God certainly will not, according to Behn's noble slave. The point is even clearer when we remember that Oroonoko's audience includes the white sea captain who has lied to Oroonoko in order to enslave him.

Equally, when Courtine in Otway's *The Atheist* says, "'Tis certainly the fear of Hell, and hopes of Hapiness, that makes People live in Honesty, Peace, and Union one towards another," Daredevil responds that mundane fears are the true source of civil peace:

Fear of Hell! Heark thee, *Beaugard;* this Companion of thine, as I apprehend, is but a sort of shallow Monster. Fear of Hell! No, Sir, 'tis fear of Hanging. Who would not steal, or do murder, every time his Fingers itch't at it, were it not for fear of the Gallows? Do not you, with all your Religion, swear almost as often as you speak? break and

prophane the Sabbath? lie with your neighbors Wives? and covet
their Estates, if they be better than your own? Yet those things are
forbid by Religion, as well as Stealing and Cutting of Throats are. No,
had every Commandment but a Gibbet belonging to it, I should not
have had Four Kings Evidences to day swore impudently I was a
Papist, when I was never at Mass yet since I was born, nor indeed at
any other worship these Twenty years.[17]

Daredevil is by no means a trustworthy guide in the play, since,
it turns out, he has more religious fear than either Courtine or
Beaugard. But Courtine makes no response, and Daredevil's comments are certainly applicable to the upper class at least, for
neither Courtine nor Beaugard appears to have any fear of consequences despite the fact they do commit the sins of which Daredevil accuses them. Something other than the fear of hell is the
source of ethical constraint in both Behn and Otway.

Clarendon himself commented on the role that Hobbes played
in fanning doubts about religion in the context of an attack on
Hobbes's views on miracles. Clarendon is by no means willing
to agree that all claims of religious knowledge are the product of
royal fiat; Hobbes's claim that miracles should be regarded as
true because a king says they are is a part of the dangerous lust
for novelty that threatens the kingdom and which invites unnecessary hypocrisy on the part of a king:

> [Hobbes] hath contributed very much to that uncontroulable spirit,
> which by the extravagance of fancy, invention and imagination, hath
> made such confusion both in the speculation and practice of Religion
> in this distracted Kingdom, and by his making that which God hath
> manifestly commanded, liable to be controul'd, or to receive aut[h]or-
> ity from the pleasure of the King, that both God and the King are
> less reverenced, and their precepts less regarded than they have us'd
> to be in this nation.[18]

Religious precepts are true and independent of temporal power,
and any attempt to ground respect for authority in merely temporal considerations is a danger to order. But Hobbes is only a
"contributor," a part of "that uncontroulable spirit" threatening
the stability of the age.

Hobbes's ethics are teleological in that moral value is determined by nonmoral values, but the value is private and unarguable: "But whatsoever is the object of any mans Appetite or
Desire; that is it, which he for his part calleth *Good*."[19] Etherege
also apparently believes that ethical decisions are personal, but

his ethics are deontological. Religious constraints, in Etherege's view, are not merely suspect because of the character of the people who make them, but they are also in opposition to Etherege's personal code of morality:

> I have ever enjoy'd a liberty of opinion in matters of Religion. 'Tis indifferent to me whether there be an other in the world who thinks as I do. This makes me have no temptation to talk of the business, but quietly following the light within me, I leave that to them who were born with the ambition of becoming Prophets or Legislators. 'Tis not amiss to see an humble Clergy. They are more like the Holymen in the primitive time, but it wou'd be very hard to be excommunicated for fornication, it being a point all the differing Churches agree in.[20]

Not only is morality not a subject for dispute (the contempt for "Prophets or Legislators" is implicit), but social consensus ("all the differing Churches") is irrelevant as well. Etherege has a moral code, as his letters about his duty to James II make clear, but it is not subject to rational evaluation.

Even Descartes, who has the option of bringing God into his discussion of how we control the dangerous passions, does not. The general problem of the passions can be solved by Cartesian rationalism. Experience informs us of what is actually a good and instills temperance in us: "C'est pourquoy nous devons nous servir de l'experience & de la raison, pour distinguer le bien d'avec le mal, & connoistre leur juste valeur, affin de ne prendre pas l'un pour l'autre, & de ne nous porter à rien avec exces."[21] Reason distinguishes between good and bad, and the will can then act without any supernatural guidance.

The skeptical crisis of the seventeenth century did create doubts about religion's adequacy to provide moral guidance. Edward Gibbon, in his memoirs, describes Bayle in a way that shows how relious controversies weakened both sides' claims for moral authority:

> In reviewing the controversies of the times, he turned against each other the arguments of the disputants: successively wielding the arms of the Catholics and the Protestants, he proves that neither the way of authority, nor the way of examination can afford the multitude any test of religious truth; and dexterously concludes that custom and education must be the sole grounds of popular belief. The ancient paradox of Plutarch, that atheism is less pernicious than superstition, acquires a tenfold vigour when it is adorned with the colours of his wit, and pointed with the acuteness of his logic.[22]

And the Cambridge Platonists, at least, knew precisely what was at stake. Ralph Cudworth begins *A Treatise concerning Eternal and Immutable Morality* by describing his opposition as those who deny God and rationality as the source of ethical belief:

> As the vulgar generally look no higher for the original of moral good and evil, just and unjust, than the codes and pandects, the tables and laws of their country and religion; so there have not wanted pretended philosophers in all ages who have asserted nothing to be good and evil, just and unjust, naturally and immutably; but that all these things were positive, arbitrary and factitious only.[23]

Cudworth's immediate reference is more likely to be Hobbes than Bayle, but he is claiming that the view that ethics are customary rather than divine or rational is common. Skepticism, of course, need not generate atheism. Richard Popkin has shown that a common response in the sixteenth and seventeenth centuries was fideism.[24] But the best example of this fideistic response, Montaigne, ultimately accepts even religious faith on the basis of custom. It is not much of a step to accept custom for its own sake. This is precisely Rochester's view, as reported by Burnet, and it is a consequence of Rochester's belief in an indifferent God, who "had none of those Affections of Love or Hatred, which breed perturbation in us, and by consequence he could not see that there was to be either reward or punishment."[25] Rochester accepts the argument from design but, like Hume, sees that religious belief and moral obligation are not entailed by that acceptance.

If Shadwell held the first belief he was not an anomaly, even if he was not an atheist, and even though some of the examples I have used tend to doubt reason or religion but not both; later in this chapter I shall discuss Hobbes in greater depth, as well as Halifax and Charleton, none of whom requires either religion or universalizable rational principles to construct ethical systems. But the second belief, which my reading of *The Squire of Alsatia* also requires, would seem to conflict with MacIntyre's claim that ethics in the seventeenth century were shifting away from teleological ethics. What I wish to argue, however, is that teleological views of morality never went away and remained the dominant tradition in England at least until the eighteenth century. MacIntyre moves smoothly from the medieval period to Hume, Kant, and Kierkegaard, while in England utilitarianism seems to spring full-formed and antecedentless from Bentham's head. MacIntyre is, of course, primarily concerned with showing the antecedents of modern ethics, and since the trend has been away from the teleological tradition, he simply ignores it. It may well be that the formulations of this tradition, which I shall describe, are philosophically untenable, but they were, nonetheless, common and influential and may still be the foundation of garden-variety moral arguments.

The second belief is so alien to the modern view of ethics that many critics may regard the entire concept as necessarily alien to seventeenth-century ethical thought as well. Shaftesbury certainly expresses something close to the modern view when he rejects the notion that one can act ethically if one's reason for doing so is to achieve heaven and avoid hell:

> There is no more of rectitude, piety, or sanctity in a creature thus reformed, than there is meekness or gentleness in a tiger strongly chained, or innocence and sobriety in a monkey under the discipline of the whip. . . . Be the master or superior ever so perfect or excellent, yet the greater submission caused in this case, through this sole principle or motive, is only the lower and more abject servitude[.][26]

In other words, if we do not choose to act virtuously for the sake of virtue alone, we are either acting under constraint, in which case the action is not virtuous because not freely chosen, or we are acting out of self-interest, which, in Shaftesbury's view, by definition cannot be an ethical action. D. P. Walker, commenting on this same section, says,

> It might be thought that Shaftesbury is here merely demonstrating an analytical truth: that we do not in fact call virtuous such actions as are motivated by fear of punishment or hope of reward, because the moral responsibility for them rests not on the doer but on the punisher or rewarder, or because we would call all such actions purely self-interested or expedient, and therefore morally neutral or bad. But this is not what he is doing; for it is very doubtful whether in his day this was an analytical truth.[27]

Walker is exactly right; Shaftesbury's position has roots in the Protestant rejection of Catholic teleological ethics, but he is, I believe, the first to make the claim without a religious grounding. And it was perfectly possible—and, prior to the eighteenth century, probable—that a philosopher of ethics would hold the reverse. Certainly Aristotle and Aquinas would have been stunned to hear that a man was not acting ethically if he was seeking the reward of happiness and avoiding the punishment of unhappiness. And this was a common Protestant view as well.

A mainline Anglican like Thomas Traherne could still say confidently that virtue is no more than a means to an end: "The Excellence of Virtue is the Necessity and Efficacy thereof in the Way to Felicity. It consisteth in this, Virtue is the only Means, by which Happiness can be obtained." Traherne specifically aligns himself with Aristotelian ethics, and says that the only problem with Aristotle is that he assumed that felicity was temporal. Traherne is not an ascetic who rejects the pleasures of this world, but simply argues that they are not the true end of virtue:

> I am not so Stoical, as to make all Felicity consist in a meer Apathy, or Freedom from Passion, nor yet so Dissolute, as to give the Passions all their Liberty. Neither do I perswade you to Renounce the Advantage of Wealth and Honor, any more than those of Beauty and Wit: for as a Man may be Happy without all of these, so may he make a happy use of them when he has them.[28]

While I shall return to the role of the passions in ethical systems, I wish to point out here that Traherne believes they are not necessarily incompatible with morality, nor are social station and temporal happiness. The natural man need not deny himself to act ethically, only control himself. And social felicities too are clearly a good, which means prudence will have a role in virtue.

Built into Richard Cumberland's view of natural law is a system of rewards and punishments:

> A law of nature is a proposition quite clearly presented to, or impressed upon, the mind by the nature of things from the will of the First Cause, pointing out an action, of service to the common good of rational beings, the performance of which is followed by adequate reward, while its neglect is followed by adequate punishment.[29]

We do not, therefore, act for the common good purely because we ought to act for the common good, but because there is a carrot and stick applied to the moral sense. Henry More says of his moral "Noema" that "they propose nothing for good, which at the same time is not grateful also, and attended with delight." Included in these delights are "external blessings" such as success in "Science, Arts and Sapience."[30]

Edward LeRoy Long, in connection with Puritanism, has argued that "Protestantism has fostered various forms of legalism in which law-embraced-as-response to the Gospel has become law-embraced-to-obtain-a-reward."[31] Further, this facet of Protestantism begins in England in the mid to late seventeenth century. His examples are casuists like Baxter and Taylor, whom he misidentifies as a Puritan. His main point is very compelling; casuists offer guidebooks through potential minefields of vice to an everlasting felicity. For example, Taylor appears to be offering a straight appeal to divine precept independent of consequences when arguing that a daughter's duty to her father takes precedence over personal attraction when choosing a husband, but the argument is presented as a refutation of claims that she can make rational judgments about personal attractions:

> For beauty is not the praise of a man, and he may be a worthy person, though of an ill shape, and his wit and manners may be better than his countenance. And there is no exception to this, but that if the daughter has used all means to endure him, and cannot obtain it, she can only then refuse when she can be sure that with him she can never do her duty; of which she cannot be sure beforehand, because his worthiness may overcome the air and follies of her fancy, therefore the unhandsomeness of a man is not alone sufficient cause for a daughter to refuse her father's earnest commands.[32]

Natural law theorists would argue that fathers have no such right, and Taylor feels obligated to show that the daughter has no real capacity to make reasonable decisions about personal desire.

Informing the argument, however, is Taylor's recognition that people do make such decisions based on factors that are ultimately not moral. Although the father does have the right to force his daughter to marry for her own good, "a good father will never use it, when it is very much against his daughter, unless it is very much for her good." Further, the daughter does have the right to refuse the morally unfit because that may lead her into sin, which will imperil her soul and risk heaven. Even more significant is the fact that the daughter can refuse those of substantially lower social station because that will affect her happiness in this world. Finally, a son is granted a great deal more leeway in choosing a wife based on the nonmoral value of personal attraction: "but a son hath in this some more liberty, because he is to be a head of a family, and he is more easily tempted, and can sooner be drawn aside to wander, and beauty or comeliness is the proper praise of a woman." The son is granted his liberty because without it he is more likely to sin; the wandering is a societal given, but since equally reprehensible, some concessions to personal attraction are necessary. Taylor is then allowing a place for nonmoral values and consequences to at least modify moral obligations, and this, it seems to me, tends to blur the separation of the grounding of ethics and the reasons for ethical behavior. What virtue is becomes inseparable from why one ought to be virtuous.[33]

What Taylor and Traherne share is a tendency to modify inherited ethical traditions in terms of what they perceive to be irreducible facts of human nature that are not society-specific. Taylor concedes that personal attraction exists whether it should or not; Traherne prefaces his ethical system with the remark "the Consideration of the End is that alone which does animate a Man to the use of the means," implying that we cannot escape from considerations of self-interest when discussing why a man ought to act in any particular way.[34] The belief that there are facts of human nature to which ethical systems must selectively adapt is perhaps the most striking fact of seventeenth-century ethical thought and is especially noticeable in the secular ethics of the period. This is why I believe it likely that Shadwell could have held the third belief, that "the passions" are ethically neutral.

Individuals in the seventeenth century were quite capable of arguing that the roles society and society's God prescribed for them were immoral; that some acted upon that belief is the whole point of Hill's The World Turned Upside Down. Since Diggers and Levellers, Ranters and Quakers were by no means the most educated people in society, it may have seemed quite plausible to political and ethical theorists that there were innate human traits in conflict with ethical systems as they then existed. Where before such traits would have been ascribed to man's sinful nature, by the Restoration there was a tendency to destigmatize such characteristics. As R. S. Crane says about the Latitudinarians,

> The passions, they insisted wth Aristotle, are neither good nor evil in themselves; they may, however, be ordered to virtue, and when so ordered they have a positive value, since they and not our weak reason are the forces which make it possible for us to act at all; to wish to eradicate them from our nature is not only a futile but a misguided desire.[35]

In other words, expecting people to restrain themselves on the basis of a proper end for man established by God or society without reference to the natural drives of the individual was analogous to expecting water to flow uphill.

Moreover, the changing economy of England inevitably affected moral perceptions of character. For instance, grain sales had traditionally been under government regulation, for if a selfish individual did not consider the greater good many would starve. As grain harvests improved over the course of the seventeenth century, commentators increasingly argued that the individual had the right to do with his property as he wished. Harvests were so good after 1662 that control of grain became a moot point. Thus grain, which once had been perceived as a reason to control man's sinful nature, became just another commodity; what once had been selfishness became morally neutral.[36]

Albert Hirschman explains the rising interest in the passions by relating it to the belief that the old order was inadequate:

> Ever since the end of the Middle Ages, and particularly as a result of the increasing frequency of war and civil war in the seventeenth and eighteenth centuries, the search was on for a behavioral equivalent for religious precept, for new rules of conduct and devices that would impose much needed discipline and constraints on both rulers and ruled.[37]

This generalization is in need of qualification—not everyone perceived a need for something other than divine precept, and many of those who did could still argue that divine precept provided the foundation of secular law. But the fact remains that many thought religion was inadequate as an ethical and political standard and attempted to conceive ethical and political systems independent of it.

If the church can no longer control restless man, the question becomes, Who can? Hobbes's political solution, as Hirschman points out, begs the question. If men need protection from each other because of an innate and insatiable desire for power, investing that power in an all-powerful monarch is simply wishful thinking; since he has the same drives, he will inevitably oppress those who gave him the power. And recent history could demonstrate that under such conditions men would rise and throw the rascal out. But implicit in *Leviathan* is a view of social exchange whereby men's interests will control their passions.

Good and evil are relational terms for Hobbes:

> For these words of Good, Evill, and Contemptible, are ever used with relation to the person that useth them: There being nothing simply and absolutely so; nor any common Rule of Good and Evill, to be taken from the nature of the objects themselves; but from the Person

of the man (where there is no Commonwealth;) or, in a Commonwealth, from the Person that representeth it; or from an Arbitrator or
Judge, whom men disagreeing shall by consent set up, and make his
sentence the Rule thereof.[38]

In other words, there are only laws, whether individually or so-
cietally imposed. The consequence of this, in the absence of a
sovereign, is that an action is right or wrong depending on
whether it is to our advantage, and whether we can get away with
it.

We are honorable or dishonorable as other people judge us or,
more precisely, wish they could do as we can do. The measure
of a man is his power: "The *Value*, or WORTH of a man, is as of
all other things, his Price; that is to say, so much as would be
given for the use of his Power" (151). That which is honorable
is that which shows power: "The measure of the value we set on
one another, is that which is called Honouring or Dishonouring.
To value a man at a high rate is to *Honour* him; at a low rate to
Dishonour him" (152). This is not limited to physical or economic power, although such a power may be the final cause;
emotional control is a power, and hence honorable: "Also, what
quality soever maketh a man beloved, or feared of many; or the
reputation of such quality is Power" (151). The greater our role
is in society, the more honorable we are.

All this does not leave much room for ethics on a personal
level; that which I want to and can do is honorable. The second
part provides the core of societal ethics. Based on past experience I make predictions on what I can get away with; if I go too
far in infringing on what others regard as theirs, either they or the
commonwealth will stop me. The drive toward self-preservation
balances the desire for power. In the absence of some sort of
social order, talk of ethics is empty. Prior to the acknowledgment
of a social order founded on a combined power, "The notions of
Right and Wrong, Justice and Injustice have there no place.
Where there is no common Power, there is no Law; where no
Law, no injustice" (188).

Along with the consideration that if we go too far society will
stop us is the restraint that the nature of sensual pleasure itself
forces on us: "Desire of Ease, and sensuall Delight, disposeth
men to obey a common Power; Because by such Desires, a man
doth abandon the protection might be hoped for from his own
Industry, and Labour" (162). Sense pleasures such as food and
drink, carpets and paintings, require aid in that we cannot get

everything by our own industry. We are no longer wholly independent and require society to regulate our affairs for our own protection.

Charleton and the marquis of Halifax are examples of thinkers who explore the possibility of rapprochement between the needs of individuals in a social context. They, like Hobbes, think that claims that something is a good have their origin in self-interest, but they also examine the extent to which custom provides sources of obligation beyond self-interest.

Charleton, in *Epicurus's Morals*, argues for a teleological system that centers around pleasure. His version of pleasure, however, shifts the terms of pleasure from Hobbes so that it is no longer an implacable enemy to order. In Hobbes, the desire for ever-more power ceases only with death, whereas Charleton regards desires as easily manageable. In fact, anxiety itself is a symptom of taking any desire too seriously: "for wherever Pleasure is, there can be nothing of pain, of anxiety."[39] Self-control is an inescapable prerequisite for pleasure, and self-control will naturally bring us into alignment with social order.

There are two primary virtues in Epicureanism. Prudence "being our Directress, conducts us to tranquility, by extinguishing the ardor of all cupidities. For, cupidities are insatiable, subverting not only single persons, but also numerous and opulent Families, yea sometimes the most potent and flourishing Common-wealths" (29). Temperance protects us from apparent pleasures with unfortunate consequences:

And hence it is understood, that Temperance is to be desired, not because it avoids some Pleasures, but because by restraining a man from them, it declines Troubles, wich being avoided, he afterward obtains greater Pleasures. And this in the meantime it so doth, as that the action becomes Honest and Decent: and we may clearly understand, that the same men are lovers as of Pleasure, so also of Decorum.

(43)

Temperance, as decorum, is good manners raised to the level of honesty and decency. Prudence is the virtue closer to the modern notion of temperance—the capacity to extinguish the ardor of desire.

A prudent man will not marry for personal reasons; the benefits are far outweighed by the risks:

You may presume, indeed, that your Wife will be sweet and Compla-
cent; that your Children will be of ingenious and tractable disposi-
tions . . . and yet you can but presume all this, nor do I know of any
God, who will oblige himself, that your affairs shall succeed according to your presumption. Wherefore, seeing the business is very
doubtful; it is far below the part of a Wise man, willingly to put
himself upon Chance, to undergo the hazard, and engage himself in
that condition, from whence, in case he should afterward repent, he
cannot withdraw himself.

(35)

Unfortunately, the business of preserving the family line or
populating a country may require you to marry and have children. Nevertheless, there is no natural moral obligation to do so.
The solution, abstinence, has much in common with the Catholics, but Charleton's objections to the "incommodities" of sex are
physical and social: "Consumption of strength, decay of Industry,
unfitness for business and labour, neglect of Domestick Prudence, impairment of Estate, Mortgages, and Forfeitures, ruine
of reputation and Fame" (51). Prudence protects one from all
these threats to personal happiness.

Temperance is virtue in its social manifestation of decorum.
The sanction against nonmarital sex is social:

[A] wise man ought not to live after the beastly manner of the Cyn-
icks, or to deport himself with Immodesty and Impudence, which
they not only shew but boast of in public. For, when they plead,
that they therein follow the directions of Nature . . . they seem not
sufficiently to consider, that they live in a Civil Society, and not
single, and at random abroad in the fields, and after the manner of
Wild Beast.

(53)

The argument is not that there is a moral imperative against sex
but a social one:

For, from the time we have given up our names to a Society, Nature
it self commands us to observe the Laws and customs of that Society;
to that end, that participating of the common Goods, we draw no
Evil upon our selves, such as is Infamy at least, or Ignominy, which
follows upon that impudence, or the want of such shamefastness,
as the Customs of Manners of Society, wherein we live, commonly
prescribe, and from the observance of which in voice, aspect, and
other seemly gestures, that Verecundity, which all virtuous persons
so worthily commend, is derived and denominated.

(63–64)

As a part of society, we are obligated to play by society's rules. When we do not, we risk societal censure, which will actually inhibit our capacity to achieve pleasure in society. Further, our worthiness is a function of our behavior in society, and acting in a manner appropriate to the customs of society provides a kind of satisfaction and hence is a virtue.

Charleton at times sounds Hobbesian. In the previous passage, we are required to observe societal strictures on voice and gesture as much as we are to eschew fornication. The two appear to be at the same level of wrong and for the same reason: they are contrary to custom. But there is a crucial distinction. A true Epicurean has already restrained his own desires to such an extent that he is unlikely ever to reach the stage of offending society, whereas for Hobbes, without an all powerful central authority we are almost certain to break social bonds. The marquis of Halifax, in his *Advice to a Daughter*, like Charleton, thinks that the individual must be aware of social restrictions in order to be happy, and that a compromise can be reached between individual desire and social constraints.

Halifax has no patience with claims of fundamental principles, as his *Political Thoughts and Reflections* makes clear:

> Fundamental is used as Men use their Friends; commend them when they have use of them, and when they fall out, find a hundred Objections to them.
> Fundamental is a Pedestal that Men set everything upon that they would not have broken. It is a Nail every body would use to fix that which is good for them: for all Men would have that Principle to be immoveable, that serves their use at the time.
> Every thing that is created is Mortal, *ergo* all Fundamentals of human Creation will die.[40]

Rather, Halifax assumes the stance of a realist appealing for evidence of assertions to ordinary reason and experience. The given of his advice to his daughter is that women are in a socially disadvantageous position: they have to make do with what they draw in the marriage market since the power of choice is not in their hands. Halifax's realism also assumes that this is the way it should be in that most men have more strength and reason than women have. But women have a weapon in their hands as well that in the social context gives them strong cards to play: "gentleness," which translates to the ability to use the forms of civil society to get men to act properly.[41]

There is no point in complaining about lack of virtue in a

husband since it will not accomplish anything and will lead to social disfavor. Moreover, anything that contributes to the individual's control of the situation is at least like virtue. For example, complaining about an unfaithful husband will only embarrass the wife:

> If he is a Man of Sense, he will reclaim himself; the Folly of it, is of itself sufficient to cure him: if he is not so, he will be provok'd, but not reform'd. . . . Besides, it is so coarse a Reason which will be assign'd for a Lady's too great Warmth upon such an occasion, that Modesty no less than Prudence ought to restrain her; since such an undecent Complaint makes a Wife much more ridiculous, than the Injury that provoketh her to it.
>
> (10–11)

Since there is nothing the wife can do about the problem of infidelity, "An *affected Ignorance, which is seldom a Vertue,*" even if it doesn't make him faithful, "Will naturally make him more *yielding* in other things" (11). Drunkeness works out the same way. Halifax argues that the seemingly paradoxical claim that it is good for a husband to have faults is proved by experience: "The *Faults* and *Passions* of *Husbands* bring them down to you, and make them content to live upon less unequal *Terms,* than Faultless Men would be willing to stoop to" (12).

Halifax's standard of judgment is social utility. He quickly concedes that religion is true, but its real justification is that it serves as a mechanism for restraining our counterproductive impulses:

> Instead of imposing unnecessary Burdens upon our *Nature,* it [religion] easeth us of the greater weight of our Passions and *Mistakes.* . . . [it] redeemeth us from the *Slavery* we are in to our selves, who are the most severe Masters, whilst we are under the Usurpation of our Appetites let loose and not restrain'd.
>
> (5)

In this view of course, religion and Epicureanism are not incompatible because they both have the same goal: "A wise *Epicure* would be *Religious* for the sake of *Pleasure; Good sense* is the Foundation of both; and he is a *Bungler* who aimeth at true *Luxury,* but where they are join'd" (5). While Halifax occasionally sounds as if he would like to maintain a distinction between virtue as ontologically distinct entity and the appearance of virtue as a maneuver for social success, the attempt is halfhearted, and the appearance of virtue is really all that is necessary for the individual to achieve success in society. When counseling his daughter about the need for reserve lest men think she is available, he says, "It is a *Guard* to a *good Women*, and a *Disguise* to an *ill one*. It is of so much use to both, that they ought to use it as an *Artifice*, who refuse to practice it as a *Vertue*" (33). Even if we regard Halifax as recommending hypocrisy, we need to remember that hypocrisy is not so dreadful a vice if it brings one to practice an appropriate role.[42]

Implicit in Halifax's advice to his daughter is the notion that she can only be truly happy playing a socially appropriate role. That role entails ethical obligation is perhaps the oldest ethical tradition in Western civilization. In the *Iliad*, it comes from the mouth of Sarpedon, explaining that what entitled men to "pride of place at table" is their willingness to go die for their people when dying is necessary (12.310–21). This has nothing to do with the "social contract," since Sarpedon's people have no bargaining rights; it is purely a statement of moral obligation based on social role. Such a view requires that the highest virtue must be attended by advantageous economic circumstances. The master of the Greek *oikos* required property because without independence he could not exercise his civic and political virtues. This position was revived by Harrington in the seventeenth century and was perceived as politically necessary in the 1670s as a counterbalance against the centralized power of the crown.[43] However, the notion of aristocratic virtue was under attack from two directions. From the Protestant belief in the equality of souls, it followed there must also be an equality of virtues. Indeed, the aristocratic ethos might well be inimical to the practice of true, Christian virtue.[44] On the other hand, the aristocratic gentleman of the Renaissance had relied for justification of his place in a hierarchy on "a conception of an order actually *cosmological*, not merely psychological or sociological, on a belief that the aristocrat was a part of God's and nature's plan for the universe."[45] As I have shown, it was increasingly difficult for some to believe that we could have any knowledge of what God's plan for the universe was, in which case it was idle to appeal to divine hierarchies to justify social ones.

Such a view was not, of course, universal. The anonymous and overtly religious *Advice of a Father* argues that social position is determined by God: "Every man hath his lot; nothing can befall us, but what was before designed; there is no such thing as chance; our Father hath appointed his children their several portions, why then am I not satisfied with what comes to my share?" And the lot of a gentleman requires that he work toward a moral society. The public sphere is the proper arena for the virtuous gentleman:

> Intend a Publick good, rather than a Private; the Gain on every side will be greater, and the greatest thine: Thou canst not effect a general good without doing thy self good; that which is beneficial to the whole, cannot be prejudicial to any part. Be not of a scanty Spirit, thy are not born for thy self; the whole Creation claims a share; it were monstrous a particular interest should outweigh the World.[46]

Richard Allestree's equally religious *The Gentleman's Calling* states that the gentleman has the advantages of education, wealth, time (by which Allestree means leisure), authority, and reputation. These combine uniquely to fit the gentleman to his work: "And here they need not fear that I mean to put the Spade or Hammer into their hands, to require them to become either Husbandmen or Mechanicks; my whole design is founded in their distinction from these, namely in those things, wherein either in Kind or degree they excel them."[47] God has placed the gentleman in his station as an instrument of his will to instill ethical notions in those dependent on him: family, tenants, and servants.

Francis Osborne, on the other hand, also sees an ethical value in acting in accordance with one's role, and a part of one's role as a gentleman is in ensuring social order; but role is referred to as a function of "fortune," and there is much less of a sense that fortune is a part of God's plan. Unlike Allestree or the anonymous author of the *Advice of a Father*, Osborne never suggests anything of the sort. Rather, one lives up to one's role by being educated to do so: "Therefore few not freely educated, can wear decently the habit of a *Court*, or behave themselves in such a Mediocrity, as shall not discover too much idolatry towards those in a superior Orb, or disdain in relation to such, as Fortune rather than merit hath possibly placed below them." Osborne's notion of a gentleman contains egalitarian tendencies precisely because position is a product of luck rather than merit:

> Keep no more *Servants* than you have full Employment for; and if you find a good one, look upon him under no severer aspect than that of a *humble Friend*; the difference between such a one and his Master residing rather in Fortune than Nature. . . . Thus by proportioning your Carriage to those below, you will the better bring your

Mind to a safe and easie Deportment to such as Fate hath set above you.[48]

Obligation remains a function of role, not merely in the absence of a divinely ordained hierarchy, but even without the psychological defense of regarding the hierarchy as a function of innate merit passed down through the bloodlines. "Fortune" is, of course, not incompatible with divine providence, but Osborne never equates the two where other authors of courtesy literature do.

Charleton, Halifax and Osborne offer a way to preserve the ethics of role independent of cosmology. The social role is a part of the smooth functioning of society. Halifax's skepticism about fundamentals of any sort, including moral principles—his favorite author was Montaigne—and his tendency to describe virtue only as a social behavior illustrate a possible solution to what I have previously described as the moral dilemma of the Restoration: if God can no longer be relied upon as the source of ethics, and if rationality is untrustworthy as a source of universal ethical principles, where do we locate ethical obligation? Halifax's position is very nearly identical to the ethical system that I have ascribed to Shadwell in *The Squire of Alsatia* on all four points of belief. Halifax assumes that ethics are a product of custom rather than reason or religion, and that ethical obligation is a function of role validated by individual happiness and the smooth functioning of society. More imporant, Halifax illustrates the continuity between very different positions and indicates both that Shadwell and his audience could have held the beliefs, or at least been capable of presenting and recognizing the beliefs, that I have used to explain the play.

3

Religion and Duty

In this chapter I shall argue that contrary to many current readings, Shadwell never suggests that ethics can rely on an innately virtuous human nature. Moreover, Shadwell, throughout his career, sees religion as having only limited utility as a source of ethical obligation, and this is plausible from what we know of his life, and apparent in the plays from his treatment of religion and in his presentation of the relationship between parents and children. Finally, I shall discuss the major development that occurs over the course of Shadwell's career, the increasing importance of the benevolent paternal figure.

Most commentators seem to accept the view that Shadwell comes to an increasingly optimistic picture of human nature over the course of his career. Donald Bruce casually remarks that Shadwell "replaced the man of mode with the man of honour, moving from the courtly ideal of the early Restoration towards the religiously based ideal of the eighteenth century." Further Bruce apparently agrees with the current reading of Shadwell, which is implicit in a subsequent (and in some versions of Christianity incompatible) statement in which he claims that Isabella in *A True Widow* shows that Shadwell thought "mankind inherently virtuous but vitiated by society."[1]

This view of Shadwell's ethics is not uncommon and is shared by Don R. Kunz. Kunz argues that

Shadwell habitually asserted that Hobbesian self-interest was only a temporary social veneer which may be stripped away during a process of self-discovery assisted by an exemplar; beneath the surface gloss lies natural goodness, which when exercised, gives the greatest sense of fulfillment to man as a social animal. But almost as a neoclassical reflex, Shadwell felt compelled to rationalize this romantic philosophy of good nature which springs from feeling: By his last comedy he could assert true social and self-love were the same; feeling and reason were not only reconciled but united in a common cause.[2]

Susan Staves offers a more sophisticated framework, but she too implies that man's nature is not merely compatible with the virtuous life, but inclines toward it: "No one suggests that [heroes in Shadwell's late comedies] should abandon their natural appetites. Instead they are converted because they recognize with Shaftesbury that the life of a sober gentlemen yields more pleasure, more freedom from pain, and more gratification of natural appetites."[3] The reference to Shaftesbury indicts that this kind of prudence is distinct from a Hobbesian prudence based on mutual insecurity, where some natural appetites are genuinely dangerous to the individual because they are dangerous to other individuals; Staves implies that natural appetites are not merely not negative, as in Hobbes, but not even neutral, as I shall argue Shadwell thought. Rather, their satisfaction is not merely an end of virtuous behavior, but the chief end.

That the tone of Shadwell's comedies changes over the course of his career is undeniable. At least part of the change is probably due to changing theatrical tastes. Scouten and Hume claim that Shadwell is "not exerting pressure on the audience; rather, he is responding to a changing climate of opinion."[4] The first claim is probably true; the success of the *The Squire of Alsatia* indicates that audiences responded favorably to the play, and, I suppose, the only historical evidence that any work put pressure on its audience would be the presence of controversy when the work was first presented—for instance, the premiere of *Waiting for Godot*. The latter claim, that Shadwell is responding to changing audience taste, is more unlikely except in the weak sense that by 1688 he could more freely present what he had always preferred. It does not follow from the fact that an audience finds the ideas embodied in a play congenial that the playwright presented those ideas because the audience would find them congenial. As J. H. Smith points out, and Hume and Scouten concede, in early plays like *The Miser* and *The Humorists* there are exemplary male leads who have either already reformed or never needed to.[5] I believe, however, that throughout his career, with the exception of *Epsom Wells* and *The Virtuoso*, Shadwell is quite consistent in his presentation of both characters who need to reform and exemplary characters who serve as examples for them. Critics have mistakenly singled out *The Squire of Alsatia* as a turning point in Shadwell's career because after 1688 other playwrights began to follow what was always Shadwell's practice.

All agree that Shadwell's earliest plays offer virtuous gentlemen (i.e., working to preserve social stability) and heroes reformed by love. Lovel, the second lead in *The Sullen Lovers*, has already repented his affair with Lady Vaine before the play begins. Bellamour, in *The Miser*, is perfectly virtuous—he is virtually indistinguishable from Endymion in Shadwell's previous play, *The Royal Shepherdesse*—and regards people who rail against marriage as possessing "the common place wit of all the young Fops on this town" (2.5.91), while the hero Theodore rejects his previous rakish life for Isabella. No courtship is necessary for Raymund, in *The Humorists*, because his virtue enables Theodosia to accept his suit the first time they are alone together: "I have so absolute a confidence in your honour, that I yield to your conduct in the affair" (1.4.234).

Waiving *Epsom Wells* and *The Virtuoso* for the moment because they quite clearly do not contain either exemplars or reformed heroes, with *A True Widow* Shadwell returns to presenting both an exemplar and a hero who reforms, although they are balanced against the successful Lady Cheatly. Carlos can say honestly, "Faith, Madam, I am a moral man, I do as I would be done by" (3.3.329). Moreover, Bellamour reforms more convincingly than either Belfond Junior or Sir William Rant, shifting from a man who "aimes but at fornication" (3.1.291), to a man who prizes mutual love: "When I made these offers, I did not know half your worth: I was a fair Chapman for your Beauty; but your Vertue, and other Perfections, are inestimable" (3.5.358). Even Sir Humphrey Scattergood, in *The Woman Captain*, is forced to reform and accept prudence, although love has no role in his conversion. Finally, Bellfort and Doubty, in *The Lancashire Witches*, are "Knight Errants" (4.2.130), willing to take Isabella and Theodosia without property. Love has eliminated their desire for socially dangerous satisfaction: "Those interviews have spoiled me for a man of this World, I can no more throw off my loose corns of Love upon a Tennants Daughter in the Countrey, or think of Cuckolding a Keeping Fool in the City" (4.1.118).

This catalog of reformations and exemplars from Shadwell's earlier plays illustrates a point previous critics have either overlooked or underemphasized. The mere fact that Belfond Junior and Sir William Rant reform need not indicate that Shadwell has taken on a load of metaphysical freight involving a belief that man is fundamentally good-natured and only immoral because of social causes. No one has ever claimed that Shadwell's plays prior to *A True Widow* (1679) illustrate such a belief, and yet both virtuous men and reformed rakes are commonplace.

Further, in all of these late plays there remain characters for whom no evidence is offered that their vice is a consequence of social corruption. Matched with Isabella in *A True Widow* is her sister Gartrude, so innocent as to be virtually a natural and a remarkably unattractive character; she fornicates consecutively with Selfish and Stanhope and is a clear counterexample to any claims that man possesses natural goodness. It would be hard to say who in *Timon*, other than Evandra, reveals man's fundamentally benevolent nature. If man is naturally good, why is it that Lord Bellamy in *Bury Fair* tells Wildish "I must think a Man a Slave, till he has conquered himself" (4.1.309)? Tope, with as much intelligence, breeding, and social position as anyone in *The Scowrers*, remains cheerfully unrepentent and unreformed at the end of the play. Mrs. Hackwell is both lascivious and greedy in *The Volunteers*, and Rose Abel Wright observes that while mellow enough in its presentations of Roundheads and Cavaliers, "the play is, nevertheless, quite ruthless in its exposure of the utter inanity of the two London fops, who give a view of the empty fashionable life of the capital city."[6] That some of the vice in society is a function of the nature of society is clear; it seems equally clear that by no means all is.

Shirley Strum Kenny, in her important article on "humane" comedy, regards hypocrisy as the most castigated vice in the transitional period of the 1690s and early 1700s: hypocrites "are treated harshly, perhaps more severely than most of their Restoration forbears, for hypocrisy is, after all, an affront to good nature."[7] This is, however, not true of Shadwell, and helps to distinguish him from, say, Farquhar. While the fop Sir Nicholas is the product of social affectation according to Major General Blunt in *The Volunteers* (5.1.164), Mrs. Hackwell and Nickum are hypocrites to disguise their illnature. Hypocrisy is not only a product of trying to measure up to corrupt social roles but also a means to achieve dangerously antisocial personal desires. Indeed, a kind of hypocrisy may actually be a good thing. Sir Timothy is actually a coward who wishes to appear brave, and discovers in maintaining the appearance that he actually enjoys fighting—the consequence is that he vows at the end of the play to turn from a beau to a "Whore-master" (5.5.224). Since a beau is presumably less dangerous to society than a Whore-Master, Sir Timothy's shift from one satisfied with the appearance of

courage to genuine valor is actually bad for society. Self-approba-
tion, even when undeserved, may be necessary for the individual
to function in society. The virtuous Theodosia and Isabella in
The Lancashire Witches claim that individuals must lie to themselves about their own qualities in order to be happy:

> *Theodosia.* I would not live without vanity for the Earth; if every
> one could see their own faults, 'twould be a sad world.
> *Isabella.* Thou sayst right, sure the world would be almost depopu-
> lated, most men would hang themselves.
>
> (4.1.112)

Honest analysis of human nature reveals that the species is seriously flawed; vanity—self-deception—makes life bearable.

Maximillian E. Novak, in response to Kenny's article, says he
likes the term "sentimental" "to describe the kind of comedy
started by Shadwell." A part of what Novak describes as charac-
terizing this drama is applicable to Shadwell: "to move the audience, to 'touch' the hearts of those viewing the plays by depicting
scenes of 'Distress,'"[8] and it is certainly true that Mr. Rant's scene
with his son could not easily be imagined in Shadwell's earlier
plays. But a later remark by Novak shows how different Steele
and Shadwell are:

> A clever, witty rascal would seem out of place in Steele's comic
> world. Even self-interest calls the moral scheme into question. After
> Shaftesbury, the self-interest that was accepted as the governing force
> in human nature gives way to a social world in which everyone, if
> rightly guided, would be capable of displaying his virtues.[9]

Presumably when the worthy Major General Blunt says, "No man
does good but to please himself" (5.3.195), this can be taken
as an example of Shaftesburian "self-approving joy," and hence
would not refute Novak's argument if it were to be applied to
Shadwell.[10] On the other hand, Mrs. Hackwell and Nickum are
clever and witty rascals in *The Volunteers* who take self-interest
as the only standard. Likewise, Tope in *The Scowrers* is a frank
hedonist who possesses wit and self-control. These characters
are carefully presented as unattractive, but then, with the possible exceptions of Bruce and Longvil in *The Virtuoso* and Rains
and Bevil in *Epsom Wells,* such characters are always presented
as unattractive in Shadwell.

Shadwell's late comedies are more "humane" than his early
comedies in that even fools such as Belfond Senior, Wachum,

and Sir Nicholas are not objects of contempt in the way that Fribble and Bisket are in *Epsom Wells*. But this is not a consequence of an altered conception about human nature; the same character types are present in plays throughout Shadwell's career, and there are neither major formal changes in the structures of the plays, nor explicit remarks in the dialogues to indicate a major shift in Shadwell's beliefs about human nature. I am not claiming that Shadwell's plays are all of a kind. In the next chapter I shall examine *Epsom Wells* and *The Virtuoso*, which are different from the rest of Shadwell's comedies in that they contain no exemplars and only dubious reformations. Moreover, as I shall discuss later in this chapter, benevolent paternal figures become increasingly important in Shadwell's plays starting in the 1680s.

Aside from not portraying ethics as founded on innate goodness or sympathy, religion has only a limited role as a source of ethical obligation for Shadwell. The conclusions of two of Shadwell's plays invite belief in a providential order. The king in *The Royal Shepherdesse* says "How mercifull is Heaven; who would be bad / When Vertue's thus rewarded in distress?" (1.5.169). Heaven brings about a happy ending where the virtuous are united with their loved ones and the wicked are punished. In *The Libertine*, after society has failed miserably in its attempts to control Don John, heaven hauls him off to perdition and the statue has the last word: "Thus perish all / Those men, who by their words and actions dare, / Against the will and power of Heav'n declare" (3.5.91).

While I would accept that both plays allow the audience a divine superego who serves as a final safeguard on virtue and vice, I would also argue that these plays have limited applicability to Shadwell's "realistic" social comedies.

The Royal Shepherdesse is Shadwell's adaptation of John Fountain's unstaged drama of 1661, *The Rewards of Vertue*. Part of the appeal of the play to Shadwell must have been its moral purity. As he says in his introduction to the reader,

> I shall say little more of the Play, but that the Rules of Morality and good Manners are strictly observed in it: (Vertue being exalted, and Vice depressed) and perhaps it might have been better received had neither been done in it: for I find, it pleases most to see Vice incouraged, by bringing the Characters of debauch'd People upon the Stage, and making them pass for fine Gentlemen, who openly profess Swearing, Drinking, Whoring, breaking Windows, beating Constable,

etc. and that is esteem'd among us, a Gentile gayety of Humour, which
is contrary to the Customs and Laws of all civilized Nations.

(1.100)

This is of course Shadwell's common refrain about the immorality of the stage and its celebration of heroes who are a threat to
civil order. Still, the play did run for six nights and, according
to Pepys, emptied the king's playhouse with its competing production of Fletcher's *The Faithful Shepherdesse*. Thus, Shadwell
is perhaps exaggerating his audience's preference for representations of vice. Moreover, Shadwell's substantive additions increase the stage time of the low plot and lessen the efficacy of
divine justice as a controlling force on the wicked, which tend
to undercut Fountain's celebration of divine providence.

Shadwell himself says about his additions that "I have added
little to the Story, onely represented that in Action, which was
expressed by him [Fountain] in long Narratives" (1.99). Thus the
plot of Neander and Geron to entrap the queen and the priest is
revealed in dialogue in Shadwell's version, while it is merely
recounted as a part of Neander and Geron's confession, read by
a Lord in Fountain's play. Shadwell also adds a sword fight between Pyrrhus and Endymion not present in the original play,
and two song-and-dance numbers: the first involving some shep-
herds, the second a sacrifice to Mars by priests. The largest casu-
alty from Fountain's play is a nine-page scene between Cleantha
and the priest in which Cleantha defends loving those of a lower
social station (she is a princess, Endymion a "worthy Lord of
small Fortune") and the priest attacks the idea as both sinful and
imprudent. Shadwell's reason for cutting this scene was no doubt
the fact that it is repetitive and dramatically unnecessary, since
one knows from the conventions of pastoral drama that when
everyone else is taken Cleantha and Endymion will marry. If a
member of the audience knew the original play, they might well
think that Shadwell wanted to limit the impact of Cleantha's
defense of virtue independent of role; there is no evidence to
suggest, however, that the original was well known and arguing
from what is not present in a play is probably a dubious proce-
dure. One element that is eliminated as well from the Fountain
version is a brief flash of anticlericalism. When the priest says
that Cleantha is acting immodestly, she rounds on him and says
"know I may love Endymion, and yet talk of Innocence and Modesty, much more than you of civility."[11] The priest apologizes for
his presumption. Since in other Shadwell plays there is a strain

of anticlericalism, it is perhaps interesting to note that he avoids an opportunity to include it here, probably because it occurs in a lengthy scene he had already decided to cut.

But the largest change in the play is the expansion of the role of Neander. In both versions Neander is a cowardly, lecherous rascal, but he is on stage much longer in Shadwell. The opening scene of both plays reveals Neander's cowardice, but Shadwell has him attack "honour" explicitly. When Pyrrhus defends their current war by saying, "The honour of our Country lies at stake," Neander replies,

> Honour! The Fools Paradise, a bait
> For Coxcombs that are poor, and cannot have
> Pleasure and Ease; but sell their Wretched lives
> (That are not worth the keeping) for that Trifle
> *Honour;* the breath of a few Giddy People.
>
> (1.1.104)

This speech would seem to enforce the necessity of belief in divine justice and punishment, since Neander is not restrained by the customary obligations of rank.

However, Shadwell also adds a scene after Neander and Geron are caught and sentenced to death that indicates Neander has no fear of divine retribution in the next life:

Priest. Peace, stupid Wretches, I command you: and confess, and repent of your most horrid Crimes.
Neander. Well, Sir, I have done; and do confess from the bottom of my heart—O you old dry, raw-bon'd, wretched, decrepit Cuckold you, to bring me to this.
Priest. Heav'n! what impiety is this?
Geron. Ay, Sir, you see his Devotion? O! Villainous wicked man.
Priest. Sir! hold your Tongue! my Lord, 'tis time now to be sensible of your sad condition.
Geron. Ay, Sir! so it is, if you knew as much as I do of his wickedness, you'd say so.
Neander. Well, Sir! I do confess, I'le torment the Rogue   [*aside*
I have many sins to repent of—First—I have been naught with that old Fellow's wife.
Priest. The Gods forgive you.
Geron. What do I hear? Hell and Furies!
Priest. Do you repent of it?
Neander. Yes, Sir; it was a horrid Crime.
Geron. O Villain! I'le be reveng'd of him! it was a horrid Crime

indeed; 'twas Incest, for he is my Son, about five or six and twenty
years ago, his Mother and I were a little familiar.
Priest. O impious men! you are too near of kin in wickedness.

(1.5.162)

The only thing Neander repents is trusting Geron. Nor does he
hesitate to add to his sins even though he expects to die shortly
(in fact, in the general happiness at the end, Geron and Neander's
sentences are commuted to banishment). The only control on a
character like Neander is the civil authority, the wise "Lord of
the Councel" who threatens the villains with tortures until they
confess (1.5.154). The claim that this scene is added for comic
effect is undoubtedly true, but that does not change the sub-
stance of their exchange; the Gods are present in pastoral ro-
mances as a generic convention, and that does not invalidate the
presentation of divine providence either. But divine providence
in this play, at least with Neander and Geron, operates through
very mundane agents.

The single most interesting addition in the play is a speech on
justice that Cleantha makes. When Evadne informs Cleantha that
the queen has been cleared of charges, Cleantha says,

> I did expect no less: the Gods had been
> Unjust to have left such Vertue in distress,
> They had injur'd too themselves, as well as her:
> For should such Innocence as hers not be
> Protected: their Altars would be empty,
> 'Tis Justice makes 'em Deities.

(1.5.156)

This is, of course, the claim made by the Cambridge Platonists
and Shaftesbury that virtue is independent of God's will; that is,
we have a notion of Justice that is antecedent to our notion of
God, for if God ordained something that was unjust, God would
be a demon rather than a deity. Thus, the proof that the Gods are
just is that the queen is cleared. If she were not, it would not be
evidence that she was in fact guilty, but that the Gods were unjust
and hence not Gods.

Shadwell, then, is rejecting in *The Royal Shepherdesse* a view
of Christianity, shared by Protestants like Luther and Catholics
like Pascal, that morality exists only because God has willed it.
Moreover, true hardened villains like Neander and Geron are
clearly not restrained by fear of divine retribution, but are
stopped by ordinary, earthly mechanisms of detection and pun-

ishment. So even within this play, the role of God is finally as a kind of overseer who assures the providential happy ending. In Shadwell's comedies it is typically the wit of the heroes and heroines that guarantees the happy ending, and God is even less important to the maintenance of ethical standards.

In *The Libertine*, however, justice is clearly left in divine hands because human hands are inadequate. The problem is that, although Rose A. Zimbardo may see the play as "a Bosch-like nightmare vision of reality,"[12] many readers have found the play comic rather than a convincing lesson in divine justice. Charles Edward Whitmore noticed that the presence of the cowardly servant Jacomo and the lack of seriousness in the presentation of the supernatural tend to destroy any capacity to take the end seriously, although he assumes that this is simple ineptitude.[13] The comic servant, of course, was not created by Shadwell, but is present in all seventeenth-century versions of the legend, from Tirso de Molina's *El Burlador de Sevilla y convidado de piedra*, through Dorimon's and Villier's identically titled *Le Festin de Pierre ou le fils criminel*, to Molière's *Dom Juan*. And the comic servant highlights an important point about the seventeenth-century dramatizations of Don Juan. All of these plays are partially comical, as Oscar Mandel points out, and the legend moved easily to the *commedia dell-arte*.[14] The seductions engineered by the seventeenth-century Don Juan are frequently closer to Flashman's style than they are to James Bond's.

Langbaine's comment on the play is interesting: "This Play, if not regular, is at least diverting: which according to the Opinion of some of our First-Rate Poets, is the End of Poetry."[15] Langbaine stresses the entertainment value of the play and, in his comment that the play is "not regular," presumably draws attention to the fact that the play does not seem much like the "tragedy" its title page says it is. Several critics have drawn attention to the comic elements in *The Libertine*. Mandel describes the play as a "bizarre comedy," although he perhaps gets carried away when he compares it to Raskolnikov's vision "of Atheism unleashing the brute passions of man." [16] Robert Hume calls the play a "sardonic mock-tragedy" and says "The result is a diverting travesty of the libertine philosophy and moral code."[17] Michael Neill argues that while the play is "nominally a tragedy . . . its furiously unstable tone is frequently closer to that of black comedy."[18] He also points out that Shadwell has included deliberately parodic elements; thus, Betterton confronting the ghost of his father is reprising one of his most famous roles as Hamlet.

Coleridge, in the *Biographia Literaria* examines the Don Juan legend, and, although his remarks have wider applicability, all his examples are drawn from Shadwell. He makes what I think is a crucial point: "nothing of it belongs to the real world." That is, Don John is an abstraction of pure materialism: "Obedience to nature is the only virtue: the gratification of the passions and appetites her only dictate." Coleridge goes on to say that no one identifies with Don John, and that he is purely a fantasy figure. This does not mean the play has no intellectual content; indeed, the "moral lesson" of the play is what I have claimed is operating in *The Squire of Alsatia:*

> In fine the character of *Don John* consists in the union of every thing desirable to human nature, as *means*, and which therefore by the well known law of association become desirable on their own account. On their own account, and in their own dignity they are here displayed, as being employed to *ends* so unhuman, that in effect, they appear almost as *means* without an *end*. . . . [Many] are ready to receive the qualities of gentlemanly courage, and scrupulous honor (in all the recognized laws of honor,) as the *substitutes* of virtue, instead of the *ornaments*.[19]

Courage is not a virtue per se; it is only a virtue when applies to a worthy end. Hence Don John's materialism bars him from virtue because the only worthy ends available to the materialist are the satisfaction of appetites. Coleridge is claiming that Shadwell's moral purpose is not to dramatize a divine justice, but to take the libertine philosophy to its logical conclusion and show that it is horrific. The best modern analysis of the play remains John Loftis's, who sees it as a reductio ad absurdum of fashionable libertinism: Don John "represents an extreme embodiment, perhaps even a caricature, of moral qualities intermittently revealed, or allegedly revealed, by a score of young sparks of Restoration Comedy who, as libertines like him, were committed to the unscrupulous pursuit of women."[20] Don John is destroyed for the audience, not through the intervention of God, but by being rendered absurd.

Nonetheless, Shadwell does provide the possibility of a divine providence that, when all else fails, can supply the believer with a final court of appeal in the face of superhuman vice. No doubt some members of the audience were comforted by the thought, although the fact that the ghost is the instrument of divine vengeance would tend to undercut even this weak version of a divine guarantee of justice; it has perhaps been pointed out often enough in connection with *Hamlet* as not to need further elaboration here, that there isn't really any room in Protestant theology for ghosts—what appears to be a ghost can only be a demon in the absence of Purgatory as a holding ground for souls of middling vice. Nor does disbelief in divine justice affect the theatrical effectiveness of the play; many disbelievers thought *The Omen* series of films very effective. In any case, *The Royal Shepherdesse* as pastoral romance, and *The Libertine* as horror show, share little affinity with Shadwell's realistic social comedies.

All classes are routinely shown using religion as a prop to mercantilist self-interest in the comedies. In *A True Widow*, Lady Cheatly willingly forswears herself when necessary, and the citizens' pairing of soul and money shows their incapacity to see any point in religion other than its pragmatic consequences:

> *Steward.* . . . Pray, Madam, consider your Soul.
> *1 Cit.* Ay, Madam, consider your Soul.
> *2 Cit.* And the payment of my money.
>
> (3.5.356)

In *The Volunteers*, Hackwell Senior, a colonel in the revolutionary forces turned stockjobber, rejects his son as vicious and regards social virtues as meaningless:

> *Hackwell Sr.* I have [a son], what then, wou'd he had Grace.
> *Welford.* I don't know what you call Grace; but he has as much Vertue and Honour, as any Gentleman living.
> *Hackwell Sr.* Vertue and Honour will bring him but to Hell.
>
> (5.1.175)

Characters in Shadwell who make explicit statements indicating religious belief are invariably the object of satire.

This presents a problem, however. Lord Bellamy, the exemplary character of *Bury Fair*, compares religious belief to social affectation, summing up what virtuous characters in Shadwell seem to believe: "There are those things in Bury [wit and breeding], but as 'tis in Religion; least among those who talk of them most" (4.1.310). The absence of positive statements of religious belief does not demonstrate the absence of religious belief, at least among those who do not deny it. Still, there are indications that Shadwell's Christian piety was a subject of debate.

As Susan Staves points out, no hero in Shadwell ever reforms after talking to a preacher: this might appear to offer at least some evidence that religion is not the foundation of moral behavior.[21] This is not a strong indication, however, since, so far as I know, no character in Restoration comedy ever reforms after talking to a preacher. There were, of course, limits as to how far Shadwell could go in expressing dissatisfaction with religion as the source of morality. He defends the presentation of the witches as possessing real power in *The Lancashire Witches*, not only on dramatic grounds, but as necessary to escape attacks from the devout:

> For the Actions, if I had not represented them as those of real Witches, but had show'd the ignorance, fear, melancholy, malice, confederacy, and imposture that contribute to the beleif of Witchcraft, the people had wanted diversion, and there had been another clamor against it, it would have been called Atheistical.
>
> (4.101)

But there is some evidence to suggest that Shadwell was not devout. He was the subject of a pamphlet war in which he was accused of being both an atheist and a papist.[22] Again, this is not reliable testimony, since it may be no more than a political attack—after all, Dryden was also accused of being an atheist by political enemies. Yet there is the tantalizing reference in Shadwell's will to the most important source in the period for a rejection of religious ethics:

> Item I give to my sonne John five pounds for mourning and my Latin and philosophicall bookes with Mr. Hobbes his workes warning him to have a care of some ill opinions of his concerning government but hee may make excellent use of what is good in him.[23]

And Tom D'Urfey's attack on Shadwell in *Sir Barnaby Whigg* presents him as changing religions at the drop of a hat.

Hume dates *The Lancashire Witches* as premiering around September 1681 and *Sir Barnaby Whigg* around October 1681.[24] If these dates are accurate, then most of *Sir Barnaby Whigg* was presumably written prior to the production of *The Lancashire Witches*. Nonetheless, D'Urfey clearly draws attention to his attacks on Shadwell, and presumably the play was modified in response to *The Lancashire Witches*. D'Urfey's dedication complains that "in this Age 'tis not a Poets Merit, but his Party that must do his business; so that if his Play consist of a Witch, a Devil, or a Broomstick, so he have but a Priest at one end of the Play, and a Faction at 'tother end of the Pit, it shall be fam'd for an excellent piece."[25] Aside from this unfavorable catalog of the dramatic elements of *The Lancashire Witches*, D'Urfey's cast list describes Sir Walter Wiseacre, one of the play's butts, as "An opinionated Fool and Cuckold: A Lancashire-Knight and in Love with Livia"; the character is typical of many conceited fools in Restoration comedy, but the fact that he is from Lancashire and is "opinionated" presumably satirizes Shadwell's Sir Edward Hartford, who, it is true, does have a tendency to lecture people on their duty.

But the chief attack on Shadwell is by way of the title character who identifies himself in a wickedly amusing song:

> Farewell my Lov'd Science, my former delight,
> Moliere is quite rifled, then how should I write?
> My fancy's grown sleepy, my quibbling is done;
> And design and invention, alas! I have none.
> But still let the Town never doubt my condition;
> Though I fall a damn'd Poet, I'le mount a Musician.
>
> I got Fame by filching from Poems and Plays,
> But my Fidling and Drinking have lost me the Bays;
> Like a Fury I rail'd, like a Satyr I writ,
> Thersite my Humour, and Fleckno my Wit.
> But to make some amends for my snarling and lashing
> I divert all the Town with my Thrumming and Thrashing.
>
> (28)

The references to Shadwell's pride in his musicianship, his drinking, his frequent reliance in his early career on sources for his plays, and MacFleckno indicate that Sir Barnaby is Shadwell.[26] He is also described several times as a "huge fat fellow" in reference to Shadwell's celebrated girth. The two male leads also comment on his political activity:

> *Benedict.* If I mistake not, this fellow values himself extremely by playing on the Musick.
> *Wilding.* Oh yes, but the Town of late has us'd him so unkindly, that he has left it off, and now sets up for a grand Politician.
>
> (10)

And Dryden's charge of dullness is reiterated when Sir Barnaby writes propaganda for the whigs:

> *Sir Barnaby.* . . . there's the Paper with all the Wise mens hands too't—Now read, and then judge; the wit and method I compos'd my self.

Wilding. —Wit—why thou double Traytor, dar'st thou assasinate
that too—thou contrary to Wit as Loyalty.

(19)

Throughout the play, then, the audience is reminded that Sir
Barnaby is a caricature of Shadwell, which makes Sir Barnaby's
attitude toward religion of particular interest.

At one point in the play Sir Barnaby turns from Puritan to
Anglican when he sees an advantage in it (39–41). But the most
amazing flexibility is shown when a servant, disguised as priest,
tells Sir Barnaby that a Bassa's widow, possessed of ten thousand
pounds, has converted to Catholicism but is in danger of
marrying a Protestant. To prevent that, the sham priest seeks a
potential suitor and asks Sir Barnaby what religion he is. Sir
Barnaby replies, "What Religion am I? hum? why, faith to tell
thee the truth, Father, I am—hum—Of what Religion am I, d'you
say?" (48). Then a letter comes saying the Bassa's widow has
reconverted and can only marry a "Musselman." Sir Barnaby is
undeterred:

> *Turk!* Well, well, since it can't be help't, I'le turn *Turk*, man, *Jew,*
> *Moor, Graecian,* any thing; Pox on't, I'le not lose a Lady, and such a
> sum for the sake of any Religion under the Sun, by *Mahomet* not I.
> (50)

Sir Barnaby is discovered in his disloyalty to the throne and
religion and is ultimately taken off to be executed. As closely as
Sir Barnaby is tied to Shadwell, it seems clear that D'Urfey
thought Shadwell's religious beliefs were an area where he was
vulnerable to satire.

As a working dramatist, however, Shadwell was limited in
what he could present on stage. Passages dealing with the role
of religion in society in Shadwell's most explicit play on the
subject, *The Lancashire Witches*, were expunged from production by Charles Killigrew, Master of the Revels, because Killigrew
thought the play was an attack on the Anglican church. This may
be the best evidence of Shadwell's heterodoxy; Shadwell's friend
Langbaine, as I shall discuss in chapter 5, also thought the play
an attack on the Anglican church.

What Shadwell could do, however, was print and dislocate.
The Lancashire Witches was printed with the expunged sections
highlighted in italics, and *The Amorous Bigotte* is set in Spain.
The latter play attacks the suppression of individual freedom
through parental authority and the power of the church. Rosania,

one of the two heroines, is threatened with the convent if she disobeys: "Must I be buried while alive with Melancholy and Green-sickness'd Nuns? (5.5.63). Further, the church has the power of the confessional to discover attempts to escape its power. Belliza, Rosania's aunt, suspecting that Rosania has fallen in love, threatens her with confession:

> *Belliza.* You Mrs. Malepert, I hear you have not been at Confession this fortnight: I will make you confess, Huswife, to Father Tegue who will be here soon: withdraw and prepare yourself for it.
> *Rosania.* Why shou'd Old fellows know the Secrets of the Young? But it must be so, I cannot help it.
>
> (5.2.32)

Some of the attacks on religion in *The Amorous Bigotte* are nontransferable to Protestantism. Fornication and its concomitants are not really something to worry about for a Catholic, in Shadwell's view, since the sins are forgivable in those who love the church. In a very amusing scene, Tegue explains why the bawd Gremia is not seriously culpable for running her brothel and, indeed, performs a social service:

> *Tegue.* I believe dou art a good Laady, and dosht love de Church, vel joy, as dou shayst every one cannot Marry; and Fornicaation is Venial but vee vil pass by some Peccadillo's as Shwearing, Wenching, and Lying and de like; in dose who love de Church indeed. Are dese young Gentlewomen handsome dat dou dosht breed up for de Occaasions of de young Cavaliers Joy[?]
> *Gremia.* The very Parragons of the City, and they Dance with Castanietto's most Charmingly and Sing to the Guittar most Melodiously.
> *Tegue.* By my Shoul, a shivil and a good Pious Voman, and I vil go vid a good Priesht my Friend a gallant Man indeed, and vee vil Fornicate and Absolve, Absolve and Fornicate by turns every day at her House.
>
> (5.2.31)

Shadwell's attack on Catholicism is, of course, not remarkable for an English Protestant. Dryden and Crowne both attack Catholicism for supposedly allowing sexual license.

In Dryden's *The Spanish Friar* (1680), the title character serves as a go-between for Lorenzo and the unhappily married Elvira. Dominic's power as a confessor to absolve Elvira of her sins is used by her as one of the justifications for her attempted adultery: "—never woman had such a husband to provoke her, such a lover to allure her, or such a confessor to absolve her. Of what am I afraid, then? Not my conscience, that's safe enough; my ghostly father has given it a dose of church-opium, to lull it."[27] Catholic casuistry justifies adultery as a venial sin in comparison to the mortal sin of allowing Lorenzo to die of love, according to Dominic: "Remember, that adultery, though it be a silent sin, yet it is a crying sin also. Nevertheless, if you believe absolutely he will die, unless you pity him; to save a man's life is a point of charity; and actions of charity do alleviate, as I may say, and take off from the mortality of the sin" (2.451). Lorenzo reduces religion to merely an artifice that enables the priesthood to achieve what priests desire: "He preaches against sin; why? because he gets by it: He holds his tongue; why? because so much more is bidden for his silence" (2.454). As with Tegue, religion does not provide moral standards but justifies before the fact whatever desires the individual has.

Similarly, in John Crowne's *The English Friar* (1690), Father Finical, attempting to seduce the maid Pancy explains at great length that Catholic teleology tolerates occasional failings on the part of the priesthood:

> 'Tis certainly most lawful to circumvent a dangerous enemy by all frauds, it has ever been a holy strategem o' priests to pretend to more power over the flesh, than perhaps mortal man can attain in this life; thereby religiously to deceive the world into a bold contest with a seeming baffl'd foe; whereas if we marry we confess the enemy cannot be conquer'd, the flesh wou'd prevail, and we shou'd fall into contempt. We therefore, to keep ourselves in veneration, carry saint-like chastity, or at least the image of it before us.[28]

Since the end of chastity is laudable despite being unattainable, priests justify their hypocrisy as a necessary lie. The play implicitly attacks priestly celibacy as leading to fraud, and Thomistic morality as claiming that the ends justify the means.

However, what got Shadwell into trouble was pairing Tegue with an Anglican chaplain, Smerk, in *The Lancashire Witches*. Tegue clearly stands as an emblem of how Catholicism has warped morality so that clerical marriage is a mortal sin while fornication is venial: "Art thou in love Joy? by my shoule dou dosht Comitt fornicaation; I vill tell you it is a veniall Sinn, and I vill after be absolving you for it; but if dou dosht Comitt Marriage, it is mortall, and dou vilt be damn'd and bee fait and trot. I predee now vill dou fornicat and not Marry: for my shaak now vilt dou fornicate" (4.4.161). Tegue has no interest in Susan, the object of Smerk's raptures due to a love potion she has given Smerk; Tegue's target is the wealthy and foolish Lady Shacklehead. Thus, Tegue's comment is a specific attack on Catholic doctrine by Shadwell rather than an example of priestly hypocrisy. But Shadwell presumably was censored for linking Smerk and Tegue through Smerk's willingness to accept Catholic teachings on purgatory, transubstantiation, and "The Presbyterian Plot" (4.3.143 and 4.4.161). Although this willingness to accept Catholic doctrine clearly makes Smerk a special case, the censored sections of the play limit not only Smerk's authority but all clergymen's authority.

The Lancashire Witches is straightforward in the limitations it would place on all religion, including the Anglican church.[29] The play begins with a censored argument between Sir Edward and his chaplain Smerk. Smerk is prying into Sir Edward's business: "You now, Sir, are become one of my Flock: / And I am bound in Conscience to Advise, / And search into the troubles of your Spirit, / To find the secrets that disturb your Mind" (4. 1. 105). Sir Edward rebukes him for his presumption: "Your Father is my Taylor, you are my Servant. / And do you think a Cassock and a Girdle / Can alter you so much, as to enable / Yo[u] (who before were but a Coxcomb, Sir) / To teach me" (4. 1. 106). Smerk regards this as "Atheistical" but Sir Edward reiterates that Smerk's job is limited to religious functions: "Your orders separate, and set you apart / to Minister, that is to serve in Churches, / and not to domineer in Families" (4. 1. 106). Interference in civil affairs is as reprehensible as interference in the family: "The other world should be your care, not this. / A Plowman is as fit to be a Pilot, / as a good Clergy-man to be a Statesman, Sir" (4. 1. 108). The real power is in Sir Edward's hands; when he lays down the law to Smerk, Smerk at least pretends to fall into line to save his job. But even a "good Clergy-man" should not interfere either in the family or the commonwealth.

When members of the clergy attempt anything more than to uphold the social order by preaching honesty to the servants, they are guilty of Catholic abuses. Sir Edward, still in the censored opening of act 1, makes the charge explicit:

> Vain was our Reformation, if we still
> Suffer auricular Confession here,
> by which the Popish Clergy rule the world,

No business in my Family shall concern you;
Preach nothing but good life and honesty.

(4.1.108)

Isabella, when Smerk is attempting to woo her, storms at his claim that personal and social equality is conferred on him by his office:

Smerk. My function yet, I say, deserves more reverence.
Isabella. Does it make you not an Ass, or not a Taylors Son?
Smerk. It equals me with the best of the Gentry.
Isabella. How, Arrogance? Can any power give honour but the Kings? This is Popery, I'll have you trounced.

(4.2.122)

Sir Edward and Isabella reject Smerk's claims partially because of his lack of social position—the repeated sneering references to Smerk's father's occupation—but also because Smerk is an ill-educated fool, with only "small Logick, and Divinity" (4.1.106). Being a preacher does not make him the equal of those of the gentry who have sense and manners, since morality is a matter of common sense rather than a religious mystery requiring special interpretation:

Isabella. And may they [divines] make love to the Daughter, without the consent of the Father?
Smerk. Undoubted, as Casuists must determine.
Isabella. Will not common sence, without a casuist, tell us when we do wrong, if so, the Law we are bound to, is not plain enough.

(4.2.121)

The clergy are not needed to interpret morality for the well-educated and well-born.

Sir Edward's desire to remove religion from affairs of state and the family leaves him open to Smerk's charge that he and the young heroes, Bellfort and Doubty, are "Hobbists and Atheists" (4.3.144). Thomas B. Stroup argues that we should regard this as Shadwell's view of the characters as well, since Stroup regards Sir Edward's final speech in the play as a Hobbesian denial of freewill:[30] "Design whate'er we will, / There is a fate which over-rules us still" (4.5.188). Stroup ignores, however, Sir Edward's denial of the charge: "Incorrigible ignorance! 'tis such as you are Atheistical, that would equal the Devils power with that of Heaven it self" (4.1.113). Further, Bellfort and Doubty do praise some clergymen who, unlike Smerk, believe in the Popish plot. Still, Sir Edward's rebuttal is an appeal to logic rather than an assertion of piety, and Doubty and Bellfort's admiration of the Church of England men who believe in the Popish plot emphasizes the praiseworthy political consequences of their actions: "the true and wise Church of England-men believe it, and are a great Rock against the Church of Rome" (4.3.144).Certainly nothing in the play indicates that any of the three male leads treats religion as anything other than a social form.

Sir Edward's attack on atheism does not necessarily indicate belief in religion as anything other than a useful aid to order. Thomas Otway's *The Atheist*, for instance, defends religion on social grounds.[31] Daredevil, the atheist to whom the title refers, is only an atheist because it is fashionable. After Beaugard and Courtine have satirized wits, Courtine inquires what Beaugard thinks of that subclass of wits, the atheists; Beaugard responds with a description of Daredevil:

> By this good Light, thou hast prevented me: I have one for thee of that Kind, the most inimitable Varlet, and the most insufferable Stinkard living; one that has Doubts enow to turn to all Religions, and yet would fain to pretend to be of none: In short, a Cheat, that would have you of opinion that he believes neither heav'n nor Hell, and yet never feels so much as an Ague-fit, but he's afraid of being damn'd.[32]

Nevertheless, Beaugard is fond of Daredevil because, "to give the Devil his due, he is seldom Impertinent; but, barring his Darling-Topick, Blasphemy, a Companion pleasant enough" (1.309).

Beaugard's tolerance for Daredevil's folly is partially explainable from Beaugard's own lack of religious belief. We know long before Daredevil is introduced that Beaugard regards religion as a social form from a conversation with his father:

Father. . . .What Religion are you of?—hah?—
Beaugard. Sir, I hope you took care, after I was born to see me Christen'd.
Father. Oh Lord! Christen'd! Here's an Atheistical Rogue, thinks he has Religion enough, if he can but call himself a Christian!
Beaugard. Why, Sir, would you have me disown my Baptism?
Father. No, Sirrah: but I would have you own what sort of Christian you are though.
Beaugard. What sort, Sir?
Father. Ay, Sir; What sort, Sir.
Beaugard. Why, of the honestest sort.

Father. As if there were not Knaves of all sorts!

Beaugard. Why then, Sir, if that will satisfie you, I am of your sort.

Father. And that, for ought you know, may be of no sort at all.

Beaugard. But, Sir, to make short of the matter, I am of the Religion of my Country, hate Persecution and Penance, love Conformity, which is going to Church once a Month, well enough; resolve to make this transitory Life as pleasant and delightful as I can; and for some sober Reasons best known to my self, resolve never to marry.

(1.301)

I have quoted this passage at length because it is, I believe, as close to a statement of agnosticism as Otway can allow a comic hero. When first questioned, Beaugard talks of his baptism. Then he repeats the question to gain time. Still attempting to avoid an argument he assures his father that he is of his sort. Finally, he avows only a positive belief in the customs of Anglicanism because they are unlikely to breed contention. He then turns his father's attention back to Beaugard's refusal to marry, which immediately sidetracks his father from his inquiries about Beaugard's religion. Beaugard loves "Conformity," the easy acceptance of his country's religion, because that is most likely to lead to a pleasant life.

This acceptance of traditional obligations in religion is mirrored in his acceptance of obligations toward honor and his father. Beaugard and Courtine recognize clearly that duels are an irrational behavior:

Courtine. Nay, when Cuckolds or Brothers fight for the Reputation of a back-sliding Wife or Sister, it is a very pretty Undertaking, doubtless. As for example; I am a Cuckold now.

Beaugard. All in good time, Ned; do not be too hasty.

Courtine. And being much troubled in Spirit, meeting with the Spark that has done me the Honour, with a great deal of respect I make my Address-as thus,—*Most Noble Sir, you have done me the Favour to lie with my Wife.*

Beaugard. Very well.

Courtine. All I beg of you, is, that you would do your best endeavour to run me through the Guts to morrow morning, and it will be the greatest Satisfaction in the World.

Beaugard. Which the good-natur'd Whoremaster does very decently; so down falls the Cuckold at *Barn-Elms,* and rises again next day at *Holborn* in a Ballad.

(2.320–21)

Nonetheless, when challenged to a duel by he knows not whom,

Beaugard's only response is to ask Daredevil if he is willing to be a second (3.336). Gentlemen fight duels because if they didn't, they would not be gentlemen.

Equally, Beaugard will monetarily support his father even though there is no obligation in nature nor has his father's behavior merited his support. Conception is done to please the father and hence confers no obligation. Further, Beaugard's father turns him out of doors at an early age penniless, because Beaugard calls his father's mistress a whore (1.299). Over the course of the play, the father even fights on the opposite side of Beaugard because Beaugard has refused him money for gambling. Yet at the end of the play, as long as the father promises to leave off gambling, Beaugard promises to supply him with money for wine, tobacco, beef, and wenches (5.397–98). Beaugard's treatment of his father is specifically tied to his attitude toward religion:

> Courtine. Methoughts, as I look'd into the Room, he [Beaugard's father] ratled the Box with a great deal of Grace, and swore half a dozen Rappers very youthfully.
> Beaugard. Prithee no more on't, tis an irreverent Theme; and next to Atheism, I hate making merry with the Frailties of my Father.
> (2.313)

Beaugard insists on respect for religion and his father, even though neither, from anything we are shown in the play, deserves it. The reason he does so is that religion and family are necessary fictions, mechanisms that help to prevent social chaos. Shadwell is by no means as bleak as Otway in his attitude toward human nature. But religion in both *The Atheist* and *The Lancashire Witches*, even though they are written from opposite sides of the political debate of the early 1680s, is valued as something that contributes to social order, and atheists are a threat because they jeopardize that order.

While it may be tempting to dismiss Tegue as a Catholic priest and Smerk as an exceptional case and hence argue that *The Lancashire Witches* does not attack the established church, we must remember that Killigrew did not see it that way and censored large sections of the play. Jeremy Collier's attack on the stage's treatment of the clergy suggests why Killigrew thought the play objectionable:

> The Satyr of the *Stage* upon the *Clergy* is extreamly particular. In other cases, They level at a single Mark, and confine themselves to Persons. But here their Buffoonry takes an unusual Compass; They

shoot Chain'd-shot, and strike at Universals. They play upon the *Character*, and endeavor to expose not only the Men, but the Business.[33]

This is true even when the attacks are made on Catholicism—Collier cites *The Spanish Friar* as an example.[34] (98–100). Indeed, Collier argues that attacks on any religion can be attacks on Christianity. Thus "The Author of *Don Sebastian* strikes at the *Bishops* through the sides of the *Mufti,* and borrows the Name of the *Turk,* to make the *Christian* ridiculous. He knows the transition from one Religion to the other is natural, the application easy, and the audience but too well prepared."[35] Collier is a polemicist and exaggerating his case, but he was an intelligent man, familiar with many of the plays of the Restoration, and his comments should be taken seriously.

Congreve made the obvious rebuttal to Collier by arguing that Collier was confusing satire on the failings of individual priests with satire on the institution. Collier responds that attacks on individuals are likely to be interpreted as an attack on their professions as well: "Though the Function and the Person are separable in Notion, they are Joyn'd in Life and Business. . . . If you make the Man a Knave, the Priest must suffer under the Imputation: And a Fool in his *Person* will never be thought discreet in his Function."[36] In the case of Shadwell, though Collier does not comment on him in particular, Isabella's and Sir Edward's repeated sneers at Smerk's birth are examples of one of the stage's worst abuses of the clergy—its refusal to accept that ordination made a clergyman a gentleman: "The *Priest-hood* is the profession of a Gentleman. A *Parson* notwithstanding the ignorant Pride of some People, is a name of Credit, and Authority, both in Religion and *Law.* The *Addition* of *Clerk* is at least equal to that of Gentleman.[37] In my view then, *The Lancashire Witches* is what Killigrew and Langbaine apparently thought it was: a rejection of organized religion as the source of ethical obligation except as it contributes to social stability.

The most frequently cited passage in all of Shadwell's works is Bruce, in *The Virtuoso,* quoting Lucretius admiringly and saying "Thou reconcil'st Philosophy with Verse, and dost, almost alone, demonstrate that Poetry and Good Sence may go together" (3.1.105). The passage in question is a denial that God concerns himself with the affairs of this world:

> Omnis enim per se Divum Natura necesse est,
> Immortali aevo summa cum pace fruator,

Semota a nostris Rebus, sejunctaque longe,
Nam privata dolore omni, privata pericilis,
Ipsa suis pollens opibus, nihil indiga nostri,
Nec bene promeritis capitur, nec tangitur ira.[38]

Alssid claims that the Lucretian reference is important because it illustrates man's inability to know nature, which is in conflict with "the Cartesian belief that nature's mysteries may ultimately be revealed, or so the wits implicitly believe; between man and nature stands an insurmountable and (in the nature of things) necessary barrier." Alssid's view is that Sir Nicholas is an object of satire partially because he is "tampering with nature's secrets."[39]

The quotation, however, has nothing to do with any such epistemological skepticism, but is a straightforward claim that God is indifferent to human concerns. Sir Nicholas is contemptible for Alssid's second reason, that he neglects the practical in favor of the speculative. As Bruce says, "This foolish Virtuoso does not consider, that one Bricklayer is worth forty Philosophers' (3.14.159). The true study of man is man, while Sir Nicholas is "One who has broken his brains about the nature of Maggots; who has studi'd these twenty years to find out the several sorts of Spiders, and never cares for understanding Mankind" (3.1.113). Shadwell does not need any Lucretian reference for that; Joseph M. Gilde argues that Shadwell is not attacking members of the Royal Society because they, too, would have regarded Sir Nicholas's impracticality as contemptible.[40] Gilde may be mistaken in supposing that Shadwell was not attacking specific members— Hooke and others certainly thought he was being attacked[41]—but Charleton was both the popularizer of Epicurus and a member of the Royal Society.

The point of Epicureanism in the play is that no providential order guarantees a happy ending due to correct behavior, and this observation is repeated throughout Shadwell's corpus. This is an issue distinct from poetic justice; the good are almost always rewarded in Shadwell's plays. The world itself, on the other hand, shows no progress. Bellamy, in *Bury Fair*, is an exemplary character of impeccable manners and upright morality, who nonetheless recognizes that he cannot control the world: "What good does Wit and Sence do you? do what you can, the Fops will be at the top of Pleasures; and the Knaves will be at the head of all Business in spite of you; and will bear down the World, that a man who has Wit can be good for nothing" (4.3.337). His response is self-control, and a retreat from the world to his estate where he invites only those who share his tastes and background. But, like Sir William in *The Lancashire Witches*, he remains flexible when fate contradicts his choice in love; he switches easily from Gertrude to Philadelphia when he discovers that Gertrude loves Wildish and Philadelphia loves him.

Fate in Shadwell's plays is the luck of the draw that man cannot control and to which, in consequence, he must adjust. For instance, Major General Blunt's daughter Teresia, in *The Volunteers* is an idiot: "What Prodigy is this? Was ever a Creature so different from Father and Mother, and Sister; by the Lord Harry, I shall begin to believe the old Tales of Fairies changing Children in the Cradles" (5.1.166–67). Rather than worrying over it, Blunt resolves to marry her off and it costs him no anxiety. The individual is not, as Stroup supposes, the passive victim of fate; rather, the individual copes with the tricks fate plays on him or her, and if any character assumes there is a providential order that provides these accidents with meaning or purpose, none of them refers to it except in *The Royal Shepherdesse.*

But if Shadwell does except a classical notion of luck as playing a role in ethical behavior, it does not imply determinism, nor does his use of humors characters. In Shadwell's first play, *The Sullen Lovers*, individual passivity in the face of untoward circumstance is flatly condemned. At the beginning of the play, Stanford and Emilia simply complain about the fools that torment them. Over the course of the play they change to taking action. When Emilia complains that fate is against her, Stanford tells her that inaction is unacceptable:

> *Emilia.* 'Twere vain presumption to hope for Liberty by Miracle; they will no more lose us, then an Attorny will a young Squire that's newly waded into Law; will be sure never to leave him, till he has brought him out of his depth.
> *Stanford.* By this rule you shou'd not resist a Man that comes to Ravish you, because he's like to be too strong for you; but if you did not use the means your honesty would be no more admir'd in that, then your Wisdom in this.

> (1.5.76)

Man's fate is not determined by his "humor"; humor limits the possibilities, but does not eliminate all possibility. Stanford in a rage tells his servant Roger to shut up, but Roger is right in summing up a key tenet in Shadwell when he tells Stanford, "Be patient Sir: *Seneca* advises to moderate our passions" (1.2.35).[42]

Indeed, Shadwell's plays could not be morally instructive if he did accept determinism. Brian Corman examines Shadwell's theory of humors and determines that Shadwell thinks a humor must be amendable to be an object of satire, although Corman argues that it is in members of the audience that this amelioration takes place.[43] I would only add that it also takes place in Stanford and Emilia. Man's freedom of action is not incompatible with Christianity, but Shadwell's indifference to providential order does not invite us to seek Christian explanations for vice and virtue in his plays.

Another indication of how Shadwell limits religion as a source of ethical obligation is that he does not regard parents as possessing a right to "dispose" of their children. Although parents and children have duties toward each other, the duties are both limited and conditional. The duty is not religious, nor "natural" in that parents or children have some sort of instinctive desire to serve each other; the plays show the relationship between parent and child to be an accident of nature where respect is earned and where duty on either side is secondary to questions of love and personal honor. That in itself is not terribly interesting; the same could be said for most playwrights of the Restoration. What is interesting is the extent to which Shadwell emphasizes it.

The nature of obligation between parents and children is an enormously complex issue in the Restoration. In outline, what happens is that parental authority is stripped of its divine sanction particularly in relation to marriage. Just as the divine right of kings is discredited, so too is the religious authority of parents, so that ultimately, a half a century later, writers as different as Fielding and Richardson assert that children have the right to choose whom they will marry based on affection.[44] But while patriarchal authority based on religious sanctions was dissipating, that same authority was reconstituted through the movement toward the companionate marriage and domesticity. As Randolph Trumbach says, "Domesticity . . . increased patriarchal control over women and children since men believed they could not love what they did not own.[45] Joseph Allen Boone in describing this shift introduces a key distinction: "On the one hand, anything *but* friendship in marriage was derided as tyranny; on the other, most contemporaries failed to realize that the shift from absolute patriarchal authority to a benevolent paternalism did not change the fundamental hierarchy of power in the marital estate."[46] Over the course of Shadwell's career, the benevolent

paternal figure becomes increasingly important, but the patriarchal figure whose authority is derived from religious obligation
is rejected.

For many in the seventeenth century, parental authority was
inextricably connected to revealed religion. After all, the fifth
commandment is "Honor thy Father and Mother." On the authority of the fifth commandment and scriptural citations, the frequently reprinted *Whole Duty of Man* states, "We owe them
[parents] an obedience in all things, unless where their commands are contrary to the commands of God."[47] When Sir Robert
Filmer in *Patriarcha* works to establish the divine right of kings,
he bases it on what he regards as an unarguable premise: "I see
not then how the children of Adam, or of any man else, can be
free from subjection to their parents. And this subordination of
children is the fountain of all royal authority, by the ordination of
God himself."[48] In *Observations on Aristotles Politiques*, Filmer
equates children with slaves: "Adam was the Father, King and
Lord over his family: a son, a subject and a servant or slave, were
one and the same thing at first; the Father had a power to dispose
or sell his children or servants" (188). Filmer was not alone in
this view. Gordon J. Schochet cites a number of examples from
Restoration political literature in which patriarchalism is pro-
posed as an alternative to Hobbes's contractual theory, which
asserts that a king's authority is derived from God bestowing
authority on Adam over his children.[49] Children are the property
of fathers according to one of Tillotson's sermons "Concerning
Family Religion": "And this certainly is the duty of fathers and
masters of families; and an essential part of religion, next to
serving GOD in our own persons, to be very careful that those
that belong to us do the same. For every man must not only give
an account of himself to GOD, but of those likewise that are
committed to his charge, that they do not miscarry through his
neglect."[50] The father's authority is so absolute that he is also
judged on the behavior of his property.

Nowhere is this insistence on a parent's divine authority more
stressed than in the case of marriage. A London broadside of
1662 entitled "An Admonition to all such as shall intend hereafter to enter the State of Matrimony Godly and Agreeably to
Lawes" lists three conditions and the forbidden degrees of marriage; the second condition is "that they make no secret con-
tracts, without consent or counsel of their Parents or Elders,
under whose authority they be, contrary to Gods Laws and mans
Ordinances." *The Whole Duty of Man* regards marriage without

consent as the chief act of disobedience a child can make: "But of all the acts of disobedience, that of Marrying against the consent of the Parent is one of the highest. Children are so much goods, the possesions of their parents, that they cannot without a kind of theft, give away themselves, without the allowance of those that have the right in them" (301–2). *The Ladies Calling* cites scripture to show that there are no acceptable excuses for marriage without consent:

> And this is one of the highest injuries they can do their parents, who have such a native right in them, that 'tis no less an injustice than disobedience to dispose of themselves without them. The right of the parent is so undoubted, that we find God himself gives way to it, and will not suffer the most holy pretense, no not that of a Vow, to invade it, as we see his own stating of the case, *Numb.* 30. How will he then resent it, to have his so indispensible a law violated upon the impulse of an impotent passion, an amorous inclination.[51]

Love is not a sufficient justification for acting in a manner contrary to parental authority. To disbelieve that parents have a divine authority does not indicate atheism; Locke claims that the tie between parents and children is a function of gratitude, respect, and the practical consideration that the father can leave his money where he pleases.[52] Locke's position is an example of religion, not being rejected, but being rendered irrelevant and this is what happens in Shadwell as well.

The title character in Molière's *L' Avare* is a greedy old fool, characteristics he shares with Goldingham in *The Miser*. But Molière provides nothing like Goldingham's closing curse on his son Theodore and new daughter-in-law Isabella:

> Goldingham.   Yes, I will give you my blessing.
> Isabella.   I shall receive it joyfully.
> Goldingham.   May all the curses e're attended Marriage fall on you.
> Isabella.   Oh impious wish.
> Theodore.   We are obliged to you Sir.
> Goldingham.   May invincible impotence possess you, raging Lust her, and tormenting jealousie both of ye.
> Justice.   For shame Neighbor, be not so wicked.
> Goldingham.   May the perpetual spirit of contention wait on ye, may ye never in your lives agree in one thing; may the name of quiet ne're be heard betwixt ye; and to compleat all, may ye never be asunder: and so Farwel.
>
> (2.5.89)

The chief reason why Goldingham's curse presumably does not carry much weight is the overwhelming power of love, the subject of Theodore's last speech in the play: "Now we have done, I must confess I have transgress'd in my duty to my Father, which I could not help; unless I would have neglected a greater, which I ought to your Beauty my *Isabella* and my Love; and I hope / My passion will a just excuse be thought / What is urg'd on by love, can be no fault" (2.5.93). This asks for a great deal of forgiveness from fathers in the audience; Theodore swindles his father out of six thousand pounds. But the play as a whole indicates that the duty of son to father is based on mutual obligation rather than any natural or religious hierarchy.

Both Isabella and Goldingham assert that a child owes a parent obedience. Isabella will not marry Theodore without the permission of her mother who, in turn, will not give it unless Goldingham bows out of his previous engagement to Isabella. Because her mother has not acted irrationally or ungenerously in the past, Isabella is obliged to act obediently; Goldingham has to be tricked by Cheatly into breaking the engagement before Isabella can marry whom she chooses. Goldingham, on the other hand, sees duty as purely extending from child to parent. He will marry Theodora to anyone who will take her without portion and regards it as "insolence" when she threatens to kill herself if he does (2.1.31). Goldingham is himself an opportunist associated with rebellion, which is how he made his fortune. Since familial obligation is limited to what his son and daughter owe him, a chance to save his fortune by disinheriting his son makes him willing to pretend loyalty to his country: "My loyalty is dearer to me than Son and Daughter, and all the Relations in the World; I will hang him, I'le to the King immediately" (2.4.70). Where obligations are not mutual, however, there is no obligation, as the parallel with the subplot of Bellamour and his brother makes clear.

Bellamour's brother, upon the death of their father, has "possess'd [himself] of the Estate, and has inhumanly put my Mother and Sister out of the house" (2.5.80). When Bellamour reveals to Isabella that he is her brother, he adds that their brother will find it out as well "To his great grief" (2.5.89). At this point Theodore finds out that his friend is also Isabella's brother, but that tie remains secondary to their real bond: "My dear brother, you are now doubly so, but friendship yet will be the stricter tie" (2.5.90). The established duties of family receive their sanction from individual obligation and responsibility. Blind acceptance leads to the plight of Tim, who woos Theodora because "'tis all one as long as my Father bid me ask you" (2.2.37); this entanglement with his bettters makes him only a convenient target for the disappointed Theodore.

The Miser is concerned throughout with what constitutes obligation. In the case of Robin and Cheatly, no more is needed than agreement:

> *Robin.* What say you Mrs. Cheatly, shall you and I marry, or continue to love on as we did?
> *Cheatly.* I am very indifferent Robin, take thy own choice.
> *Robin.* Why then as you were.
> *Cheatly.* Contented.
>
> (2.5.93)

Only the lower class can ignore social forms entirely, but that the relationship between parent and child is not founded on religion is emphasized very early in the play by Theodore:

> *Theodore.* Hold, Sister, I know as well as you that I depend [Scomatically] upon a Father, and that the name of Son, carries an inviolable Duty along with it.
> *Theodora.* But Brother—
> *Theodore.* And that I ought not to engage my heart without the consent of him who gives me breath.
> *Theodora.* Do you hear—
> *Theodore.* And that heaven has made our Parents disposers of our wills, and that they are in a condition to see more and be less deceived than we.
>
> . . . .
> . . .
>
> *Theodora.* Not one of these wise things would I have said to you, but tell me are you engaged to her you love?
> *Theodore.* No, but resolv'd, in spight of all opposition, and I conjure you, give me no reasons.
>
> (2.1.26)

Shadwell explicitly draws attention to religious claims of filial obligation, but neither Theodore nor Theodora sees any need to refute them. They are simply ridiculous when compared with the claims of love. This is a common position in Shadwell, in that love tends to take precedence over any kind of restraint. Even when the parent is intelligent and virtuous, as is Sir Edward in *The Lancashire Witches*, Isabella follows her own heart rather than Sir Edward's wishes. P. F. Vernon argues that in *Timon*

Shadwell adds the two females' roles to show the debasement of love by the mercenary concerns of marriage;[53] thus social form is less important than love as well.

But it is also true that even when love is not an issue, children reject the wishes of parents. Lady Cheatly, in *A True Widow*, attempts to make her daughter Isabella amenable to being kept by saying "'tis now adays, more like Marriage than Marriage it self" (3.2.305) because there is no cost in reputation or company. Isabella refuses but there is no reason to believe Lady Cheatly is wrong, for her own success at the end of the play indicates she understands the world better than any other character. The audience presumably thinks Isabella should reject the wishes of her mother because what her mother asks is immoral (I shall argue in the next chapter that Isabella's morality is still teleological in nature despite her mother's teleological argument). Similarly, Clarinda and Miranda in *The Virtuoso* must distance themselves from Sir Nicholas because their uncle (and guardian) is a fool. Theodosia in *The Lancashire Witches*, Theodosia with her Aunt Lady Loveyouth in *The Humorists*, and Philadelphia in *Bury Fair*, all have to disobey parents or guardians because the person they have an obligation to obey is unworthy of obedience because of either stupidity or moral turpitude. My point here is that in Shadwell we have repeated examples of parents who are vicious or foolish and who therefore make nonsense of the notion that adults have an obligation to obey their parents beyond what springs from gratitude for kind and intelligent guidance.

In an exactly parallel manner, there are examples of children whose parents need have no obligation to them, beyond, as Sir Edward in *The Lancashire Witches* says, the simple claim that "there's a Duty from a Father to make what he begets as happy as he can" (4.5.179). In Sir Edward's case, this is an unhappy duty that has nothing to do with natural affection. He says to Isabella, "Thy Brother has been still my tender care, / Out of my duty, rather than affection" (4.7.109). Sir Edward has arranged a marriage for his son with Theodosia; when the son remains cheerful over the fact that Doubty has married Theodosia, Sir Edward rounds on him: "Eternal Blockhead! I will have other means to preserve my Name" (4.5.187). The repeated evidence of worthlessness and an irrational unwillingness to be guided to a happy and useful life renders the family tie null. I am not arguing that there is no obligation between parent and child. Major General Blunt, in *The Volunteers*, has no affection for his daughter Teresia—indeed, he has "much ado to forbear kicking her" (5.1.166)—but he allows her to marry whom she wishes because she has committed no offenses. But the duty is not a high-level obligation. Blunt allows Teresia's choice of Sir Nicholas Dainty partly as a favor to others who might get stuck with them: "what a rare match 'twoud be, better one House than two troubled with them" (5.1.166).

In neither of the preceding cases is duty connected to affection; affection is equally possible without any corresponding duty. It is true that Mr. Rant, in *The Scowrers*, forgives his son's crimes repeatedly until the "prodigal" reforms; Paul E. Parnell regards J. H. Smith's remark that there is no philosophical statement justifying this repeated tolerance as a "quibble": "Mr. Rant clearly loves his son on principle."[54] But the principle that Parnell regards as operating in all of Shadwell's late plays is anything but clear in *The Scowrers*: the belief that mankind is innately good and if allowed proper freedom will reform. Parnell himself concedes that the skepticism of the women in the play and the backsliding of other characters tends to undermine the reformation,[55] but this misses the point. Tope, despite having birth, breeding, and wit, never reforms, and it is Sir William's love for Eugenia, not his father's remonstrance, that begins Sir William's reformation. Moreover, because Sir William is in love, his reformation is not really in doubt. Mr. Rant does not continue to forgive his son because of a sense of duty, or a belief that his son will reform, but because he loves his son, and that love is not based on any principle; before his son tells him of his love for Eugenia, he doubts Sir William's repentance, but the expression of repentance alone is enough to sway the doting father: "Oh *Will*, that this conversion were but perfect; / Yet, as it is, I cannot but embrace / And weep over thee" (5.5.140). The point of the biblical parable is that love forgives beyond principle, and that is true in this play of Mr. Rant with his prodigal son.

Nonetheless, benevolent paternal figures who guide the young to approved social roles become increasingly important in Shadwell's works starting with *The Lancashire Witches*. While love ultimately converts all of the characters who need to reform in Shadwell's plays, father figures stand for public responsibility and the acceptance of duty. Benevolent father figures exist in Shadwell's early plays, but they are not developed. Emilia's father in *The Sullen Lovers* is only briefly annoyed that Emilia has married Stanford rather than the "Countrey Gentleman" to whom he has planned to give her: he bows to the situation with a perfunctory, "Well! Heaven bless you together since you have

don't" (1.5.91). Sir Richard Loveyouth, in *The Humorists*, protects Theodosia and Raymund from the wrath of Lady Loveyouth
and ensures their future happiness by making Theodosia, his
niece, his heir. But his chief dramatic function is as the final
check on Lady Loveyouth, and he does not deliver the lengthy
speeches on duty that characterize Sir Edward in *The Lancashire
Witches*, Sir Edward Belfond in *The Squire of Alsatia*, Lord Bellamy in *Bury Fair*, Mr. Rant in *The Scowrers*, and Major General
Blunt in *The Volunteers*. It must also be stressed that in no way
does the increasing importance of benevolent paternal figures
commit Shadwell to a view that people are innately benevolent
or that parents have a divine authority. In all of these plays, the
paternal figure is contrasted with another paternal figure who is
rendered contemptible through either vice or foolishness: Sir
Jeffery Shacklehead in *The Lancashire Witches*, Sir William Belfond in *The Squire of Alsatia*, Mr. Oldwit in *Bury Fair*, Sir Richard Maggot in *The Scowrers*, and Colonel Hackwell Senior in
The Volunteers. Deference is paid to these fathers out of good
manners (an example of how the late plays differ from the early
plays), but their wishes are politely ignored.

There are two features of interest about the list of admirable
paternal figures. The first is that only Mr. Rant is actually the
father of a rake who needs to be instructed. Sir Edward in *The
Lancashire Witches* delivers his speeches chiefly to the suitors
of his daughter and the daughter of Sir Jeffery Shacklehead; they
do not need education in their duty, and he fails miserably in
explaining duty to his son. Sir Edward Belfond is the uncle of
Belfond Junior, and Lord Bellamy instructs his friend Wildish
and his servant Charles/Philadelphia. Major General Blunt, like
Sir Edward, discourses on patriotism to the suitors for his daughter and the daughter of Colonel Hackwell Senior, who again, do
not need instruction. The right of paternal authority is not a
consequence of nature or religious sanction, but an honor ac-
corded a figure whose own examples of virtue demonstrate his
right to instruct. There is no benevolent paternal figure in *The
Amorous Bigotte* precisely because in Catholic, priest-ridden
Spain, Bernando sees no need to prove his worthiness to command his son Luscindo, but assumes it—mistakenly—as an in-
alienable right.

The second point of interest is that all except Sir Edward Belfond live in the country. Sir Edward is a worthy Lancashire
knight who praises the housekeeping of a country gentleman
over the wage slavery of the city: "For my part, I love to have my

Servants part of my Family, the other were, to hired day Labourers to wait upon me; I had rather my Friends, Kindred, Tenants and Servants should live well out of me, than Coach-makers, Taylors, Embroiderers, and Laceman should: To be pointed at in the Streets, and have Fools stare at my Equippage, is a vanity I have always scorn'd" (4.3.136). Lord Bellamy explains the true difference between city and country life to Wildish:

> *Wildish.* . . . I thought you had been so retir'd, I had lost you.
> *Bellamy.* That was your fault: I have as pleasant a House and Seat, as most in *England*, that is thine as much as mine, *Ned.*
> *Wildish.* But 'tis in the Country; a pretty Habitation for Birds and Cattel: but Man is a herded Animal, and made for Towns and Cities.
> *Bellamy.* So many Pens of Wild Beasts upon two Legs, undermining, lying in wait, preying upon, informing against, and hanging one another: A Crowd of Fools, Knaves, Whores, and Hypocrites.
> (4.1.308–9)

Mr. Rant only comes to town to try and reclaim his son from his dissipation, and they will then return to the country to "live a sober Country Life" (5.5.147). Major General Blunt comes to London to marry off his daughter. Blunt could speak for all of these exemplars when he says, "For you I have left my dear Country Life, my sweet and fragrant Air; with plain, natural and honest Company, for essence of Sinks and Common-Shoars, for subtle Artificial Knaves, Ambitious Covetous Villains, who wou'd sell their very Country for Money, or a Title added to that of Villain" (5.1.164). The importance of the country to most of these figures indicates Shadwell's fundamentally political motivation in emphasizing these characters.

The type of the benevolent paternal figure in Restoration comedy is created long before *The Lancashire Witches* by Sir Robert Howard and the duke of Buckingham in *The Country Gentleman* (1669). Sir Richard Plainbred stands for good English food and benevolent treatment of his country servants: "begon and get me a great peece of beef, a lusty leg of mutton, and a large fat capon with white legs and spurs; my country servants must eat. I hear your Pages and Lackyes are kept here with the smell of meat and cabige-porriges."[56] His former servant Trim has moved to the city, and he and Sir Richard discuss sadly the difference between the city and the country:

> *Sir Richard.* I do abhor a place, where the most estimed crafts are cheating; and the most admirable policy word-breaking; where

most people spend all they have, and some more than theyr own. Greatnes is now to be judg'd by outside, and interest chang'd for-grandeur. Your Countrymen scarce know theyr Landlords, and are grown too poor to care for 'em. Fy upon't Trim, in former time we liv'd by one another, and now we live upon one another.

Trim. Sir I cannot but remember, when I was but a stripling, how your honest tenants and neighbors would rejoyce, to show their good wills; here Sir is nothing but "Your servant," and a mouth made.

(5.149–50)

Opposed to country honesty is city vice, to country sincerity city dissimulation, and, most important, to the country's sense of community and interdepedance, the city's cannibalistic destruction of its own citizens. The irony is that the city can corrupt anyone; Trim is now as much the con man as any native.

Not merely is Sir Richard identical to the Shadwellian paternal figures in his preference for the country, his treatment of his children is also similar. His daughters, Isabella and Philadelphia, marry without his permission, but since they marry two worthy gentleman, he is pleased nonetheless: "Now by my life, my heart's eas'd: blesse me Girle; thou hast chosen with my eyes: but you should have asked my consent child; but I am too well pleas'd, to chide" (5.152). Disobedience is not a vice when it leads to a worthy end, and parental authority is limited to that which gratitude requires.

The play ends with Sir Richard returning to the country with his daughters and new sons:

For my self, Worthy, and Lovetruth, we'l to the Countrey with our Wifes; where we'l cheerfully spend what we have, and wast nothing that our Ancestors left us; We'l not expose our content to noise, nor our fortune to crowds; we'l doe good to all, that desire, and hurt to none that deserve it; we'l love our King, and be true to our Country, wish all well[.]

(5.154)

Intimately linked with country virtues are patriotism and loyalty. The editors of the play, A. H. Scouten and Robert Hume, are surely right when they suggest that Sir Richard is presented as a positive figure because politically Howard and Buckingham wanted the support of the country party in Parliament at that time.[57] And surely Shadwell is attempting to make Whiggism more palatable to Tories by suggesting that the Whiggish country virtues of Sir Edward in *The Lancashire Witches* are closer to their interests than the fashionable city rakes in Tory plays like Crowne's *City Politicks* and Behn's *The City Heiress*. After the revolution, Shadwell's plays show the country as loyal to the crown to reinforce the lesson of patriotism that a faithful whig laureate must inculcate. But as I shall show in the next chapter, it is also true that the country gentleman of the second half of Shadwell's career represent a virtuous ideal of gentlemen living in accordance with their role, a role not incompatible with the virtuous city gentleman of *The Humorists*, *A True Widow*, and *The Squire of Alsatia*.

To this point I have argued that Shadwell's plays indicate that God provides only a limited guarantee of morality, and that organized religion may well be used as a tool by the unscrupulous. Further, and possibly as a consequence of this (although nowhere is it explicitly stated), the obligations that exist between parent and child—or siblings—are extremely limited; the plays undercut any claims of divine sanction for parental authority, and what "natural" duty there may be is extremely limited, which is shown by the repeated examples of children tied to foolish or vicious parents and guardians or vice versa. Further, intelligent characters in Shadwell's plays tend to deny or ignore the existence of providential order in the universe. Also, I have argued that Shadwell does not think we can rely on natural goodness. What then is the source of ethical obligation in Shadwell, if one can rely on neither God nor an assumption of innate virtue to provide ethical obligation? Other possibilities are social forces or rationality's capacity to provide universalizable principles. In the next chapter I shall argue that both of these sources contribute to man's capacity to act morally, but neither is adequate in the absence of love.

4

Public Order and Private Attraction

In this chapter I shall argue that Shadwell's plays consistently affirm that ethics are a product of social custom based on the individual's perception of the appropriateness of his actions to his role in society (the fourth belief). Further, that the consequences of virtuous (appropriate) behavior are the smooth functioning of society and the happiness of the individual (the second belief). But I shall also argue that Shadwell presents romantic love as playing an important role in drawing men from nonconstructive behavior while allowing women some relief from too restrictive social roles; love creates a dialectic between personal desires for freedom and social roles.

J. R. Jacob has explored Robert Boyle's rejection of the aristocratic ethic to which he was heir because the dislocations of the revolution made it seem inadequate. Still, this standard of morality is of interest in a discussion of Shadwell, because it offers a plausible system of moral obligation that requires neither a divine standard nor any assumption of a human nature naturally inclined to benevolence:

> The primary characteristic of this ethic was "the close-knit alliance of honor and virtue. . . ." Gentlemen proved their moral worth by conforming their behavior to the specifications of a code of honor. This standard of conduct was binding upon all men who were by birth or wished to become gentlemen. The ultimate determinant of the satisfaction of this standard was also public: the judgment of one's peers. So neither the terms of the code nor the fulfillment of its requirements was a matter of private conscience.[1]

This is a classical teleological system. A gentleman measures himself against a standard of behavior, because that standard supplies the definition of who he should be; independent of that standard, he could not know himself to be a gentleman. While I shall argue that there is more to Shadwell's ethics than the public component, the social role of honorable gentleman remains a compelling telos and, indeed, influences judgments about virtuous behavior at every social level and in both genders.

On a low level in *The Miser*, Hazard has the true gambler's reliance on skill and the house odds. When Ranter suggests that they carry the drunken Tim into the next room and pick his pocket, Hazard replies, "No pox, our way is a little more honourable" (2.3.54). His contempt for women and marriage indicates he is not capable of higher virtues—Theodore explains this by referring to his "ill company, and your leud lives" (2.2.43)—but this does not alter the fact that on his level he is a more virtuous man than Ranter, in that Hazard's behavior is more appropriate for a gambler.

Prostitution provides an interesting example of the gender politics of role. The Puritan emphasis on the dignity of marriage and the legitimacy of sexual pleasure within its bounds made nonmarital sex even more reprehensible than it had been under Catholicism. Nonetheless, the double standard remained firmly in place, and it was assumed that young men would fall.[2] Thus, while prostitution might well be regarded as a necessary evil, prostitutes themselves remained contemptible. Mandeville in 1724 sardonically defended a legal and publicly sponsored prostitution because it would prevent young men from making marriages that threatened the distinctions of social rank:

> If young men were to live entirely chaste and sober, without blunting the Edge of their Passions, the first fit of Love would turn their Brains Topsy-turvy, and we should have the Nation pestered with Love Adventures and Feats of Chivalry: By the time a *Peer's* Son came to be Sixteen, he would be in danger of turning Knight-Errant, and might possibly take a Cobler's Daughter for his *Dulcinea*; and who knows but a sprightly young *Taylor* might turn an *Orlando Furioso*, and venture his Neck to carry off a Lady of Birth and Fortune.[3]

It follows then that there must be prostitutes to defend the true dignity of marriage as the preserver of noble families.

Even bawds justify their actions with claims that they fill a socially useful role that has its own ethical standards. The bawd in *The Woman Captain* is typical in her desire for respect based on recognition of her diligence:

> *Sir Humphrey.* . . . Oh honest Bawd! How dost thou do?
> *Bawd.* Do! why I am e'en worn out in your Worships Service; I have gotten a hoarseness will never leave me, with rising a Nights, to

let in your Worship, and your unseasonable Company to save my
Windows: Well, I cannot live long.

Sir Humphrey. Thou wilt dye nobly then, in the Service of thy
Countrey.

Bawd. Nay, Heaven be prais'd, I have been diligent in my Calling,
very diligent to supply the Necessities of young Gentlemen.

(4.1.24)

The audience presumably does not think that the bawd is virtuous, but what is of interest here is the line of defense that both
she and Sir Humphrey take. Her occupation is justified by custom and necessity, and her hard work in corrupting young girls
is, in its way, a kind of service to the well-being of the country
and therefore virtuous. The Bawd illustrates the pervasiveness
of an ethic based on social roles.

On the next level up, servants fill a necessary role and are
virtuous when they do it well. Sir Humphrey's steward's honor
is offended when Sir Humphrey presses him into service as his
pimp: "Does not your Worship mistake me? I am your Steward"
(4.1.23). A part of Sir Humphrey's madness is that he neither
recognizes such distinctions nor regards the advice of the honest
steward who would have him restrain his expense. Sir William
in *The Scowrers* is reprehensible for an identical insult to his
servant Ralph:

Sir William. Well, thou art a faithful Bawd.
Ralph. Bawd, Sir?
Sir William. Yes Bawd Sir, what a Devil dost thou think I keep thee
for thy neat parts? Indeed thou art a little stout.
Ralph. Any man but my Master, should find I were a great deal so,
if he talk'd thus to me.

(5.1.88)

As a loyal servant, Ralph will not turn on his master, and in so
acting he is virtuous and entitled to respect. Master and servant
are not equals, so there can be no mutual obligation to provide
a reason for Ralph's loyalty; but loyalty is a virtue especially
important to the role of servant, and Ralph lives up to that role.

Further, an honest servant who fulfills his role can even be
promoted to the level of gentleman. Hernando, the witty servant
of Luscindo in *The Amorous Bigotte*, lies and fights for his master as he did for his master's father. These are not vices in a
servant; in fact, Luscindo says that these actions have earned
friendship: "Put on thy Hat *Hernando*, thou hast been too long

my Fathers good Servant, not to be my Companion, and art to have the next Commission that falls in my Flanders Regiment" (5.1.22). Likewise in *Bury Fair*, Lord Bellamy responds to Phila-delphia/Charles's service and gratitude with a promise of ad-vancement: "I'll breed thee up to be my friend" (4.1.308). The virtuous performance of duty is admirable, although further edu-cation is necessary for a transition from one sphere to another. In servants, and as we shall later see in their masters, no one has an instinctive or innate nobility. All must learn their role and must act it to be virtuous.

The privilege of being born English confers a dignity on ser-vants and peasants and requires respect. Sir Humphrey in *The Woman Captain* has "provided a set of *French*-fellows to serve me" (4.1.19) because they do not have any dignity to stand on, as the steward recognizes: "They are [fit] for Slavery, They are born and bred to it" (4.1.19). A gentleman knows that indepen-dence is a sturdy English virtue and honorable on any social level, as is clear in the contrast between France and England in *Bury Fair*:

> Count. I voud be glad to putte my Cutto into de Body of de Peasant, dey have fright de Lady.
> Bellamy. But, Monsieur le Count, our Peasants have Quarter-staves; and if Gentlemen go to run 'em through, they will knock 'em down: and we commend 'em for't.
> Count. De Peasant! begar, de Peasant be de Slave, de Dog, morbleu.
> Bellamy. Our Peasants wear Shooes, and Stockins, and lye warm; and have good Meat and Drink in their Houses.
> Wildish. Your King is a King of Dogs then: but how much greater is ours, who is a King of Men and Free Men! Ours governs the will-ing, he the unwilling.
> Count. Your King great as our King! Jerny, your King can do noting, dere is de Law, de Parliament, I dont know vat begar: my King can send for my Head wen he pleas; yes indeed, hum.
>
> (4.2.328)

Both high roles and low roles have rights and limits. Admitting the worth and honor of lower social levels ennobles one's own state; a gentleman or a king is worthier when he has worthy people below him. Finally, it is also honorable to accept that one has superiors, for one of the merits of the English peasants is that they freely accept their rulers and accept their own place in the social hierarchy. The English gentleman regard their system as superior because there is more general happiness.

The consequence of this view for women is, to a modern audience, unattractive. Gertrude, in *Bury Fair*, is in some ways one of the most appealing heroines in Restoration comedy. Witty, beautiful, and virtuous, she is more than a match for Wildish in any intellectual exchange. But despite her avowed independence in deciding whom she will marry, her sense is shown by her willingness to accept the limitations society places on the arena in which a woman's abilities can be applied. She argues with Lady and Mrs. Fantast about what a woman can properly do when they put forth their ability to speak poor French and Latin as an example of "breeding": "I know no breeding necessary, but Discretion to distinguish Company and Occasions, and Common Sence, to entertain Persons according to their Rank, besides making a Courtesie not awkwardly, and walking with one's Toes out" (4.2.314–15). Her answer is a definition of breeding that emphasizes utility and acceptance of existing roles.[4]

Nor need a woman be widely educated, since a virtuous woman's obligations do not require education:

> Gertrude. A Lady may look after the affairs of a Family, the demeanour of her Servants, take care of her Nursery, take all her accounts every Week, obey her Husband, and discharge all the Offices of a good Wife with her Native Tongue; and this is all I desire to arrive at; and this is to be of some use in a Generation, while your Fantastick Lady with all those Trappings and Ornaments you speak of, is good for no more than a Dancing Mare, to be lead about and shown.
>
> (4.2.315)

A woman is "good" when she is of use to her husband. This is reiterated at the end of the play when she accepts Wildish: "And know, for all my vapouring, I can obey, as well as e're a meek, simpering Milksop on 'em all; and have ever held *Non resistance* a Doctrine fit for all Wives, tho for nobody else" (4.5.368). Obedience in a wife is virtuous because society requires it, however unnatural Gertrude is for the part.

Although gentleman, because of their social position, are allowed more flexibility in the roles they explore than anyone else, they, too, are barred from some activities. In *The Sullen Lovers*, Sir Positive renders himself ridiculous through his attempt to portray himself as an adept at all roles—even those which are inappropriate for a gentleman. To Lady Vaine, he insists that he is the best pimp in London:

Sir Positive. Sorry! Well! if I would bend myself to't, I would starve all these Pimps, they should not eat bread, but I am not thought fit.
Lady Vaine. Surely you railly all this while.
Sir Positive. Railly! ha, ha, ha. Why, there is not a Lady of Pleasure from *Blackwall* to *Tuttle-Fields* that I am not intimately acquainted with, nay that I do not know the state of her Body from the first entring into the Calling.

(1.2.40)

Emilia could be commenting on all the fools in the play when she criticizes Sir Positive's vain desire to make a reputation as a playwright:

Would it not distract one to see Gentlemen of 5000 *l.* a year write Playes, and as Poets venture their Reputations against a Sum of Money, they venture theirs against Nothing? Others learn Ten years to play o' the Fiddle and to Paint, and at last an ordinary Fiddler or Sign-Painter that makes it his business, shall out-do 'em all.

(1.3.45)

Sir Positive is contemptible for two reasons: first, he is unlikely to surpass those who must make their livings as poets and painters, and second, his income makes it unnecessary to compete in such lowly occupations. What playwriting, painting, and pimping share is that they are equally excluded from the code of gentlemanly behavior—unless one needs the money, as did Shadwell. Conceivably, superior genius on the order of a Sedley, Buckingham, or Rochester would constitute an exception to the restrictions of role, but no useful end is served by Sir Positive's behavior.

And just as the code excludes some activities as immoral because ungentlemanly, it will allow a gentleman to lie as a means to a worthy end. In *The Humorists,* Raymund deceives Lady Loveyouth by pretending to be in love with her, but this deception is necessary, because he cannot otherwise escape with Theodosia. Sir Richard Loveyouth's response indicates how we should regard this deception; when Lady Loveyouth complains that "this base Villain *Raymund* has stol'n away my Niece," he remarks in an aside, "I see *Raymund* is a man of honour" (1.4.239). As a gentleman, Raymund's obligation is to aid Theodosia to whom he has engaged his honor. Although he wishes "to make peace with Lady *Loveyouth,* whom I really have used ill" (1.5.248), this is a consequence of good manners rather than of any sense that his means were unjustified, since circumstance allowed him no other. The play ends with a public celebration of Raymund and Theodosia's marriage; Sir Richard's approbation puts the seal of approval on Raymund's machinations. Likewise, Wildish, in *Bury Fair*, disguises La Roche to punish Lady and Mrs. Fantast for their folly. There is nothing wrong with the gag per se, but when it threatens social order because La Roche actually plans to marry Mrs. Fantast, Wildish steps in to stop it: "My Lord, I must take off this Rogue, my Honour may be question'd: for, tho I hate the Affected Creature, I wou'd not have this go on to a Marriage, or a Contract" (4.4.350). He can torment the Fantasts legitimately, but when a French tradesman threatens to marry into the gentry, he has to intervene to reestablish correct social relations.

In *The Lancashire Witches*, Sir Edward is explicit in his statement of what constitutes a gentlemen. Just as tennant farmers are "the strength and sinnews of our Country" (4.5.185), gentlemen fill the role of guardians of family, civilization, and country. He berates his son for enjoying the pleasures of rank and position without deserving them: "None but the vilest men will make their sports their business; their books, their friends, their kindred and their country should concern 'em: such drones serve not the ends of their Creation, and should be lopt off from the rest of men" (4.5.180). In *The Scowrers*, one of the arguments that Mr. Rant uses on Sir William to try and reclaim him is an explanation of how his vices make him ineligible for the proper employments of a gentleman:

> By Drunkeness you are useless at the best,
> Unless as Flys or humble Bees, meer Drones.
> What Office is there in a Common-Wealth,
> A Drunkard can sustain? Unless it be one,
> To be a Strainer through which Claret runs.
> Your Nerves you weaken, and you drown your Minds;
> You're all meer Sops on Wine, your Brains are Bogs;
> A Toast is equal to a common Drunkard:
> You'll say you have Courage, No, it is not Valour;
> Valour is joyn'd with Vertue, never prostitute,
> But sacred and employ'd to just Defence
> Of Prince and Country, and the best of Friends,
> With necessary vindication of our Honour:
> Yours is a brutal Fierceness that annoys
> Mankind, and makes 'em fear and hate you too.

(5.5.139)

Sir William does not respond that he does not desire an office in the commonwealth; he accepts that such responsibilities are a part of being a gentleman. Note as well that courage is not a virtue unless it is used as a means to a worthy end, and that the ends listed are all public in nature. Even Longvil and Bruce in *The Virtuoso* forget their private pleasures to restore order when the lower classes threaten a gentleman's residence.

In *The Volunteers*, Shadwell's last play, private affection remains secondary to public obligation; indeed, Hackwell Junior says "Honour is the Out-work to Love, without winning one, there are no Approaches to the other" (5.3.196). Eugenia is not impressed by this argument: "Wou'd you have me make my self so miserable, as to set my heart upon one who may be lost in every Recountour or Attaque[?]" (5.3.197). Hackwell Junior's response is not all that much to the point in that he does not address the issue of personal happiness with which Eugenia is concerned:

> *Hackwell Jr.* Does not our Royal Mistress do the same and bears it with a Princely Magnanimity; She and our Country have the greatest Stake in Europe, who will be sure to hazard himself with the bravest.
>
> *Eugenia.* She is to be reverenc'd and admir'd, but hard it is to Imitate so Glorious an Example; and methinks a private Lady may be happier.
>
> *Hackwell Jr.* We cannot in Gratitude pretend to be happier than those from whom we have our Happiness; in them our Countreys Cause, and yours, and all's at stake.
>
> (5.3.197)

All he has done is reaffirm obligation to country over private happiness. While obviously someone has to fight the country's wars, the contemptible Sir Timothy is an example of one who can be perfectly happy freeloading on the general sacrifice, so there is no practical reason why Hackwell Junior must go to war. The difference between Sir Timothy and Hackwell Junior is that the latter is a gentleman while the former has only the social position of a gentleman; Sir Timothy does not act in a gentlemanly way, while Hackwell Junior follows the glorious example of William. Even the fop Sir Nicholas becomes admirable when he tells Teresia that he must volunteer even if it means losing her—Major General Blunt says that is the first time he has ever agreed with him.

A part of ethical behavior for a gentleman, then, is his willingness to act as a gentleman ought, and virtue is shown in his ability to defend and preserve the social structure, maintain personal dignity, and employ himself in gentlemanly occupations like reading and entertaining friends. Is this, however, all that there is to being a virtuous gentleman? Stephen D. Cox has already analyzed how Shadwell's heroes are usually skillful in dealing with riotous situations: Longvil and Bruce in *The Virtuoso*, for instance, show their gentlemanly qualifications by driving off a mob of proto-Luddites angry at Sir Nicholas under the false impression that he has invented a power loom.[5] On the level of personal honor—a subject that Cox does not examine but which is equally dependent on social constructions—Bevil and Rains in *Epsom Wells* uphold virtue in the face of great temptation; Rains will even turn down sex with Mrs. Woodly because he is bound in honor to fight for Bevil. All four of these characters are also "epicureans" in the sense of being moderate hedonists. W. R. Albury regards Longvil and Bruce as embodying the "sensible hedonism of the moral Epicurean" in contrast to "the seemingly ridiculous pretensions of the natural philosopher,"[6] and one could place Bevil and Rains in similar opposition to the moral absolutism—as opposed to the epistemological absolutism of the virtuosos—of Justice Clodpate. If gentlemanly virtue is only the defense of order and conformity to social mores, then we must regard all four characters as virtuous.

On the other hand, if these libertines are admirable, then Shadwell has shifted his emphasis from his earlier plays. J. H. Smith's analysis of Lovel in *The Sullen Lovers* could be applied equally well to Theodore and Bellmour in *The Miser* and Raymund in *The Humorists*: "Shadwell's hero, however, is an honest lover from the start, any phase of revulsion from matrimony on his part having passed before the play begins."[7] Bruce concedes in *The Virtuoso* that the misanthrope Snarl is "sometimes in the right" (2.131), and Maximillian E. Novak points out that Clodpate is not incorrect in his description of the vices of the age in *Epsom Wells*, while adding that Shadwell's position on libertinism was ambiguous in the 1670s.[8] As a popular playwright, Shadwell is adapting to the seventies' vogue of sex comedies. Nonetheless, there is an undercurrent of dismay at the libertine threat to mutual love that the plays before and after *Epsom Wells* and *The Virtuoso* affirm as the force that draws men to appropriate social roles. If we look at Bellamour's reformation in *A True Widow*, the comedy that follows *Epsom Wells* and *The Virtuoso*, we can see where the ambiguity of Shadwell's two problem plays lies and the importance of mutual love to a society that seeks individual happiness.

In a scene of which Shadwell was justly proud, Lady Busy attempts to make Isabella amenable to being kept by arguing that morality is subordinate to the necessities of social station:

> *Lady Busy.* Nay, Heaven forbid I should persuade you to be dishonest: Vertue is a rare thing, a heavenly thing. But I say still, be mindful of the main—alass a Woman is a solitary, helpless Creature without a Man, God knows—good—how may this Man be had in Marriage say you?—very well—if you could get a fine Gentleman with Money enough, but alas! those do not Marry, they have left it off. The Customes of the World change in all Ages.
>
> (3.2.304)

Self-interest is the primary obligation, and premarital chastity is a custom that is fading. If God cares He'll understand what necessity forces a woman to. But Isabella does not respond with a defense of virtue predicated on God or a universalizable principle of chastity. Keeping brings a gentlewoman to the level of loose women at the playhouse, and bars her from associating with her own kind: "A very Comfortable thing, for a Gentlewoman to bring her self into a Condition of never conversing with a Woman of Quality, who has Wit, and Honour, again; but must sort with those Tawdry painted things of the Town" (3.2.304).

Gartrude, Isabella's whorish, half-witted sister, chimes in at this point with the response that Isabella can keep company with her and Lady Cheatly, and this response makes clear what the standard of honor is; moral choices under the social code are fundamentally aesthetic in the sense that good breeding renders some roles distasteful. That is, women, obligated to preserve their chastity to ensure that bloodlines are clear and hence their value as medium of social exchange is undamaged, internalize the political and economic value of chastity as a judgment on whom is a social equal and therefore a plausible mate. Isabella's taste and wit determine what constitutes an appropriate social role. Utility is not an issue here: Gartrude after copulating successively with Selfish and Stanmore can still be married off to young Maggot; Lady Cheatly can repair her fortunes by marrying Maggot Senior. But these are unattractive alternatives, and Isabella must maintain her right to a life that is not merely materially prosperous but which weds her to a social equal. The precondition for such a right is that Bellamour has to be converted from regarding

Isabella as purely an object. Custom and utility as the only standards of judgment are, according to Isabella, inadequate. Inflamed
by Isabella, Bellamour makes an argument similar to Lady Busy:

> *Isabella.* Can you pretend to love, and tempt me from my Honour?
> *Bellamour.* 'Tis no dishonour, custom has made it otherwise.
> *Isabella.* When a Man of Honour can turn Coward, you may prevail
> on me; the case is equal.
> *Bellamour.* On the contrary, Kindness in Woman is like Courage in
> Men.
> *Isabella.* Did not the general license of the time excuse you, I ne'er
> would see you more.
> *Bellamour.* What, will nothing down, but to have and hold? I'll
> marry nobody else, and when my inclination dies, leave you its
> wealthy Widow, you may marry after it.
>
> (3.3.319)

Custom justifies keeping, and utility makes it worthwhile. Indeed Bellamour's argument implies that both courage and pli-
ability are virtues because society regards them as such, and
Isabella's response indicates that his is the majority view. Ultimately, Bellamour will not marry because it is an unfashionable
sort of thing to do.

Although aware that this kind of argument pairs him with
Lady Busy, Bellamour cannot disassociate himself from it: "Pox
on this Bawd, I love the treason, but I hate the traytor" (3.3.320).
His first doubts then are aesthetic in that he of necessity must
associate himself with a woman who is distasteful to him. The
play within a play requires further self-recognition. In the farce,
two lovers are hidden in the wife's chamber when the husband
comes home. After the play, Gartrude, dressed as Isabella, has
her adventures with Selfish and Stanmore; Bellamour assumes
she is Isabella and confronts her in a jealous rage. But what right
does he have to do so? He claims that Selfish is unworthy of her,
but that should make him contemptuous, not jealous. The social
picture that Bellamour believes in, and that the farce depicts,
reveals the endless suspicion to which sex without fidelity assured by mutual love is likely to lead.

Individuals lose when they treat marriage as only a custom
justified by utility. Sex is not something the virtuous do for
money because that would violate one's social station. Isabella
angrily rejects the offer of being kept: "And I the while shall be
but a part of your Equippage, be kept; what is it but to wear
your Livery, and take Board-Wages" (3.3.319). Sex without love is

service, and hence inappropriate for Isabella who is a gentle-woman. Desire may not last forever, but love creates a bond that will assure happiness: "If you ever loved, you can never hate, and I shall be content where I have had the best, to keep the rest, and if you love me less, shall lay the fault of Nature, not on you" (3.3.319). Natural desire is not rational, but women cannot be regarded as objects, and Bellamour's final proposal shows how his views have changed: "When I made these offers, I did not know half your worth: I was a fair Chapman for your Beauty; but your Vertue, and other Perfections, are inestimable" (3.5.358). Bellamour realizes that sex is not merely another kind of mer-chandise. The only price for love is mutuality, and mutuality is the only guarantee of fidelity.[9]

Shadwell's major defense of romantic love in the main love plot is to show the consequences of denying it by comparing Bellamour with the lovers in the farce, and by showing the happy union of Bellamour and Isabella when he accepts her premises. In the subplot between Theodosia and Carlos, Shadwell portrays selfish vanity as the major threat to romantic love. Carlos is a virtuous man interested in marriage from the very beginning. Theodosia, despite her love for Carlos—apparent to the audience by her concern when he is in danger and her jealousy when he is trying to attract other women through her command—is not offering either marriage or sex.

Vanity and selfishness, of course, are the principle motivations for all the fools in the play. Lady Cheatly can cheat the steward and Maggot because their vanity allows them to believe she loves them. Moreover, their pure self-interest makes morality no more than a catchphrase for them. The steward claims love because, "I have in your Service lost my honesty, lay'd by my conscience" (3.3.323); his shrewdness evaporates when she agrees to marry him, claiming that she wanted to do so all the time. The steward is the prime example of how powerful a force vanity is: "that I should be so credulous, to believe her to be true to me, when I was an hourly Witness of her falshood to others" (3.5.348). Maggot is trapped the same way, but determines to retrieve the situation, because morality is for him no more than self-interest:

> *Lady Cheatly.* If you will go on, and maintain what I have done, I shall have a good Estate yet, though it belongs of right to other People.
> *Maggot.* Right? 'Tis no matter for Right: I'll show 'em Law.
>
> (3.5.361)

The problem is that vanity and selfishness are the chief motives for the intelligent, witty, and charming Theodosia. For instance, she wants Carlos to court Isabella because she wants her admirer to be universally admired, and thus imperils Carlos's virtue as well, since he knows the attempt is wrong:

> *Theodosia.* Make *Isabella* slight *Bellamour,* little *Gartrude* sacrifice *Selfish:* Be the third word in every Ladies mouth, from fifteen to five and thirty; and you shall find what I'l say to you.
> *Carlos.* To attempt this, were great vanity, and no less dishonesty, to my friend *Bellamour.*
> *Theodosia.* If you love, you'l think anything lawful: This must be done, I dare not trust my own judgment; I will have you in vogue, e're I favour you in the least.
>
> (3.2.311)

Isabella and Carlos do not think that everything is lawful in love, and neither does Bellamour by the end of the play. The root of Theodosia's view is self-love, of which she is most guilty when accusing Carlos: "Vanity and ingratitude are as inseparable as old age and ugliness; they that think too well of themselves, ever think too ill of others; and I will give you no temptation of any kind" (3.3.329). The criticism cannot be applied to Carlos; he is capable of neither ingratitude nor vanity. Theodosia, however, must be loved by one whom everyone loves, and is ungrateful when Carlos, following her instructions, attracts Gartrude.

Self-love is not wrong; it just should not be a bar to mutuality. Carlos is a genuine paragon and knows from the beginning what it takes Bellamour the entire play to learn: "True Beauty, Madam, can no more be bought than true Love; in me behold the one, while I admire the other in your self" (3.2.310). And Carlos has self-love, which does not interfere with his loving Theodosia: "My love of you . . . began so early in my Heart, self-love was scarce before it" (3.2.310). But Theodosia cannot understand this because she views love as a contest:

> *Theodosia.* Suppose I should answer you in your whining strein, and say, my love were as true as yours, my flame as great, and all your wishes mine.
> *Carlos.* Then were *Carlos* the happiest man on Earth.
> *Theodosia.* No, then the Game were up betwixt us, and there were no more to do but to pay the stakes, and then to something else.
> *Carlos.* We might play Set after Set for ever.
> *Theodosia.* No, one of us would be broke.
>
> (3.2.311)

Her dialogue would be at home in Etherege, but Carlos's would not. Or rather, Bellair's speeches are characterized by the same insistence on fidelity and virtue, but Bellair is only "the most tolerable of all the young men that do not abound in wit," and even Emilia says of his protestations of eternal devotion, "our love is as frail as is our life, and full as little in our power, and are you sure you shall outlive this day."[10] Carlos is an exemplar: witty, honorable, and the complete gentleman. Yet to get an engagement, he has to trap Theodosia into a wager that his persistance will make her love him and even then Isabella has to adjudicate the bet to keep Theodosia from welshing. Shadwell could easily have had the two marry at the end of the play, as do Isabella and Bellamour, but even though she has lost the wager, Theodosia still delays and requires more time. Carlos relies on her "good Nature" (3.5.362), but, in the midst of all the vanity of the play, is it likely that Theodosia can reform and that marriage can become what Carlos wishes, a place of comfort and security? I think the answer is no, although by closing this way Shadwell allows the audience a happy ending if they wish it. In this subplot, vanity and self-love stand as a real threat not only to Theodosia but to the paragon Carlos, and thus Shadwell stresses the need for mutuality in love. Nevertheless, whatever doubts the audience has about Theodosia, Carlos, as virtuous gentleman, will presumably make the best of whatever happens.

There is reason to believe then that the male leads of *Epsom Wells* and *The Virtuoso* are not necessarily admirable, if only because they are so different from the exemplary heroes of his previous comedies and so similar to Bellamour, who is required to reform in the immediately subsequent comedy. That does not, of course, prove anything; Shadwell had to have his plays performed and was not above pandering to audience taste; the epilogue of *The Woman Captain* admits forthrightly, if petulantly, that because *A True Widow* did badly, Shadwell "made this Low, so to your Level fit" (4.17). Along these lines Hume expresses doubt that although *Epsom Wells* claims to be a satire, "whether the 'satire' outweighed the appeal of the behaviour satirized we may wonder."[11] The behavior to which Hume refers is presumably that of Rains and Bevil who are witty, swaggering cuckold makers. But, minus the wit, this sort of activity pervades the plot, which makes the activities problematic, unless one assumes, as Kathleen Lynch does, that Shadwell was converted to an admiration of libertinism through his admiration for Etherege's *She Wou'd if She Cou'd*.[12]

Vice is universal. Justice Clodpate repeatedly attacks the immorality of London, and there is no reason to believe he is wrong;
his mistake is not to recognize his own complicity and that what
he attacks is the general condition of England. Lucia's view is
the correct one: "I believe there is no Village but sins as much,
in proportion to the bigness; only your Country sins are something the more block-headed sins" (2.2.121). Alssid's reaction to
the general decadence is to see the wells as providing a natural
liberation from social restraints on every level: "Epsom is, sym-
bolically, the site of freedom, where people unmask and where
truths are revealed."[13] If this is true, however, what is revealed is
a cuthroat competition at a place where the foolishness of the
country and the viciousness of the town can meet in the dissipation of both. Like Alsatia, the fashionable resort threatens established customs—marriage most of all.

If you're a cit, you're contemptible. An interesting inversion in
this play is that the wives, as well as the husbands, debate about
the best way to manage a spouse. Mrs. Fribble claims control by
being submissive, whereas Mrs. Bisket is imperious. This ar-
rangement is mirrored in Fribble who is imperious and Bisket
who is submissive. These roles, however, are not choice but fate.
When the submissives attempt to reverse roles with their dominant mates, they are beaten off the stage. All claims of control
are entirely illusory, because it turns out that neither brutality
nor uxoriousness can control a wife.

Morality is reducible to property. In a very amusing scene that
converts the audience to secondhand voyeurs, Fribble and Bisket
discover their wives in the act with Cuff and Kick. Cowards to
the bone, their only recourse is law. But the cits merit no pity,
for they will use the adultery to show a profit:

> Bisket. If we order our business wisely and impannel a good sub-
> stantial Jury, of all married men, they'll give us vast damages.
> Fribble. I have known a man recover 4 or 500 l. in such a Case, and
> his Wife not one jot the worse.

> (2.5.179)

Honor has no meaning here; their wives are possessions. If they
receive value for their possessions, then they are satisfied. Nor
do the wives merit any compassion. At the end of the play, both
are crawling to their husbands. They are never presented as victims of forced or unsatisfactory marriages, but simply enjoy vice.

In the low plot then, virtue is irrelevant because there is no concept of honor. Vice can be translated without remainder into damage to property. Among the higher social ranks in this play, women remain an exchange item, but ethical values distinct from property are invoked to complicate the matter. In the high plot, there is great deal of talk about honor, usually in conflict with love, but no compromise can be achieved between the two. Even in the last act, when Rains must decline to commit adultery with Mrs. Woodly because he is honor-bound to fight for Bevil, Rains is still claiming "those old Enemies Love and Honour will never agree" (5.174). Indeed precisely from the conflicting demands of honor and desire—which is all Bevil, Rains, and Woodly think love is—flow the plot complications.

Desire creates a series of conflicts and claims, where the truth must continually be asserted to be false because honor requires it: "A Gentleman ought in Honour to lye for his Mistress" (2.3.143). The "for" in this statement can be read in two ways: first as an obligation to protect a current mistress, and second as a way to obtain a mistress one desires. Thus, because Woodly desires Carolina, Woodly tells Lucia and Carolina that Bevil and Rains have been spreading their names all over town, and Mrs. Woodly, jealous of Bevil's love for Carolina, forges a note from Carolina to Bevil to arrange a meeting and entrap Bevil in the duel. The only way for the quarrel between Woodly and Bevil to be resolved is for Bevil to assert and Woodly accept a lie that they both know perfectly well to be a lie:

Bevil. Your Life—
Woodly. Take it—I deserve to lose it Since I defended it no better.
Bevil. No, Sir—live—and live my Friend if you please; and know your Lady's innocent: I had not gone so far, but that you were pleased to make a question to *Rains*, whether I durst meet you or no.

(2.5.174)

The duel is a consequence of the conflict of honor and desire because Mrs. Woodly, at least, has no misconceptions of what the code entails: "I know he [Woodly] has too much honour not to meet him [Bevil] singly; if he kills *Bevil*, I am reveng'd, if *Bevil* kills him, he rids me of the worst Husband for my humour in Christendom; but I'le to Mr. *Rains*, he's a Gentleman indeed" (2.5.173).

Attempts to reconcile honor and desire lead only to sophisms. For instance, when Rains chaffs Bevil over his affair with his friend Woodly's wife, even Bevil sounds unhappy with his defense:

> *Rains.* Art thou not a Villain to Cuckold this honest fellow, and thy friend *Ned?*
> *Bevil.* Gad it's impossible to be a man of honour in these Cases. But my intrigue with her began before my Friendship with him, and so I made a friend of my Cuckold, and not a Cuckold of my friend.
> *Rains.* An admirable School distinction.
>
> (2.1.109)

Early in the play we are led to believe that Rains, at least, is upright. He does not wish to be introduced to Lucia by Woodly because, "I love thee and thy Family too well to lye with her, and my self too well to marry her; and I think a Man has no excuse for himself that visits a Woman without design to lye with her one way or other" (2.1.117). The veneer of superiority dissolves soon. Love for Lucia will not keep him from meeting Mrs. Jilt: "I love *Lucia* even to the renouncing of Wine and good Company; but flesh and blood is not able to hold out her time without some refreshment by the bye" (2.4.152). He does not in fact achieve Jilt's conquest, because she wants the security of marriage. But the incident is repeated more seriously later. Mrs. Woodly writes to him requesting an assignation, and he jests about himself as being reprobate: "good Devil, do not tempt me, I must be constant, I will be constant: nay, Gad, I can be constant when I resolve on't, and yet I am a Rogue. But I hope I shall have Grace, and yet I fear I shall not; but come what will, I must suffer this tryal of my Vertue" (2.5.171). The only thing that saves him this time is seeing Bevil and Woodly about to fight; that takes precedence.

The conflict is between what society allows a man yet requires of a woman. Woodly is able to enrage Lucia by merely quoting Rains's remark that the only reason to see a woman is "to lye with her." Despite the quotation's imperfect representation of Rains's feelings—Rains makes the remarks before he knows Lucia—the remark is, nonetheless, indicative of Rains's and Bevil's view of Women as merely sexual objects. Lucia protests that Bevil and Rains use their wit around women only for the purpose of seduction: "For love I bar you, can't we converse without remembring we are of different sexes[?] (2.2.134). But Bevil and Rains can't:

Rains. How prodigal soever I have been, I am resolv'd to take up in my expenses, and reserve all my love for you.

Lucia. For me? I am as hard to be fixt as you: I love liberty as well as any of ye.

Rains. Say you so? Faith let's make use on't.

Lucia. Not the lewd liberty you mean: Come, to divert us better, go a little further, and try the Eccho, here is an extraordinary one that will answer you to as much purpose as I can.

(2.3.147)

Rains will not understand her plea to be regarded as an equal, because his love sees her as an object of enjoyment. He might as well talk to the echo, since everything he hears is translated by his narcissism into a statement of his own desires.

When Bevil and Rains discuss matrimony, we see none of the desire for mutuality and affection that characterizes the lovers in Shadwell's early and late plays:

Bevil. I love these women the more, for declaring against Fools, contrary to most of their Sex.

Rains. I hate a Woman that's in love with a fulsom Coxcomb, she's a foul feeder, and I can no more have an appetite to her, when I think of her diet, than to a tame Duck when I think it feeds on Toads.

Bevil. Well, I love Carolina beyond all sense of modesty, so much, that I am resolv'd if she will, to turn recreant and marry her, let what will be the consequence.

Rains. To forbear pleasing our selves to day, for fear of being troubled to morrow, were to adjourn life and never to live.

Bevil I am sure of the present pleasure, and but venture the future pain.

(2.4.155)

Unlike the male characters in earlier plays of Shadwell who foresee close harmony based upon more than just physical attraction, Bevil and Rains subordinate everything to physical attraction. The *carpe diem* theme that they elaborate, and which is associated with vulgar epicureanism, links them with Woodly who, when his marriage turns sour, attempts to force himself on Carolina. The women's intelligence and wit makes them attractive only because it makes them exclusive; as objects they are compared to ducks worthy to be devoured because of appropriately restricted diets.

The women are in a difficult situation. Bevil and Rains are

attractive and clever men, and Carolina and Lucia cannot help being drawn to them:

> Carolina. 'Tis a shame that a company of young, wall-fac'd Fellows, that have no sense beyond Perruques and Pantaloons, should be the only men with the Ladies, whilst the acquaintance of witty men is thought scandalous.
> Lucia. For my part, I am resolv'd to redeem the honour of our Sex, and love Wit, and never think a Fool a fine Gentleman.
>
> (2.1.113)

The women's desires are complicated by their determination to maintain their own honor, which requires marriage. Woodly does not speak for Bevil and Rains, but he speaks as they would when he tries to seduce Carolina moments after Rains's misinterpretation of Lucia's statement of equality:

> Carolina. Can I suffer this any longer without prejudice to my virtue and honour; let me hear no more, you will not suffer me to use you like a Gentleman.
> Woodly. I am too loyal to rebel against you, but I may attack your evil Counsellors, your virtue and honour.
> Carolina. You'll find them impregnable.
> Woodly. Virtue and Chastity unsociable foolish qualities! I hope to live till every Woman shall be thought vicious, or at least as much scandalous as a Lawyer with a tatter'd Gown out of practice: We are a fair way to it.
>
> (2.3.147)

Carolina's pun on the word impregnable cuts two ways. First, her social position is maintained by not being impregnated through a lapse of virtue, which would damage her value as exchange item. Second, she believes her honor and virtue to be unconquerable, which indicates she is used to having them attacked.

Women are, according to a later dialogue between Woodly and Rains, fortresses under siege, and all that distinguishes Woodly from Rains is his expectations of success:

> Woodly. Your Mistresses? you are men of dispatch, you take Women as fast as French Towns; none of 'em endure a Siege, but yield upon the first Summons to you.
> Rains. You are in the wrong, such as we can buy or corrupt the Gouvernours of, may be easily had; but there are your Nimmegen Ladies that will hold out, and pelt damnably.
>
> (2.5.165)

Both accept the metaphor of women as objects to be conquered. Rains claims that his intentions toward Lucia are honorable, but all his actions in the play indicate that Woodly's response is an accurate statement about what protects Lucia: "That's as she pleases; for you have no more honour in love than needs must" (2.5.165). The "foolish" honor that hinders women from sex and of which Woodly has accused Carolina never hinders Rains; only bad luck keeps him out of bed with Mrs. Woodly, and Mrs. Jilt's desire for marriage prevents him in that adventure.

All of which leaves the women in an awkward position. To maintain honor, as Carolina says, "I see we must condemn our selves to the conversation of dull sober Fools" (2.4.154). At the end of the play, Lucia and Carolina do accept Rains and Bevil as "servants" seeking by good behavior to show that they have reformed:

> *Lucia.*   And if you should improve every day so, what would it come to in time?
> *Rains.*   To what it should come to, Madam.
> *Bevil.*   'Twill come to that, *Jack*; for one Fortnights conversing with us will lay such a scandal upon 'em, they'll be glad to repair to Marriage.
> *Woodly.*   To show you, that there was never so decent a Divorce, I have fiddles to play at it, as they used to do at Weddings.
>
> (2.5.181)

The dramatic juxtaposition of Woodly celebrating his divorce highlights the tenuousness of the probable marriages. Carolina and Lucia will accept because the alternatives are fools or scandal. Bevil and Rains have not changed, and their similarity to Woodly seems to imply a similar fate to their marriages.

In his apparent accommodation to changing theatrical tastes, Shadwell actually takes the libertine hero to what must have appeared to Shadwell to be his logical conclusion. Libertine hedonism, in the form of Bevil and Rains, is discredited by linking it to Woodly whose marriage is in ruins at the end of the play. Neither Woodly nor Mrs. Woodly is upset since theirs is a marriage of libertines. Bevil and Rains cannot appreciate what they have in Lucia and Carolina, and the women seem likely to be able to cope with their husbands only if they become Mrs. Woodlys. As long as virtue and wit are incompatible, and as long as socially generated concepts of honor deny a place for mutual love, marital happiness is impossible. The alternative that the play depicts is Woodly's unattractive celebration of new-found independence.

In *The Virtuoso*, Shadwell presents a pair of libertines who self-consciously assert sense over any kind of speculative or non-material value. They are philosophical libertines, chatting happily about the principles that Bevil and Rains only enact. The play opens with Bruce quoting Lucretius on the indifference of the divine to man, about which Bruce says happily, "Thou reconcil'st Philosophy with Verse, and dost, almost alone, demonstrate that Poetry and Good Sence may go together" (3.1.105). Certainly Lucretian materialism and the Epicurean view that knowledge is of value only as it leads to pleasure are superior to the alternative views of the fools in the play. Sir Formal is a rhetorician whose words lack referentiality and hence are deceitful: "Is there so great a Rascal on earth, as an Orator, that would slur, and top upon our Understandings, and impose his false conceits for true reasoning, and his florid words for good sense" (3.1.110). That sense and utility are the final criteria for any activity is most apparent in the satire on Sir Nicholas, the virtuoso. His interest in knowledge for its own sake is held up to ridicule throughout the play. For instance, he is learning to swim in his study by imitating a frog and having a swimming master in to comment on it:

> *Sir Nicholas.* I content myself with the speculative part of Swimming, I care not for the Practick. I seldom bring any thing to use, 'tis not my way, Knowledge is my ultimate end.
> *Bruce,* You have reason, Sir; Knowledge is like Vertue, its own reward.
> *Sir Formal.* To study for use is base and mercenary, below the serene and quiet temper of a sedate Philosopher.

> (3.2.127)

What Bruce says about Sir Nicholas could be applied to any of the fools in the play: "No Phanatick that has lost his wits in Revelation is so mad as this Fool" (3.5.165). Their enthusiasm draws them beyond common sense, both in terms of empirical verification and ordinary garden-variety intuition.

Arguably Bruce and Longvil are the sage philosophers they think they are because they have a keen grasp of facts. Alan Fisher claims that Shadwell always asserts facts and denies the imagination.[14] But this is not entirely true. For instance, in *The Lancashire Witches*, Sir Edward's rational evaluation of social facts will result in his daughter's marriage to an idiot, and she has to deceive him to achieve her marriage to an equal. Alssid points out that the witches are only another kind of mystery in the same play, and that the rational Sir Edward, Mellfort, and Doubty are playthings in the hands of women's magic.[15] Sir Edward's closing speech acknowledges the limitations on rational planning for happiness: "How shallow is our foresight and our prudence!" (4.5.188). Common sense and facts do not account for all of experience.

Nor is it the case that Shadwell was uniformly scornful of the new philosophy. Bellfort and Doubty, also in *The Lancashire Witches*, comfort themselves in a violent storm with theories of equilibrium:

> *Bellfort.* The tempest is so violent, it cannot last.
> *Doubty.* New Philosophy helps us to a little Patience.
>
> (4.1.117–18)

Shadwell's skepticism is not dogmatic but methodological. Confronted with genuinely strange events, the men confess ignorance but not epistemological despair:

> *Bellfort.* 'Tis a little odd; but however, I shall not fly from my Belief, that everything is done by Natural Causes, because I cannot presently assign those Causes.
> *Sir Edward.* You are in the right, we know not the powers of matter.
> *Doubty.* When anything unwonted happens, and we see not the cause, we call it unnatural and miraculous.
>
> (4.4.166)

Knowledge is the process of being able to assign more and more natural causes "presently." J. M. Armistead's sensible evaluation of *The Lancashire Witches* argues Shadwell's awareness of the limitations of human knowledge: "Like most Restoration men and women, Shadwell seems to have been sure that there was more to life than meets the empirical eye. But he was equally sure . . . that the best mental disposition for limited, fallen beings was empirical and pragmatic."[16] The wise are therefore cautious in both what they assert and deny, which is not the case with Bruce and Longvil.

When confronting Bruce and Longvil's admiration for Lucretian materialism, one needs to remember that in Shadwell's immediately prior play, *The Libertine* (1675), the villain Don John asserts a very narrow materialism:

> Nature gave us our Senses, which we please:
> Nor does our Reason war against our Sense.
> By Natures order, Sense should guide our Reason,
> Since to the mind all objects Sense conveys.
> But Fools for shaddows lose substantial pleasure,
> For idle tales abandon true delight,
> And solid joys of day, for empty dreams at night.
>
> (3.7.26)

Thus notions such as conscience and love are empty because they have no foundation in sense. Possible ethical restraints are social in the Hobbesian sense that if you get too far out of line, society will restrain you. This is not an option in *The Libertine* since Don John is too fearless, powerful, and skilled for any society to hold him in. His end comes when, contrary to his expectation, a just heaven allows hell to haul him off. But it seems odd to see Bruce and Longvil as admirable figures when they repeat the same kind of sensationalism that makes Don John a villain.

Outside of the Saturday matinee horror show of *The Libertine*, society can function with a moral system that reduces all moral claims to reputation, utility, and pleasure. The difficulty is that the resulting explanation of ethics remains unattractive to people of wit and taste, such as Isabella in *A True Widow*. Sir Humphrey, in *The Woman Captain*, praises a song that argues the same kind of sensationalism that Don Juan and Bruce and Longvil use to discredit alternative moral systems, and he too is clearly not admirable:

> Let some great joys pretend to find
> In empty Whimsies of the mind;
> And nothing to the Soul can come,
> Till th' ushering Senses make it room.
> Nor can the Mind be e're at ease,
> Unless you first the Body please.
> Life is, what e're vain Man may doubt,
> But taking in and putting out.
>
> (4.2.31)

In such a system man is just the animal machine who seeks to perpetuate a state of pleasure. All knowledge is founded in the senses, and anything that claims to do more than please the senses is "vain." Specifically, virtues are empty: "In that how can they Pleasure take, / Of which no Image Thought can make" (4.2.31). Logical positivism has ancient roots. We can visualize virtuous actions but not the virtue they represent, and those actions, to be accounted virtuous, must have a cash value in terms of our senses.

Morality in any sense other than prudence is no more than a social construction. The cheerful rakes claim that the words and social circumstances that surround a person or activity comprise morality:

> *Sir Humphrey.* Fy, fy, Whores! That's a naughty word. They are Ladies; there are no Whores but such as are poor and beat Hemp, and Whipt by Rogues in Blues Coats.
>
> *Bellamy.* They are brave Magistrates to commit Adultery themselves, and whip poor Wenches for simple Fornication.
>
> *Wildish.* There's no Law to whip but that of Vagrants, and when a poor Wench has laboured in her Calling seven years in the same Parish; These Fellows will whip her for a Vagrant.
>
> (4.1.25)

A prostitute becomes a vagrant when she is too worn out to remain attractive, while a fine lady is not a whore because she dresses well. No one is losing any sleep over this. Celia, protesting her loyalty to her keeper Sir Nicholas, talks about honor and conscience and worries ostentatiously about what will become of her soul. She says, "Shall it ever be said that I am false to my Keeper?" to which Bellamy responds, "No it shall never be told" (4.2.33). Hers is a formulaic appeal to honorable fame; his response, what she actually means, is that unless the betrayal is noised abroad, it does not have anything to do with morality because it does not have any consequences.

Hedonism is not wrong in itself. Gripe criticizes the "damn'd senses" (4.1.29), but his alternative is worthless for he seeks only more money. As Mrs. Gripe says, "They [misers] are such Fools to choose the worst part of life, and are yet greater Fools, and prefer it to Death, which is far better: to be dead is to be insensible; but to have sense and deny 'em all is worse" (4.3.54). Not having senses is an evil, but not as evil as having them for nothing. Even Sir Humphrey is aware of real Epicureanism, although he does not live the modified asceticism of Epicurus: "I do confess I am an *Epicurean* in this, and in every thing. I'd go no further than the pleasing of my Senses: I would have just so much Wine, as would give me an Appetite to Woman, and just so much Woman, as would give me a desire to Wine" (4.5.69). He is talked out of this temporary moderation, of course, and his excesses provide the necessity for reformation.

Sir Humphrey's repentance is strictly prudential and comes from a recognition that his unrestrained hedonism has denied the fact that one cannot be independent of society while one depends on society to provide the things that please the senses. When the money runs out, Sir Humphrey marries his mistress on whom he has settled a great deal of money. But the merely prudential view of morality that informs *The Woman Captain* is unattractive. Sir Humphrey realizes that his friends are his friends only because they enjoyed the pleasure he could provide and his only way to repair his fortune is to marry his whore. In the consequentialist view that he expouses throughout the play, this is not a problem since he has all that he wants. It is unlikely, however, that an audience can see this as a happy ending since self-interest remains unleavened by either romantic love or male friendship. The central scene of the play may well be the episode where Chloe, Celia, and Phyllis all attempt to seduce the disguised Mrs. Gripe, the woman captain of the title: in a strictly materialist, hedonist, and prudentialist moral world, the unnatural becomes the natural.

No *deus ex machina* resolves *The Virtuoso*, nor are the heroes threatened by the consequences of unrestrained hedonism, yet Bruce and Longvil share some characteristics with Don John and Sir Humphrey. They are attractive, witty men, who spout materialism, and who can drive off an entire mob of Luddites.[17] Moreover, they at least begin the play by observing a Lucretian indifference to society's ills. After Bruce catalogs the follies of the age, they congratulate each other on their own self-sufficiency.

> Longvil. These are sad Truths: but I am not such a fop to disquiet my self one minute for a thousand of 'em.
> Bruce. You have reason; say what we can, the Beastly, Restive World will go its way; and there is not so foolish a Creature as a Reformer.
> Longvil. Thank Heav'n I am not such a publick spirited fop, to lose one moment of my private pleasure for all that can happen without me.
> Bruce. Thou art a philosopher.

> (3.1.107)

There are several reasons to think that Bruce and Longvil's pretensions are being satirized here. First, Bruce has said about forty-five seconds earlier that "Perhaps good *French* may be spoken with little sence; but good English cannot" (3.1.106). Yet when Bruce agrees with Longvil's claim that the wise man is indifferent to society's problems, he resorts to the French construction "You have reason"—*vous avez raison*. Later in the play, when Bruce mocks Sir Nicholas's belief in the value of pure knowledge, he uses the same phrase in a context that clearly indicates the satire: "You have reason, Sir; Knowledge is like Vertue, its own reward" (3.2.127).[18]

A more compelling reason for doubting the possibility of self-sufficiency is the fact that Bruce and Longvil have just fallen in love—an event that Lucretius warns the wise man to guard against at all cost.[19] Their comments about this indicate they are not terribly concerned about it: "'Tis a little strange that we, that have run together into all the Vices of Men of Wit, and Gentlemen, should, at last, fall together into the Vice of Fools and Country Squires, Love" (3.1.107). But unless we are to see love for Miranda and Clarinda as a foolish act, Bruce and Longvil's admiration for Lucretius must be undermined. And while common sense is surely held up as a normative force in Bruce and Longvil, their tendency to reduce things to the purely physical is more doubtful.

That common sense has a positive value even in love is apparent. Romantic bombast is ridiculous because it has no content, as Bruce and Clarinda agree:

> *Bruce.* Come, I see this way will not do: I'll try another with you. Ah, Madam! change your cruel intentions, or I shall become the most desolate Lover, that ever yet, with arms across, sigh'd to a murmuring Grove, or to a purling Stream complain'd. Savage! I'll wander up and down the Woods, and carve my passion on the Bark of Trees, and vent my grief to the winds, that as they fly shall sigh and pity me.
> *Clarinda.* How now! what foolish fustian's this? you talk like an Heroic poet.
> *Bruce.* Since the common down-right way of speaking sense would not please you, I had a mind to try what the Romantick way of wining [*sic*] love cou'd do.
>
> (3.3.134)

Ordinary language and action should be able to express love, and poetic embellishment identifies the lover with the empty words of Sir Formal or Sir Samuel. The word love has referentiality, and metaphors and laments only serve to disguise this.[20]

But love itself is not really a fit object for a commonsensical toting up of assets and liabilities, which is the way Bruce and Longvil would like to treat it. The complication that they attempt to deal with reasonably is that while Bruce loves Clarinda and Longvil Miranda, Miranda loves Bruce and Clarinda Longvil. When Bruce and Longvil find this out, they cheerfully switch for good, solid reasons and regard it as nonsensical to invest any emotion in the decision:

> Bruce. 'Tis too evident we have plac'd our Loves wrong: They are both handsome, rich, and honest, three qualities that seldom meet in Women.
> Longvil. 'Tis true: and since 'twill be necessary, after all our Rambles, to fix our unsettled lives, to be grave, formal, very wise, and serve our Countrey, and propagate our species. Let us think on't here.
> Bruce. Let us walk and consult about this weighty affair.
>
> (3.4.156)

Bruce and Longvil may be a step up from Bevil and Rains in that they suspect that they have roles in society that they will have to fill, contrary to their initial statements in the play when they claim that they take no interest in what society requires, and this helps to stress the social importance of love.

But their flippancy rings false here nonetheless. This is actually a weighty affair, and their gay references to being wise and settled do not really measure up to what is necessary if they are to avoid becoming aging rakes no longer up to the part. Young rakes may be attractive because it is a natural thing for a young man to be, but old rakes are always ridiculous. And their low-grade hedonism (neither temperate like Epicurus nor stoic like Lucretius) brings them very close to disaster. In act 3, both attempt to commit adultery with Lady Gimcrack; Bruce justifies this by linking his love for Clarinda with Sir Nicholas's impractical experiments: "I shall forget the Speculative part of Love with Clarinda, and fall to the practick with her [Lady Gimcrack]. But I shall ne'r hold out that long journey, without this or some other bait by the way" (3.3.135). No lucky accident intervenes the second time they are tempted, and they each copulate with Lady Gimcrack, believing that they are making it with the other's beloved. After accusations of treachery, they fight; their hedonism and narcissism brings them into the only danger that society can have for them—each other.

Aside from the risk that they may kill each other, this almost costs them Clarinda and Miranda. They are justly offended that Bruce and Longvil could believe they would engage in premarital sex:

Miranda. This malice is beyond example, and your baseness, so soon to entertain such thoughts of us.

Clarinda. That senseless vanity, that makes them think so well of themselves, makes 'em think so ill of us.

(3.5.176)

Virtue is not a speculative idea for Clarinda and Miranda but has real consequences. That Bruce and Longvil think otherwise is "*senseless vanity*" (emphasis mine). Their roles as virtuous women allow them to say "I'd lose my life and Love a thousand times before my Virtue" (3.5.177).

Bruce and Longvil, confronted with consequences, are jarred into a firm switch from their initial attractions. As I mentioned already, they discussed this earlier. There, however, the emphasis was on the women's honesty, beauty, and wealth; in other words, things that make women attractive and exclusive objects in marriage. As objects, they could be evaluated like property. Here the emphasis shifts to a recognition that women have to have a mutual affection for love and marriage to be satisfying:

Longvil. Our case is plain, we have no hopes of succeeding in our intended Loves; or if I had, I wou'd not have the body without the Mind.

Bruce. A man enjoys as much by a Rape as that way. But I am so pleas'd to find that *Miranda* loves me, that I'd not change for any but *Clarinda.*

. . . .

Longvil. Love like the Sun-beams, will not warm much, unless reflected back again.

(3.5.177)

Love as a mutual event may be subject to verification, but it will not reduce to sense in the form of physical pleasure. This is a long way from Lucretius's view of love as a destabilizing force. Lucretian indifference to women as inferior beings is no longer a tenable proposition to the heroes. Morality remains teleological in that it is to one's advantage to care for the feelings of others, but love has a force that transcends the purely physical.

Epsom Wells and *The Virtuoso* are, I think, best understood as Shadwell's attempt to illustrate the potential conflict between two ideas. The first is the individual's moral responsibility to preserve society by fulfilling one's role in it. The second is the instinctive human desire to act freely, which has the status of a right because attempts to deny it are counterproductive and doomed to failure in most cases anyway. Bevil and Rains, Bruce and Longvil elevate libertinism to a socially approved role even though the consequence is to endanger potential relationships with the most attractive (physically, intellectually, morally) women available. The relationships are endangered because libertinism is not even a possibility for virtuous women, who, nonetheless, have the drive to act freely and will do so when they are not allowed a suitably attractive role as respected wife. Men and women must learn through experience that pleasure and self-interest, while motivating, will not lead to the highest pleasure.

The potential conflict is present even in *The Sullen Lovers* where Emilia has to choose Stanford because the alternatives are a country fool or solitude: "If I shou'd be so mad as to Joyn hands with you, 'twould not be so much an Argument of Kindness to you, as Love to my self; since at best I am forc'd to choose between great Evils, either to be quite alone, or to have ill Company" (1.5.83). Her choice is clearly better, in that Stanford is her match in temperament and virtue, but both she and Stanford recognize the possibility that marriage can turn out to be a disastrous yoking of ill-suited individuals:

> *Stanford.* Why there's no necessity we should be such Puppies as the rest of Men and Wives are, if we fall out, to live together and quarrel on.
> *Emilia.* The Conditions of Wedlock are the same to all.
> *Stanford.* Whatsoever the Publick Conditions are, our private ones shall be, if either grows a Fopp, the other shall have liberty to part.
> (1.5.83)

Presumably the option under discussion here is separate maintenance, which is what Sir Richard allows Lady Loveyouth in *The Humorists*.[21] While such a solution is better than the marital warfare of Otway's comedies, we see exactly how unpleasant an option this is in the separation of the Woodlys in *Epsom Wells*. But as Jean Gagen points out, "Such a proviso is, of course, a tacit admission that Emilia's right to happiness in marriage is as important as Stanford's.[22]

What Stanford and Emilia have to achieve is what the heroes and heroines of *The Miser* and *The Humorists* have before the play begins: a view of marriage as the highest kind of felicity. Theodore has already passed through the stage of sex as contest and chides Hazard and Ranter for maintaining it: "No more of your senseless Railing against Marriage, 'tis dull and common"

(2.5.92). But Hazard's view of the consequences of marriage is close to the libertine views of the next two plays: "Farewel *Theodore*, thou art no more a man of this World" (2.5.92); that is, he is no longer the dashing rake that his friends admired.

When women are treated as objects, they will respond in kind. Lady Woodly embroils her husband with Bevil to satisfy her desire for Rains. Even in the farcical *The Woman Captain*, Shadwell offers a series of justifications for Mrs. Gripe's deception of her husband. It was a forced marriage and is sexually inactive and cruel: "my Mother betray'd me in my Youth to the slavery of thy Age. Thou didst promise to be a Father to me; thou canst not be a Husband, and wilt not be a Father—but a cruel Tyrant" (4.2.38). Mrs. Gripe asks only "the same Christian Liberty that others of my quality have" (4.5.19).

Love as contest is particularly attacked in *The Amorous Bigotte*. As a consequence of the unnatural confinement of children and their inability to choose whom they will marry, at the beginning of the play love is presented as a degraded battle of wills between courtesans and courtiers:

> *Hernando.* Oh fye Sir; Your true Lover sighs and pines, and seeks out shady Groves, and muttering Brooks, and tells his mournful tale, with Arms a cross to Eccho, and never thinks his Mistriss is a Woman but a Goddess.
> *Luscindo.* No where but in Romances, why there's no diversion or conversation in Madrid, but with a Curtezan. The men are too grave (not to be uncivil and say dull) and the honest Woman are lockt up; besides none in Spain are so well bred as your Curtezans no more.
>
> (5.1.23)

One cannot take Luscindo's rebuttal either too lightly or too seriously. When he meets Elvira he reacts just as Hernando has said he will, calling her an "Angel" (5.4.59). But for the meetings of the male and female leads to occur, Elvira and Rosania have to resort to statagems that they know to be both risky and indecorous. The alternative object of attraction is Levia, a courtesan, who is beautiful, intelligent, and well bred.

Angelica, the courtesan in Aphra Behn's *The Rover*, is the victim of loving Willmore too well and losing control of the situation. Levia, on the other hand, is contemptible precisely because she regards love as a struggle for control:

> *Levia.* Luscindo began to cool upon my fondness, and seek out new Adventures; and I am resolv'd to plague him for't.

Gremia. You say you Love him?
Levia. Yes, with such madness as admits no rest.
Gremia. And will you anger him?
Levia. Yes, therefore, if we don't season our love with anger some-
    times, 'twill be too luscious, and men will surfeit of it.

                                                        (5.1.24)

Love is compared to food, good if well prepared; the metaphor
reduces love to a matter of taste, literally and figuratively. And,
before falling in love with Elvira, Luscindo regards love the same
way: "Pain is b[u]t a relishing bit, to make us taste our pleasure
better; she has made me jealous, which spurs up my restive Love,
that wou'd have Jaded otherwise[;] whilst she lov'd only me, I
cou'd have lov'd another, but now she loves another, I can love
none but her" (5.1.23). When love is a contest, difficulty in ob-
taining the object is enjoyable. And love for the unreformed Luscindo (and Levia) is merely enjoying people as if they were
objects: "Thou art no Philosopher Hernando, prithee what is
Love? why nothing but great Lust" (5.1.23).

But Luscindo and Doristeo, the other male lead, realize over
the course of the play that real love is incompatible with this
view. Levia is inferior to the pure Elvira and Rosania because,
as a whole, she is inescapably an object according to Doristeo:
"There's no comparison betwixt an adventure and a purchase,
especially where the Mistriss seems the Aggressor" (5.2.29). Love
is different from going to the store, but the latter claim is false
since Rosania and Elvira both declare their love for their respective gallants the first time they get the chance. Rosania and Elvira
differ from Levia in that they do not seek to control the affection
of those they love, while the desire for control that Levia, Luscindo, and Doristeo all share brings the men into danger; the
men almost duel over Levia and nearly lose Elvira and Rosania
as well. Luscindo sums up the consequences of intrigue in love:
"O Heaven, what fatal accidents have hurried me even to the
brink of ruine" (5.5.70).

Desire is not distinct from love, nor is pleasure. Rosania tells
Tegue that she looks forward to marital sex when he asks her if
she desires Doristeo: "Not for the World unless I were Married
to him, and then I must confess I shou'd desire it" (5.3.43). What
the virtuous women convert the men to is the belief that love
must be mutual rather than a power struggle; Luscindo closes
the play acknowledging his conversion: "Now dear Elvira, may
our mutual Love shine clear, without one Cloud upon it" (5.5.76).

What he comes to see is that love leads to virtue: "a man can no more love Elvira with dishonour, than he can love heaven and be vitious; it were a contradiction" (5.4.60). Levia, on the other hand, cannot be redeemed and continues to see love as a weapon, cursing Luscindo with "violent Love, and invincible impotence" (5.5.75). Her view of love, the rakish view, is self-defeating and leaves her a raging and disappointed termagant.

Mutual love mediates between the chastity society requires of women and the rakishness it allows in men. For men, the pleasures of mutual love with the right women are superior to the natural but unproductive pleasures of libertine youth and draw men toward their necessary role as preservers of order. For women, mutual love offers a chance of satisfying their equally natural desires without being forced to renounce their dignity and become objects of exchange. Love is an irrational force that acts providentially to the benefit of society and individuals, although love possesses rational attractions as well. Prudence draws men to mutuality, while women see it as the only way to assure recognition of their rights to self-determination. Thus mutual love serves a sociopolitical function by preserving bloodlines and assuring that wives and children will be supported.

Perhaps Shadwell's clearest statement of the importance he places on love occurs in an isolated song about love and beauty:

> Who er on these fix their desires
> Goe right in Naturs way
> All others are but wandering fires
> Which lead mankind astray
>
> (5.384)

Women and men acknowledge that they have a natural propensity toward love both for companionship and sex. In *The Sullen Lovers*, Carolina tells Emilia to leave her idle talk of nunneries since they are an unnatural fate for sensible, healthy women: "Doe you Think that any Women that have sense, or Warmth of Blood, as we have, wou'd go into a Nunnery?" (1.2.30). Theodore in *The Miser* insists that love is the better part of life: "Love, when inclinations meet, is the only condition to be enjoy'd. Love! there is no life without it; we do but sleep, and dream we live, when we are not in love" (2.4.63). In *The Volunteers*, Major General Blunt tells Hackwell Junior that love is natural for men: "Blush not my brave Stripling to be in Love, 'tis a Manly Passion, and none but beasts, or beastly fellows are without it" (5.2.180). To his daughter Blunt emphasizes that not to love is unhealthy: "By the Lord Harry, a brave Wench, blush not, 'tis not shame to love a Gallant Fellow, 'tis natural to love, and 'tis a Disease not to be subject to it" (5.1.168). The paragon Lord Bellamy in *Bury Fair* explains the agency of the happy resolution to Oldwit as "Love and Fate, that Govern Everything" (4.5.367).

Despite its naturalness, love remains fundamentally irrational. In *The Amorous Bigotte* Elvira falls in love with Luscindo at first sight and immediately begins to make assumptions about body and mind that even she knows to be unjustifiable: "Hah, what Madness is this to fall in Love with one I know not! Nor does he know me, or my Love! Oh, if his mind be like his Body (and certainly it must be so) 'twill justifie my passion to the World" (5.1.20). However realism is irrelevant in love, and when Luscindo rhapsodically claims that Elvira transcends her sex in every way, Elvira recognizes the inaccuracy but regards it as unimportant: "I know my self too well to apply this; all my hope is, that you have love enough to deceive your self; and since all happiness is but imagination, 'twill serve your turn as well as truth" (5.4.59). Lovers need not be correct in the qualities they assign to the beloved; even if their love deceives them, they can still be happy. Perhaps this irrationality accounts for why some critics have regarded the conversion of Shadwell's heroes as unlikely. Charles O. McDonald, for instance, claims that Shadwell's heroes are more "'fanciful,' unrealistic, than any figures presented by the major playwrights as well as less satirized and comic."[23] But McDonald argues that the satire of the Restoration is fundamentally "rationalistic," whereas Shadwell, as I have argued, repeatedly dramatizes the limits of rationality.

I am not arguing that rational considerations do not play some role in love since the wisest characters are aware of a dynamic between custom and love. In *The Scowrers*, Clara laments the fact that she has fallen in love with Wildish, and Eugenia chides her for complaining:

> *Clara.* Oh Eugenia! 'tis against my will, I sooner would have chosen to have been blasted with Lightning: Love struck as fiercely through my heart, and as little could I resist it; But prithee do not triumph over my Misfortune.
>
> *Eugenia.* Misfortune: why Loves the greatest blessing upon Earth, Life is nothing but a Shadow, Love is the Substance: Methinks I should be nothing but a moving clod without it: Besides he loves thee as furiously too, what wouldst thou have?

Clara. Not him of all the world.

Eugenia. Nor I the other, till I see a full Reformation in his Life, and Manners; if they think us worth that, they will soon shew the change, if they do not, sure we will have sense to think them not worthy of us.

(5.4.120–21)

Love makes life worth the living for a Shadwellian woman, which does not mean she is prepared to sacrifice her self-respect. The moral responsibility remains with the individual. However, even if love fixes on an unworthy object, rational considerations do not take precedence until it is clear that it is a question of one or the other; Clara could conceivably have to reject Wildish, but not until he becomes a threat to her own honor.

Men of sense recognize that the consequences of not reforming under the influence of love are dangerous. First, health is endangered by the use of women one can have easily. Bellamy tells Wildish that "he who uses publick ones, is a Fool, and hurts himself" (4.1.309). Mr. Rant warns Sir William that "The use of common Whores is most pernicious, / By which, the least you venture is your Nose" (5.5.139). The disease-ridden Crazy in *The Humorists* is living proof of the consequences of general debauchery. Even women who are presumably sound carry their own punishment with them. Lovel spends much of *The Sullen Lovers* fleeing Lady Vaine whom he has already enjoyed, because the prospect of a repetition has no allure for him. Sex without love grows tiresome, but an affair, once begun, is difficult to end, as Bellamy tells Wildish: "those that were worth the having were hard to come by, and harder to put off" (5.1.309). The result of this is "anxiety." Thus mutual love is justifiable on epicurean grounds in that it is conducive to health and avoids displeasing mental states.

Men have it easier than women in that when they love they can usually control choice. For mutual love to mean anything, however, women have to have free choice as well. Antipathy to forced marriages is, of course, one of the commonplaces of Restoration drama, but it is restated again and again in Shadwell. In *The Humorists*, Theodosia insists on the right to marry whom she pleases. Her aunt, Lady Loveyouth, allows her as suitors Crazy, Briske, and Drybob about whom she says, "They Husbands, why a Nunnery were more tolerable, to be mew'd up with none but musty old Women, or your melancholy young Eaters of Chalk" (1.2.208). This is not a rejection of marriage, just mismatched marriage; the institution is fine if the right couple is paired as Raymund's deception of Lady Loveyouth allows.

By *The Lancashire Witches*, and in all subsequent plays, women are stating flatly that individual rights have priority over other obligations. Isabella and Theodosia identify the imposition of a husband with Catholic oppression:

> *Isabella.* Well, we are resolved never to marry where we are de-
> signed, that's certain. For my part I am a free English woman, and
> will stand up for my Liberty, and property of Choice.
> *Theodosia.* And Faith, Girl, I'le be a mutineer on thy side; I hate
> the imposition of a Husband, 'tis as bad as Popery.
>
> (4.1.111)

Their position is that a rational individual has the right to choose for herself. Love becomes a part of a program for independence from a too rigid hierarchy. Happiness in love is a right justified by, as Doubty says, "self-preservation, the great Law of Nature" (4.2.130). An unhappy marriage is a kind of death, indicating how important mutual love is in Shadwell's idea of social relations.

Gertrude, in *Bury Fair*, makes the same political argument to Wildish: "for my Father is no Outwork of mine: you may take him, but you are ne'r the nearer to me. I am a free Heiress of England, where Arbitrary Power is at an end, and I am resolv'd to choose for my self (4.3.339). Her position is untouchable; she need not consider the social restriction of a father at all, since she is independently wealthy. Eugenia and Clara in *The Scowrers* are in the same situation. As Clara says, "We are true English woman, Co-heirs of two thousand pounds a year, and are resolv'd to assert our Liberty and Property" (5.2.97). When woman have sufficient social position and material wealth, the path to mutual love is dependent only on men who have to reform to recognize love's importance.

Even when this is not the case, intelligent parents allow their daughters' freedom of choice or at least accept it when it occurs. In *The Sullen Lovers*, Emilia and Carolina marry without their father's permission, but wise and affectionate, he is easily reconciled:

> *Carolina.* Sir, I beseech you be not offended, their Births and For-
> tunes are not unequal to ours, and if they were, 'twere too late for
> it to be redrest.

. . . .

Father. Well! Heaven bless you together, since you have don't.
(1.5.90–91)

The fait accompli is accepted as such without recriminations or punishment. The same pattern occurs in many of Shadwell's plays. Sir Richard in *The Humorists*, Sir Edward in *The Lancashire Witches*, Oldwit in *Bury Fair*, and Major General Blunt in *The Volunteers* all accept their children's or ward's choices and are clearly admirable when they do so.

On the other hand, for parents not to accept their children's choices is a sure mark of stupidity or viciousness. John Wilcox mentions that Shadwell shifts the emphasis of *The Miser* from Harpagon in *L'Avare* to the tricks of the children; as usual, Wilcox regards this as a typical English debasement of the divine original.[24] But Wilcox fails to notice that Shadwell is operating with a different assumption about the rights of children to choose where they will love, and in consequence Goldingham is made vicious as well as dense, while the cleverness of the children is correspondingly emphasized to create the conflict of custom versus love. Lady Loveyouth in *The Humorists*, Lady Gimcrack in *The Virtuoso*, the Shackleheads in *The Lancashire Witches*, and Hackwell Senior, in *The Volunteers* all reject, at least temporarily, their children's desires in love, and all are associated independently with some other kind of failing. One symptom of how dangerous the social system of Spain is in *The Amorous Bigotte* is the refusal of Bernando and Belliza to forgive their respective children Luscindo and Elvira; Bernando and Belliza end planning to marry each other so that they can disinherit Luscindo and Elvira. Whether or not the parents can succeed at their age, the lead couples must accept love as its own reward and "fly to a distant place" (5.4.60). In the absence of freedom of choice, power and wealth are left to those who cannot use them either for their own satisfaction or society's betterment.

Consistently then throughout Shadwell's career, the terms of morality take their meaning from social definitions of correct roles. These roles are more attractive aesthetically to the "well bred" than the alternative of complete independence and are desirable on teleological grounds since, if the roles are not upheld, society will not run properly nor can the individual live happily. Also, morality is dependent on individuals' capacity to recognize their roles and conform to them. What rescues the ethical system that informs Shadwell's plays from an incessant warfare between the sexes caused by the conflict between the youthful exuberance society allows men and the rigid chastity it insists on for women is the desire that men and women have for mutual love. Mutuality is both more attractive than animalistic hedonism and more likely to lead to comfort and felicity. Shadwell substitutes for God, universalizable principles of rationality, and a natively benevolent human nature, an aesthetic sense that serves as a moral guide: people choose between available roles through a perception of appropriateness, and prospective mates through the very nearly providential force of love.

John Traugott claims that Restoration comedy in general denies universal verities. In particular he examines Etherege for a potential solution to the problems this creates for ethical belief:

> When all the demands of will are known, when the necessity of the masks of manners are understood, love and honor are reinstated, founded not as formerly in natural law or religious sanction but in the demands of personality. The self becomes curiously selfless.[25]

Obvious objections come to mind when reading Traugott's analysis. First, he offers no contemporary evidence that the seventeenth-century concept of self is compatible with the Nietzschean idea of the isolated will that seems to inform his descriptions of Dorimant. In other words, the demands of will he perceives in Dorimant are more likely to be simple passions. Further, even Traugott concedes that Dorimant remains potentially dangerous despite his supposedly dissolved self. Still his point is very appealing; *The Man of Mode* ends with Harriet and Dorimant drawn together by competitive tension based upon mutual recognition that each is incomplete without the other, who is their only equal. Shadwell's plays present a similar situation, except his heroes and heroines arrive at a view of love where the recognition of incompleteness becomes not a ground for endless further competition but a way to escape the competition that a purely social construction of ethical obligation entails. Problems remain for such a view, however, but that is a subject for another chapter.

5

The Unwilling, the Unlovable, and the Unimpressed

Shadwell's plays, I have argued, require an ethical system that presupposes individual responsibility and recognition of one's role in society, the latter being a consequence of birth, education, and talent. Further, the plays are an example of the movement toward mutual love, and mutual love provides the necessary dynamic for change when the available roles are unsatisfactory. Neither God nor universalizable principles of rationality are necessary for claims of moral obligation to have meaning; only free will and society's capacity to create meaning are required.

There are, however, internal tensions within Shadwell's ethics that are apparent in the plays. I discussed earlier the repeated references in Shadwell's plays to the fact that fate or random events largely control our possibilities; a wise man or woman accepts this and makes the best of it. But sometimes the roles to which we are doomed are so much in conflict with the human desire for self-determination Shadwell posits that strains in the fabric of Shadwell's ethics appear, and although he honestly presents such conflicts, he can offer no real solution. Moreover, an ethics of role can well be an unconscious justification for existing privilege. Since "ethics itself . . . is the ideological vehicle and the legitimation of concrete structures of power and domination"[1] that which is called "right" justifies the control of someone who is "the other," and therefore inherently weaker, more stupid, and yet simultaneously a threat to the interests of the dominant class.

This is most obvious in the plight of women in the Restoration society. Elizabeth Cowie argues that women characters cannot be discussed by contrasting them to a "real" world since as "signs" they take their meaning only from the context in which they are created: "One cannot speak of 'a' sign—women—without speci-

fying the system in which it has signification—exchange. Signs
are only meaningful within the system of signification in which
they are produced, and not as discrete units."[2] Thus, we need to
consider what meaning "woman" has as sign in Shadwell's plays.
Individuals are presented in Shadwell's plays as having the right
to act freely, and this is true of women as well. Nonetheless,
ethical values are social constructs, and the value that society in
Shadwell's plays assigns women is as objects of exchange that
cement class and kinship structures. "Woman" as sign is valuable precisely as she accepts her position as object within a system. But that leads to a conflict with the system since Shadwell
also recognizes "woman" as capable of generating social values.[3]

Helen M. Burke describes Alithea in The Country Wife as a
sign that refuses complete integration into the patriarchal space
of the play: "She both is, and is not, where she should be in the
system of male desire, her own desire operating outside the system designed by the male protagonist."[4] Shadwell's women cannot go that far. They can imagine a realm of alterity where they
would not be at risk of sacrificing their capacity as independent
creators of value, but ultimately they all yield to patriarchal values. To be happy they have to marry men who are at least their
social, intellectual, and moral equals. Outside of marriage they
cannot have dignity, but inside it they are threatened with loss
of control. From The Sullen Lovers on, the women characters
display, more seriously than men, an awareness of what they risk.
Emilia is designed by her father to be married to an uncouth
country neighbor, and the alternative of Stanford offers little
comfort because she trusts no man: "O no! I dare not think of
that [marriage], if he should grow troublesome, then 'twould be
out of my power to cast him off" (1.5.83). Carolina, although in
love with Lovel, still doubts his integrity and fears marriage will
become a prison; at the same time, she desires liberty as much
as he can: "Fie; fie, 'tis such a constant condition of life, that a
Woman had as good be profest in a Nunnery, for she can no
sooner get out of one than t'other" (1.2.28). Marriage is a tremen-
dous risk, according to Carolina, and cannot be entered into in
haste: "To speak gravely; let us first take the advice of our pil-
lows: since sleep being a great setler of the brain, may be an
enemy to Marriage, for one wou'd think that few in their right
Wits wou'd undertake so unseasonable an action, as you call it"
(1.5.82). But in this play the danger is abstract rather than real,
since Stanford is virtuous, Lovel reformed, and the father of the
women rational and compliant.

In *The Humorists* and *The Miser* the women are safe only because the men they love are clever and virtuous. Goldingham in *The Miser* and Lady Loveyouth in *The Humorists* are real threats in that they desire to tie the women to fools. The women are saved only by the tricks that Raymund, Bellamour, and Theodore execute to rescue them from the tyranny of those who have a right in the disposing of them. I have already discussed at length how the heroines of *Epsom Wells*, *The Virtuoso*, and *A True Widow* are conscious of their constricting social roles and jeopardized by men too well aware of the freedom of theirs. Mrs. Gripe in *The Woman Captain* is not so lucky and must arrange her own freedom after marriage.

Even in the pastoral romance *The Royal Shepherdesse*, Urania is endangered when promoted out of her proper sphere. The king desires her, and she bewails the fate that has left her without the possibility of virtuous marriage or any hope of successful resistance.

> . . . my choice
> Is either to be wicked, or to die.
> Oh Heaven! what black, what fatal Star
> Gave sad Misfortune at my birth?
> How happy had I been had I still dwelt
> With those who wear poor Cloaths, and honour vertue?
>
> (1.2.115)

This sounds like something similar to Boyle's rejection of the aristocratic ethic in that she is claiming noble birth actually works against virtue.[5] But in fact the key point is that the great, both men and women, have greater potential for vice. Urania is saved when it turns out that she has royal blood. As either shepherdess or princess she can easily be virtuous; as shepherdess who attracts the lust of a king, she is threatened with dangerous consequences through no fault of her own. Role is destiny, and Shadwell seems, in this play, to want to claim that virtue should be independent of role. He does not, however, dramatize that possibility, and Urania's resistance is rewarded because her true social status is discovered.

In *Timon*, Evandra is very much the victim of forgetting the social requirement of chastity, although in this play that requirement is founded upon an assumption about human nature; if women do not remain chaste, men will discard them after using them because of a desire for variety. Timon recognizes Evandra's superiority to Melissa, but cannot stay away from Melissa:

Why should I not love this Woman best?
She has deserv'd beyond all measure from me;
She's beautiful, and good as Angels are;
But I have had her Love already.
Oh, most accursed Charm, that thus perverts me!

(3.2.227)

But if Timon's greatest weaknesses are his lack of prudence and
temperance, then, despite her justification of true love, Evandra
must be regarded as guilty also. Women may be able to remain
sexually faithful outside of marriage, but men cannot, as Timon's
speech makes clear.

Timon comes to see that the social judgment on Evandra is
pernicious:

> *Timon.* . . . thou [Melissa] boast'st that thou art honest of thy Body,
> as if the Body made one honest: Thou hast a vile Corrupted filthy
> mind—
> *Melissa.* I am no Whore as she is.
> *Timon.* Thou ly'st, she's none: But thou art one in thy Soul.
>
> (3.4.260)

Alan S. Fisher argues that in this play, "the point is relentlessly
driven home that true love is a pact of loyalty between two con-
senting adults and is, if anything, profaned by marriage."[6] Although Fisher's observation that true love should be a pact of
loyalty is true, that is because marriage is a social bond and this
is a corrupt society. The alternative of love in the woods cannot
work either, for men and women are social creatures. As P. F.
Vernon points out "It would be a mistake to assume that Shadwell is here seriously advocating free love as an alternative to
monogamy."[7] The problem is that society has an insufficient
value for mutual love in marriage. Evandra's chastity is her only
trump card; when she loses that, she loses her appeal to Timon
who values Melissa precisely because she is unobtainable. There
is no appropriate role for a woman in the Athenian society, because love counts for nothing, and love is the only way in Shadwell a woman can improve her lot.

After 1688, however, female characters become increasingly
vocal about the disadvantages inherent in being born a woman.
In *Bury Fair*, Wildish claims he will be Gertrude's slave, to which
she responds, "Yes, you can act a Slave for a time, in hopes
of making me one ever after" (4.3.333). Even when Gertrude is

mocking Lord Bellamy, there remains an undercurrent of anger at her situation:

> *Bellamy.* Cou'd I incline your gentle Heart to Love, then no Discourse of it wou'd seem so.
> *Gertrude.* I can't tell that; but as things stand now, indeed it makes me smile, to think of a grave Mother, or, for want of her, a wise Father, putting a daughter into a Room, like a Hare out of a Basket, and letting him loose; that is, to act the Part of a Lover before Marriage, and never think of it afterward. . . .
> *Bellamy.* But, madam, a Lady of your Wit and Sence, knows 'tis the great end that Woman is designed for; and 'tis in vain for you to speak against Love; for every look, and every word of yours, inflames me more.
> *Gertrude.* There's a word now, Inflames, and Chains, and Fetters! I warrant you; One wou'd think a Man were a Martyr, or a Slave at *Algiers* at least. What conversation might Men and Women have did not this foolish Love interpose!
>
> (4.3.339)

The end of which Lord Bellamy speaks is correct, as far as the play reveals, as even Gertrude admits in her love for Wildish; but this view of women requires that to be fulfilled they have to find their being in a man. This presents two problems.

First, women become game, pursued and harried into marriage by parents and lovers, under the assumption that they have worth only as they are marriageable. While it is to men's advantage to be married in that they will be happier, women have no real value if they have no likelihood of being married. Second, however much Shadwell wants to believe in mutual love, the conventions of society undercut any real equality. Men, while wooing, are "slaves" and afterward are masters. Conversation between men and women as equals is not a possibility, granted a view of woman's end as being the beloved of a man. Lord Bellamy willingly accepts Philadelphia (who has been disguised as his servant Charles) instead of Gertrude because, "I was Passionate to Marry the other Sister, because I lov'd her; but I think it more reasonable to marry this, because she loves me" (4.5.367). We need to recall that earlier in the play Lord Bellamy has said to Charles, "I'll breed thee up to be my Friend" (4.1.308). With an adoring wife properly trained by himself, there is no potential conflict between the individual's right to choose for herself and the proper subordination of women in marriage. This clearly is not going to be the case with Gertrude and Wildish; both love equally, but Gertrude has a clearer eye to Wildish's faults (of which there are many) than Philadelphia can have of the nearly faultless Bellamy. If Wildish cannot reform, how can Gertrude obey, which she regards as the duty of a wife?

In *The Volunteers*, Eugenia pleads with Clara to be truthful when talking to her: "Let's dissemble with Mankind: but prithee let's be honest one among another" (5.3.196). Eugenia's request is a part of her recognition that men and women have to act differently because that is the way society makes them behave: "Unequal custom, that shou'd thus impose upon our Sex, the worst of tasks, Dissembling" (5.2.186). They have to lie because modesty requires it, yet that lying is itself contrary to the spirit of love:

> *Clara.* . . . but we are now alone, and are not forced upon the Drudgery of dissembling.
> *Eugenia.* 'Tis very hard that honest Women must be tyed to that as well as Wenches.
> *Clara.* Indeed a little lying is a necessary quality in our Sex!
> *Eugenia.* That's but convenient policy—for us to use with Men; Fiction in Love and Poetry is lawful.
> *Clara.* That's a very civil word, for lying; but there is no pleasure in Conversation, when hearts are not open to one another.
>
> (5.5.216)

Social conventions not merely allow for dishonesty, they require it of women. But conversation, the discourse between equals that characterizes mutuality, is impossible when the communication is suspect, and it must be in a society that forces women to lie. And women must lie because they remain a subordinate class, which must repress their resistance to patriarchal domination.

The conflict is between individual desire and social role. The advantage that Aquinas, for instance, has over Shadwell is that it did not occur to the previous Thomas that the individual had some kind of existence separate from society and God. Shadwell does think so—hence the repeated claims that the individual has the right of free choice and an innate tendency to pursue goals that are not the product of social conditioning—but nonetheless thinks that value is largely a social construction. Although love tends to solve the problems in Shadwell's plays as men and women escape the social coil through mutuality, fortune does play a role in the possibility of virtue; bad fortune may be an inducement to vice and limits virtue. In the absence of some underlying source or principle of obligation like God, or a belief that moral claims are rationally determinable, Shadwell needs to claim that a person has no value independent of society. In other words, when the women complain that they have fewer choices, he needs to be able to say that that is the way it must be for society to operate, and Shadwell is unwilling to do anything of the sort, probably because that would deny men the right to throw off rulers and rules that don't suit them. The rise of individualism conflicts with his attempt to establish social relativism, and can lead only to emotivism. Shadwell seems to recognize the conflict in the speeches of the women, but his only real response is to say that love will provide freedom through a loss of the will to be unsocial. That is, love will cause women in particular to accept their status as objects who possess the value patriarchal society has assigned them, rather than generating a social system in which they are manipulators of values rather than just a value manipulated by men.

This response requires that love solve a great many problems, and completely disregards the possibility that one may be, either naturally or through habit, unloving or unlovable. That sort of nagging difficulty shows up early in Shadwell through Snarl in *The Virtuoso*. Snarl is, according to Bruce, "sometimes in the right" (3.2.131). He is, moreover, a man of wealth. But despite his intelligence, perception, and social position, he has degenerated into the match of Sir Formal and Sir Samuel, repeating his stock phrase "in sadness" whether he is angry or gleeful at another's discomfiture, until the term has no meaning attached to it. His other tiresome reiteration is that "The last Age was the Age of Modesty." The problem is not merely that this tag phrase indicates a failure to recognize that the values of the last age were equally a social construction; no meaning attaches to this phrase for Snarl either. For instance, he uses the phrase when asking his whore Mrs. Figgup to beat him, apparently their standard form of sexual activity because Snarl "was so us'd to it at Westminter-School I cou'd never leave it off since" (3.3.139).

Habit is not the only problem, although masochism scarcely makes him a lovable sort of person. Snarl has become so self-centered that he can no longer recognize his participation in the vices of the age. At the end of the play he marries Mrs. Figgup to preserve his pleasure and keep Sir Nicholas from his fortune. Bruce points out that this is a rather inconsistent thing for Snarl to do:

> *Bruce.* Did Gentlemen and Men of Honour marry Whores in the Last Age?
>
> *Snarl.* In sadness they have much ado to avoid it in this; if I have marri'd one, she is my own; and I had better marry my own, than another mans, by the mass, as 'tis fifty to one I shou'd, if I had marri'd elsewhere in sadness.
>
> (3.5.179)

Whatever the weaknesses of the current age, Bruce, who agrees that the current age has many, cannot see them as a justification for Snarl's marriage, as his mockery makes clear. But Snarl's personality, unlovable and unloving, is his fate and has led him to his marriage. Position and intelligence are not enough to guarantee a happy and virtuous life. Shadwell examines this possibility in much greater detail later, again offering inadequate explanations for what went wrong and what the solution is.

Critics who claim that Shadwell converts to some kind of "benevolism" in his later plays always overlook the character of Tope, the aging unreformed rake. Tope is an anomaly in that he is just one character in one play and nothing like him appears in the other late plays. But he is sufficiently developed to show that Shadwell was aware of another potential conflict between social role and personal desires. This awareness may be a consequence of the actor who played the part, since Anthony Leigh was famous for playing characters who are at odds with social values, such as Sir Edward Belfond, Tegue, and, the most extreme expression of an inversion of social order, Lady Addleplot in *Love for Money*, in which a male actor plays a woman who conspires against the political structure.[8] But whatever the genesis of Shadwell's conception, the character reveals another internal weakness of the ethics I have ascribed to Shadwell.

Although in his fifties, Tope is still the friend of Wildfire and Sir William, the heroes who must reform, as he was the friend of Mr. Rant previously. As such, Wachum's description of the perfect scowering gentleman is applicable to him: "You shall see him, oh if did you but hear him swear and curse you'd be in love with him! He does 'em so like a Gentleman, while a company of ye here about Town, pop out your Oaths like pellets out of Elder Guns" (5.2.101). It is not what you do, it is the style with which you do it. This is a view with which the gentlemen scowrers are in complete agreement, and why they see themselves as different from Whachum, Dingboy, and Bluster:

Sir William.   Well said, Jack Tope, thou art in the right, he [a true scowrer] must be of Mien and Person not ungraceful, of pleasing Speech, sharp must his Wit be, and his Judgment solid.

Wildfire.   He must be cheerful, easie, and well temper'd.

Tope.   He must be well bred[,] have seen the World; learn'd, knowing, and retentive of a secret: He must have Truth and Courage.

Sir William.   In short, he must be just such a fellow as thou art, if it be possible; while all the Contemporaries have either Dyed, or left off, and grown sober Sots, thou still perseverest in generous Lewdness.

(5.2.101)

The crunch, of course, is the last line. Sir William and Wildfire discover over the course of the play that "Lewdness" is not "generous"; Tope remains unrepentant.

We are offered the possibility of seeing him as victim of stupidity and habit when he refuses to settle down at the end:

Tope.   Ha, ha, ha, fine Fools, turn sober Sots, give over all Vanities, as you call 'em, for the greatest Vanity on Earth, Matrimony! you may leave any other vanities when you please, but that will stick to you with a Vengeance. Matrimony ha, ha, ha, there's nothing in the world worth being in earnest, I am sure not being sober, 'tis all a Farce.

Mr. Rant.   I hope for, old Acquaintance, you will embrace this motion, reform, and live a sober Country Life, then we shall be Neighbors.

Tope.   Reform, quoth he, 'tis a pretty age, at Five and Fifty to begin to lead a new Life: No, no, I have gone too far to retreat, I must charge through, I'll drink like a Fish these Fifty years, these fellows will be Asses Milk, within six Months, and dye o'th' Pip soon after.

(5.5.147–48)

He leaves calling Sir William and Wildfire "Apostates." But the problem is that his claim about marriage is true; there are no convenient, unrealistic divorces in Shadwell. Further, it is of no use pointing out that whoring and drinking will ruin his health. Tope is capable of great restraint and in the first act reproves Sir William and Wildfire for drinking in the morning while he has been out walking for two hours in the Park; he claims, and we have no reason to doubt him, that "I have buried two hundred Mornings Draughts-men of My Acquaintance" (5.1.90).

Moreover, the early death of Wildfire's father shows that virtue and domesticity do not guarantee health either:

> *Tope.* . . . but thy Father, Tom, was a sober sot, a consumptive
> Scoundrel, and we could make nothing of him, he married like a
> Puppy, and grew most pitifully uxorious, but the comfort is that
> few of that sort get their own Children: Thou art not like him at
> all.
>
> (5.1.90)

Moreover, a final explanation for Tope's isolation will not fly. Mr.
Rant's last words claim that Tope is the victim of his habits and
his limited intelligence:

> Old Habits are with Difficulty Broken,
> And Fools are ever found most obstinate;
> But the least Seeds of Wit with Understanding,
> Will in some time spring up, and grow and thrive,
> And bear down the rank Weeds of Vice and Folly.
>
> (5.5.148)

Object lessons exist of the positive claim that wit and understanding will eventually compel reformation, in Sir William,
Wildfire, and even Mr. Rant, who had a wild youth as well. The
negative claim is demonstrated by Wachum. It simply cannot
apply to Tope, however. He is not a fool, or, if he is, he has done
an impressive job of fooling both of the Rants and Wildfire for
years.

Tope, like Don John, is rendered unattractive in his refusal to
reform, because like Don John his position and talents render
him unassailable. He is ugly from his drinking—Lady Maggot
describes him as an "old Red nos'd, battered Drunkard"
(5.2.103)—which may account for the fact that Tope has not
"cuckolded an Alderman these 7 years" (5.2.104). Still, neither
of these things make him unhappy; there are always whores,
which is all Tope needs anyway. For the audience, it is apparent
that Sir William and Wildfire are better off at the end than he
because he has never felt the reforming power of love. But therein
lies the problem.

Love is fate. Clara does not wish to love Wildfire, nor he her,
but once it happens Wildfire can reform. Likewise, Sir William
is appalled when he falls in love: "But the worst of all is that I
am in love, most desperate most abominable love, the worst of
all love, I am afraid honest love" (5.1.89). The pre-Clara Wildfire
responds with doubt about the existence of the state: "Love! Faith
I could never believe there was any such thing: I have had a
furious Appetite to a new Face, like a greedy stomach to a new

Dish, but I never made a very full meal, but I wish'd it off again" (5.1.91). Tope, on the other hand, has never loved: "I have had as many Whores as any of you; but never I had one whom I car'd if she were hang'd or no" (5.1.91). His skepticism about woman's virtue is at least partially justifiable—witness Lady Maggot—and his epicureanism is the genuine Lucretian version. When Sir William ascribes virtues to Eugenia based only on his having fallen in love with her, Tope speaks of mutability:

> *Sir William.* Hence all such profane thoughts, this is a Lady, who has all the Beauty and Vertue of the Sex.
> *Tope.* Pish, Sex sayst thou? I warrant she is not overstock'd neither if she has; but Beauty is Frail, and vertue is more Frail, Will.
>
> (5.1.91)

The point is that Tope has never been in love, nor, as far as we know, has any one loved him.

This poses a contradiction for Shadwell in that love guides us to appropriate roles. But if we cannot control love, and love is the reforming power, then we cannot control reformation. If unreformed individuals are a danger to the smooth functioning of society, and the activities of the scowrers prior to reformation indicate that they are, then it may be necessary to restrict the individual freedom of those who are unloving and unlovable. But mutual love means something only if individuals have free choice to act upon their love. Between individual freedom, which Shadwell clearly believes in, and the necessity for love to provide the dynamic that keeps social roles fluid and draws individuals to socially approved roles, lies a potential gap: if you are by nature unlovable, as is Tope apparently, you could become a danger to society and lose the right to individual freedom. If you are as well bred, wealthy, and talented as Tope, it is far from clear how society can ever control you. And a disrupted society may fail to construct any kind of value.

The superiority of love is apparent to those who feel its effects. Clearly there is a positive cash value of pleasure in reforming for Sir William and Wildfire, and a positive result accrues to the rest of society when they do. But since Tope does not know any better he cannot be unhappy about not reforming. By remaining self-centered, he has the tangible value of continuing pleasure while acting in a way that the heroes and heroines regard as immoral. Tope is immoral only on aesthetic grounds; his role is unattractive to us. But is that enough if he is a danger to a society? At some point or another, Shadwell needs either to restrict individual freedom on the grounds that when that freedom is a danger to society it is immoral, or claim that the well-being of society must give way when individual freedom is at stake. In either case, one or the other must be privileged; that is, he is going to have to claim that one or the other has priority.

And Shadwell has no consistent way to make such a claim. Empirically in the plays, it turns out that society cannot control some individuals. On the other hand, values take their meaning from social constructions. When Tope cannot see the validity of the social role of gentleman because he has never been in love, both social value and individual freedom become equally valuable and valueless. There is no rational way to weigh the respective claims, and the result is likely to be the destruction of society, and hence the destruction of value. What Shadwell avoids, with the exceptions of Don John and Tope, is that if one denies both God and rationality's capacity to adjudicate between moral claims, to say some things are always right and some always wrong, and that if one assumes the individual's capacity to act freely, there remains the possibility that an exceptionally powerful individual may simply reject any social claims whatsoever and arbitrarily will some thing to be right at the expense of every one else. Perhaps Shadwell did not see this as a major problem since the individual has a limited capacity to affect society as a whole, and that may be why he feels free to present the potential problem with Tope; after all, he had survived two revolutions and seen society remain relatively stable. On the other hand, there were no nuclear weapons in the seventeenth century.

Shadwell's plays did no worse from a commercial standpoint in the eighteenth-century than most of his competitors from the Restoration. *Epsom Wells* had its last eighteenth-century performance in 1726, *The Lancashire Witches* in 1728, *The Libertine* in 1740, *The Woman Captain* in 1744, and *The Squire of Alsatia* in 1767, an impressive stage history of eighty years.[9] Although his popularity in the eighteenth-century is in no way comparable with that of Congreve, Cibber, Steele, Vanbrugh, or Farquhar, his plays did at least as well as those of contemporaries such as Behn and Crowne.[10] Still, a kind of derision attaches to Shadwell's plays that others from the period have escaped. After all, Behn and Crowne were not singled out to be heroes in *The Dunciad*. Despite the fact that Shadwell was poet laureate, he was left out of Johnson's *The Lives of the Poets* (although this may just be a consequence of the fact that Shadwell did not write much poetry, and even a Shadwell fan would have to admit that what there is is very poor). In modern times, John Traugott refers to *The Libertine* as "a perfectly insane product of that undeviatingly senseless mind."[11]

A part of the problem may well be, as Don R. Kunz argues, the fact that more people have read Dryden than Shadwell and take *MacFlecknoe* as a serious evaluation of Shadwell's drama,[12] ignoring the genesis of the poem in an aesthetic debate and the fact that as late as 1679 Dryden wrote a prologue for *A True Widow*. While this is undoubtedly a factor, Kunz ignores the defensive tone that appears in Shadwell's admirers, starting in the 1690s. Shadwell is acknowledged as a great comic playwright with two major flaws: a careless attitude toward religion and the inability to portray a true gentleman.

The former accusation is presented straightforwardly by Langbaine. Langbaine acknowledges that he is a friend of Shadwell's and prefers Shadwell's comedies to Dryden's. But he is too sensitive a critic to overlook the attacks on religion in Shadwell's plays:

> However, I wish our Author for his own sake, had left out the Character of *Smirk* [in *The Lancashire Witches*], notwithstanding the Defence he makes for it in the Preface, and his Protestation of having a true value for the Church of *England*: for 'tis evident that her Sons, the Clergy, are abused in that Character; particularly in the first scene of the second Act: and therefore Mr. *Shadwell* must allow me a little to distrust his sincerity, when he makes such large Professions of Respect to Gowns-men; to whom I believe his Obligations are greater then Kindness: otherwise, he would not have suffered such reflections to have passed his Pen, as are to be met with in his *Squire of Alsatia*, and the Epilogue to the *Amorous Bigotte*, etc. If Mr. *Shadwell* would take a Friend's Counsel, I would advise him to treat serious things with due Respect; and not to make the *Pulpit* truckle to the *Stage*.[13]

Shadwell attacks religion too boldly for Langbaine to be comfortable with it. Indeed, writers should never meddle with religion, as Langbaine goes on to say; Dryden "never miscarried more, than when he intermeddled with Church Matters." Langbaine is not accusing Shadwell of atheism, but Shadwell's anticlericalism has the effect of limiting the moral authority of organized religion, and Langbaine objects to that very much.

Langbaine was not unique in suspecting Shadwell's religious

views. Nicholas Brady, although he says very little about Shadwell in Shadwell's funeral sermon, feels obligated to say that Shadwell possessed "(however much the World may be mistaken in him) a much deeper Sense of Religion, than many others have, who pretend to it more openly" (Summers, 1: cclxiv). But Brady admits that his acquaintance with Shadwell, although "intimate," was "short." If Shadwell reconverted at the end of his life, he would not have been the first, and the fact that Brady goes out of the way to address doubts about Shadwell's religious beliefs indicates that they must have been widespread. Montague Summers, much as he would like to rehabilitate Shadwell's reputation, cannot absolve Shadwell so easily: "it is to be feared that his religious sentiments—for the greater part of his days at all events—were gravely reprehensible" (1: ccxlviii). The Reverend Summers may not be a wholly reliable judge, but he was familiar with the texture of Restoration comedy in a way few have ever been, and his perceptions should not be lightly disregarded.

It is possible that after Shadwell's death audiences wanted the religious foundation of ethics to be explicitly stated, at least in drama that purported to be morally instructive. Consider dueling, for instance. Since the obligations of role are the source of ethics for Shadwell, an honorable gentleman not only may duel, he must duel when called upon; it is, as Welford says in The Volunteers, "a Duty Gentleman owe to one another" (5.3.199). In Steele's The Lying Lover (1703), the justification of dueling as a requirement of honor is a Satanic ploy and an offense against heaven:

> Honour! the horrid Application of that sacred Word to a Revenge 'gainst Friendship, Law and Reason, is a damn'd last shift of the damn'd envious Foe of [the] Human Race. The routed Fiend projected this but since th' expansive glorious Law from Heav'n came down— Forgive.[14]

Equally in The Conscious Lovers, Bevil Junior expressly states that the sanction against dueling is divine in origin: "I have often told you in Confidence of Heart, I abhorr'd the Daring to offend the Author of Life, and rushing into his Presence.—I say, by the very same Act, to commit the Crime against him, and immediately to urge on to his Tribunal" (4.1.122–26). Duels are, of course, common in other Restoration comedies that remained popular after the turn of the century. But Shadwell's plays, more than those of his contemporaries, insist on a moral evaluation of such activities, and his tendency to accept duels when religion disallowed them, could not, perhaps, be as easily disregarded as no more than good, clean fun.

The other recurring criticism of Shadwell is that he could not present a convincing gentleman. Exactly what this means seems ambiguous, at least to me. When Etherege makes the charge (1688), what he means is clear: "his [Shadwell's] witty men will scarce pass muster among the last recruits our General made for the Dog and Partridge."[15] This is a fair evaluation coming from Etherege; certainly Belfond Junior has neither the wit nor fascination of Dorimant. But when Charles Gildon, revising Langbaine, makes a similar remark (1699), what he means is not so obvious: "if he cou'd have drawn the Character of a man of Wit, as well as that of a Coxcomb, there would have been nothing wanting the Perfection of his Dramatic Fables."[16] Gildon's objection seems to be that there is insufficient difference between the coxcombs and the gentlemen, or that Shadwell could not properly conceive of what a gentleman should be.

By 1719 when Giles Jacob makes the accusation, the wording has changed critically: "[Shadwell] well understood Humour, and could draw a Coxcomb in perfection; but he seem'd deficient in perfecting the Character of a fine Gentleman."[17] Even if Jacob is just regurgitating Gildon's judgment, a normative claim has entered that was not present in Gildon. Gildon's criticism is aesthetic; Shadwell could not "draw" a gentleman properly and that affects the "Perfection" of the "Fable." Jacob's criticism has ethical overtones; Shadwell could not "perfect" a "fine Gentleman." Seventeenth- and eighteenth-century definitions of perfect carry an ethical sense for an ethics of role. Henry Cockeram defines perfect as "absolute."[18] John Kersey defines the noun as "compleat, entire; excellent, accomplished" and the verb as "to make perfect, to finish."[19] Johnson defines the noun as "Complete; consummate; finished; neither defective nor redundant," and his third definition is explicitly connected with morality: "Pure; blameless; clear; immaculate. This is a sense chiefly theological."[20] Shadwell's gentlemen lack something that prevents them from being "perfect" gentleman; something is missing from them that keeps them from being "excellent, accomplished." And since ethics are dependent on role in Shadwell, when the eighteenth century found Shadwellian heroes ungentlemanly, they were, perhaps unconsciously, attacking his depiction of virtue. In other words, Shadwell's gentlemen do not progress in morals to the status of "fine"-ness.

Even if this distinction is ingenious, both Gildon and Jacob illustrate that the early eighteenth-century audience thought that Shadwell was better at presenting the lower class than the upper class. This view was apparently shared by Richard Steele as well. He says about *Epsom Wells* in *The Tatler* that "The whole comedy is very just, and the low part of human life represented with much humour and wit."[21] But he also printed John Hughes's attack on the supernaturalism and morality of *The Lancashire Witches* even though he remarks that he wishes Hughes had discussed Shadwell's comic strengths. Hughes's reason for writing the critique is of interest:

> I shou'd not have troubled you with these Remarks, if there were not something else in this Comedy which wants to be exorcis'd more than the Witches. I mean the Freedom of some Passages, which I should have overlook'd, if I had not observed that those Jests can raise the loudest Mirth, tho' they are painful to right sense, and an Outrage upon Modesty.
>
> We must attribute such Liberties to the Taste of that Age, but indeed by such Representations a Poet sacrifices the best Part of His Audience to the worst, and, as one wou'd think, neglects the Boxes, to write to the Orange Wenches.[22]

It is not the earthiness of the play that bothers Hughes—that he can account for as a product of the play's theatrical origin in a different age.

What bothers Hughes is the fact that Shadwell's "freedom," his anticlericalism, his acceptance of self-interest and sex, and his presentation of morality as largely a matter of custom, is popular. The difference between good men and bad men in Shadwell is a function of their willingness to play a socially appropriate role, and the orange wenches and apprentices in the audience probably agreed—they were as moral as their betters, but they just could not afford the sort of ethical niceties available to "right sense" and modesty. When virtue becomes deontological, a standard that is supposed to apply to the orange wench as well as the gentlewoman, it becomes easy to lose sight of the fact that there are some economic advantages to using ethics as a method of social exclusion. If I am a gentleman not merely because I was born one and can play the part, but also because I am morally superior to the masses, then I am entitled to sit in the boxes and insist that the playwrights dramatize an ethical view that supports my right. This is not to say, however, that ethics must be the product of economic forces. Hughes was not prepared to accept the idea that society creates its moral systems to enable and justify the continued existence of society, and that moral worth does not exist independent of social judgment. He was not alone in this; the French and American revolutions professed the belief that individual worth is not a function of social role and exists prior to and independent of social circumstance. Shadwell, on the other hand, would presumably subscribe to the view of role that Douglas Patey attributes to Pope: "Right doing takes on the aspect of passivity (and immobility) because it consists finally in submission to role: thereby the self realizes its proper end, so that in virtuous *doing* the self is *being* what most truly it is."[23] Patey argues that Pope is maintaining a fading belief; Shadwell's plays are among the last that embody this belief on the stage.

Again the contrast between Shadwell and Steele is instructive. In *The Conscious Lovers*, Indiana's worth is not linked to her social status; Bevil Junior would have been as happy to take her if she had not proved to be Sealand's daughter, except as the fortuitous discovery serves to placate his father: "I hear your Mention, Sir, of Fortune, with Pleasure only as it may prove the Means to reconcile the best of Fathers to my Love—Let him be Provident, but let me be Happy" (5.3.221–23). When Sir John Bevil suggests that virtue is contingent on social role, Mr. Sealand contradicts him sharply:

> Sir John. Sir, I can't help saying, that what might injure a Citizen's Credit, may be no Stain to a Gentleman's Honour.
> Mr. Sealand. Sir John, the Honour of a Gentleman is liable to be tainted, by as small a matter as the Credit of a Trader.
>
> (4.2.28–31)

Where Sir Edward in *The Squire of Alsatia* could defend Belfond Junior's keeping on the grounds that he did it discreetly, the manner is entirely irrelevant to the matter for Mr. Sealand:

> Sir John. My Son, Sir, is a discreet and sober Gentleman—
> Mr. Sealand. I never saw a Man that wench'd soberly and discreetly, that ever left it off—the Decency observ'd in the Practice, hides, even from the Sinner, the Iniquity of it. They pursue it, not that their Appetites hurry 'em away; but, I warrant you, because 'tis their Opinion, they may do it.
>
> (4.2.39–45)

The shift in views of morality from Shadwell to Steele is indicated by the fact that Sir Edward is a normative character in *The Squire of Alsatia* while Sir John is a blocking figure—albeit a good-humored one—in *The Conscious Lovers*. Bevil Junior might not approve of Mr. Sealand's manners, but he would not disagree with his moral claims. Honor, as Michael McKeon says, "as a term of denotation shifts [during the seventeenth century] from 'title of rank' to 'goodness of character.'"[24] The requirements of honor are the same for a merchant or a baronet because virtue is no longer regarded as contingent on social factors. Steele has not eliminated the distinctions of rank; even though Indiana's worth is presented as independent of her financial situation, dramatically the marriage of Bevil Junior and Indiana merely shows a consolidation of control by the aristocracy through the incorporation of the new aristocracy of the merchant class. Nonetheless, virtue is presented as deontological and not a social construction.

But where Steele and Hughes could possibly rely on God, rationality, or, perhaps, a moral sense, to supply moral standards independent of society, Shadwell apparently did not. And if Shadwell's attempt to wrestle with the ethical problems that skepticism creates falls on the basis of its internal contradictions, it is, at least, an ambitious ruin.

Notes

Introduction. The Complexity of Restoration Ethics

1. See Patrick J. Kearney's *A History of Erotic Literature* (London: Macmillan, 1982), pp. 19–52, for an overview of pornography in the period.

2. David Foxon says that this is a free adaptation of Aretino's *Ragionamenti*; see *Libertine Literature in England, 1660–1745* (New Hyde Park, N.Y.: University Books, 1965), p. 27.

3. Dwight C. Miller, "Benedetto Gennari's Career at the Court of Charles II and James II and a Newly Discovered Portrait of James II," *Apollo* (January 1983): 24–29.

4. Harold Love, ed. *The Penguin Book of Restoration Verse*, (Harmondsworth: Penguin, 1968), p. 26.

5. *Players' Scepters: Fictions of Authority in the Restoration* (Lincoln: University of Nebraska Press, 1979), p. 192.

6. *The First Modern Comedies: The Significance of Etherege, Wycherly and Congreve* (Cambridge: Harvard University Press, 1959), p. 119.

7. *An Approach to Congreve* (New Haven: Yale University Press, 1979), pp. x, 33.

8. *Politics and Poetry in Restoration England: The Case of Dryden's Annus Mirabilis* (Cambridge: Harvard University Press, 1975), p. 147.

9. *Etherege and the Seventeenth-Century Comedy of Manners* (New Haven: Yale University Press, 1957), p. 29.

10. Ibid., p. 16.

11. Ibid., p. 29.

12. *Restoration Tragedy: Form and the Process of Change* (Madison: University of Wisconsin Press 1967), pp. 118–21.

13. Wolfgang Bernard Fleischman, *Lucretius and English Literature: 1680–1740* (Paris: A. G. Nizet, 1964), p. 91.

14. Reprinted in Thomas Franklin Mayo, *Epicurus in England: 1660–1725* (Dallas: Southwest Press, 1934), p. 44.

15. *Scepsis Scientifica*, in *The Vanity of Dogmatizing: The Three Versions*, introd. Stephen Medcalf (Hove, Sussex: Harvester Press, 1970), p. 137.

16. *Epicurus's Morals* (1670; reprint, London, 1926).

17. See Margaret C. Jacob, *The Cultural Meaning of the Scientific Revolution* (Philadelphia: Temple University Press, 1988), p. 81.

18. See Charles T. McCracken, *Malebranche and British Philosophy* (Oxford: Clarenden Press, 1983), p. 49.

19. *Oeuvres*, ed. Geneviève Rodis-Lewis and Germain Malbreil (Dijon: Editions Gallimard, 1979), p. 444. "Because pleasure is a reward, it is an act of injustice for us to produce movements in our body that oblige God, as a result of the general laws He has established, to make us feel pleasure when we do not deserve it. . . . Before his sin man could, with justice, partake of sensible

pleasures in his ordered actions. But since the sin, there are no more completely innocent pleasures, or pleasures which are incapable of harming us when we enjoy them, for often we become enslaved by them just by enjoying them." From *The Search after Truth*, trans. Thomas M. Lennon and Paul J. Olscamp (Columbus: Ohio State University Press, 1980), p. 308.

20. For the Catholic view of the rise of asceticism, see Pierre Pourrat's *Le Spiritualité Chrétienne* (Paris: Libraire Lecoffre, 1947), esp. vol. 3.

21. In any case, it was possible for Protestant theologians to borrow from Catholic sources when it suited their purpose, which indicates that some Protestants were still reading Catholic writers. Jeremy Taylor does it frequently, and there are other examples. See Phillip Harth's *Contexts of Dryden's Thought* (Chicago: University of Chicago Press, 1968), p. 104.

22. "Mixed Feelings: The Enlightenment and Sexuality," in *Sexuality in Eighteenth-Century Britain*, ed. Paul Gabriel Boucé (Totowa, N.J.: Barnes and Noble, 1982), p. 2.

23. *The Puritan Conscience and Modern Sexuality* (New Haven: Yale University Press, 1986), p. 3.

24. *Calvin's New Testament Commentaries: Corinthians*, trans. John W. Frazier, ed. David W. Torrance and Thomas F. Torrance (Grand Rapids, Mich: William B. Erdmans, 1960), 9:135, 140. The emphasis is mine.

25. *The World Turned Upside Down* (1972; Harmondsworth: Penguin, 1975; reprint, 1982), p. 358.

26. *Sex and Sensibility: Ideal and Erotic Love from Milton to Mozart* (Chicago: University of Chicago Press, 1980), pp. 39–42.

27. In *The Complete Prose Works of John Milton*, ed. Ernest Sirluck (New Haven: Yale University Press, 1959), 2:268.

28. *Tetrachordon*, in *Complete Prose Works of John Milton*, 2:591.

29. *One Flesh: Paradisal Marriage and Sexual Relations in the Age of Milton* (Oxford: Clarendon Press, 1987), p. 196.

30. *The Marriage Ring* (London, 1883), p. 8.

31. "The Apples of Sodom: or The Fruits of Sin," in *The English Sermon: 1650–1750*, ed. C. H. Sisson (Cheadle Cheshire, England: Carcanet Press, 1976), 2:30, 26.

32. Lawrence Stone, *Marriage, Sex and the Family: England 1500–1800* (New York: Harper and Row, 1977), pp. 498–99; William Haller and Malleville Haller, "The Puritan Art of Love," *Huntington Library Quarterly* 5 (January 1942): 235–72.

33. Edmund Morgan, "The Puritans and Sex," *New England Quarterly* 15 (December 1942): 591–607; Edward Shorter, *The Making of the Modern Family* (New York: Basic Books, 1975), p. 250.

34. Stone, *Marriage*, p. 498.

35. For instance, Harold Weber recognizes that attitudes toward sexuality were changing—"after the Restoration, sex remains a dangerous and unpredictable passion, harboring a potential for destruction, but a power no longer seen invariably in terms of the divine or demonic (in *The Restoration Rake Hero* [Madison: University of Wisconsin Press, 1986], p. 19)—but still insists that "that this central quality [the rake's sexual impulses] generates the manifold complexities of his personality" (5). I shall argue that sexuality is sometimes a central issue in considering ethical positions in the plays, and at other times largely irrelevant. Thus, while Weber's thesis is admirably supported by his persuasive readings of Behn, Congreve, and Otway, it is not generalizable to Crowne and Shadwell, among others.

36. *Love Letters Between a Nobleman and His Sister*, introd. Maureen Duffy (New York: Penguin Books/Virago Press, 1987), p. 16. Subsequent references in the text are to this edition.

37. *The Dramatic Works of John Crowne* (Edinburgh, 1874; reprint, New York: Benjamin Blom, 1967), 2:113. Subsequent references in the text are to this edition.

38. See *The Development of English Drama in the Late Seventeenth Century* (Oxford: Clarendon Press, 1976), pp. 97–104; "William Wycherley: Text, Life, Interpretation," *MP* 78 (1981): 399–415.

39. "William Wycherley: Text, Life, Interpretation," 410.

40. Laura Brown argues that Shadwell is in fact atypical and unlike "contemporary social satire"; *English Dramatic Form, 1660–1760: An Essay in Generic History* (New Haven: Yale University Press, 1981), p. 196. Because Shadwell's humors characters "dominate the stage, with the result that local replaces formal satire" (63), she reaches the startling conclusion that "his early plays are not formally moral in themselves" (196). I suspect that the genre distinctions that Brown creates ex post facto were not widely recognized by the Restoration theater audience. In any case, the claim that Shadwell is outside the mainstream of comedy seems curiously at odds with contemporary evaluations such as Rochester's pairing of Shadwell and Wycherley as the writers of "true comedy"; "An Allusion to Horace, 'The Tenth Satire of the First Book,'" in *The Complete Poems of John Wilmot, Earl of Rochester*, ed. David M. Vieth (New Haven: Yale University Press, 1968), p. 120. It certainly is not clear that Shadwell himself was aware of such a distinction. In the preface to *The Humorists*, he calls *She Wou'd if She Cou'd* "the best Comedy that has been written since the Restauration of the Stage." Rochester may be wrong, and Shadwell may have misunderstood Etherege, but even if both of these are the case, their observations still cast doubt on the exclusivity of the categories that Brown wishes to propose.

Chapter 1. Ethics and Drama

1. *The Works of Aphra Behn*, ed. Montague Summers (London, 1915), 1:222–23 and 3:186. Robert Hume says that Behn's remark that drama neither instructs nor is written to instruct is unique in the period. See *The Development of English Drama in the Late Seventeenth Century* (Oxford: Clarendon Press, 1976), p. 34.

2. "A Defense of an Essay of Dramatic Poesy," in *The Works of John Dryden*, vol. 9, ed. John Loftis and Vinton A. Dearing (Berkeley: University of California Press, 1966), p. 12. The role Dryden assigns the didactic is limited; in the preface to *An Evening's Love* he argues that "the first end of Comedie is delight, and instruction only the second"; *The Works of John Dryden*, vol. 10, ed. Maximillian E. Novak and George Robert Guffey (Berkeley: University of California Press, 1970), p. 209. Nonetheless, even here instruction remains an end of drama.

3. *The Dramatic Works of John Crowne* (Edinburgh, 1874; reprint, New York: Benjamin Blom, 1967), 2:102.

4. *The Ethos of Restoration Comedy* (Urbana: University of Illinois Press, 1971), p. 5.

5. *Development of English Drama*, pp. 31–62.

6. *The Ethos of Restoration Comedy*, pp. 84–85.

7. *Critics, Values, and Restoration Comedy* (Carbondale: Southern Illinois University Press, 1982), p. 52.

8. Ibid., p. 137.

9. Ibid., p. 136.

10. "The Etiquette of the Sentimental Repentance Scene, 1688–1696," PLL 14 (1978): 207.

11. *Topics of Restoration Comedy* (New York: St. Martin's Press, 1974), p. 77.

12. "The Values of Shadwell's *Squire of Alsatia*," ELH 39 (1972): 385.

13. *The Gay Couple in Restoration Comedy* (Cambridge: Harvard University Press, 1948), pp. 125–27.

14. "The Significance of Thomas Shadwell," SP 71 (1974): 238.

15. *Development of English Drama*, pp. 78–85; and with Judith Milhous, *Producible Interpretations: Eight English Plays, 1675–1707* (Carbondale: Southern Illinois University Press, 1985), p. 19.

16. *The Drama of Thomas Shadwell*, Salzburg Studies in English Literature, no. 16 (Salzburg: Institut für Englische Sprache und Literatur, 1972), pp. 396, 300.

17. *Thomas Shadwell*, (New York: Twain Publishers, 1967), p. 146.

18. *The Ornament of Action: Text and Performance in Restoration Comedy:* Cambridge University Press, 1979), pp. 170–203.

19. Cited by Hume in *Development of English Drama* p. 80.

20. See Summers's theatrical history of the play, in *The Complete Works of Thomas Shadwell* (London: Fortune Press, 1927), 4:197.

21. *Fiction and the Shape of Belief: A Study of Henry Fielding, with Glances at Swift, Johnson, and Richardson* (Berkeley: University of California Press, 1964), p. 28.

22. *The Great Cat Massacre and Other Episodes in French Cultural History* (New York: Basic Books, 1984), p. 5.

23. *The Designs of Carolean Comedy* (Carbondale: Southern Illinois University Press, 1988), pp. 6–20, 180.

24. "The Values of Shadwell's *Squire of Alsatia*," p. 28.

25. "Public Virtue and Private Vitality in Shadwell's Comedies," *Restoration and Eighteenth-Century Theatre Research* 16 (1977): 13, 15, 11.

26. For a further explanation of this distinction see William K. Frankena's *Ethics*, 2d ed. (Englewood Cliffs, N.J.: Prentice-Hall, 1973), pp. 12–33.

27. "The Values of Shadwell's *Squire of Alsatia*," p. 384.

28. *The Puritan Conscience and Modern Sexuality* (New Haven: Yale University Press, 1986), p. 44.

29. In *Toward an Anthropology of Women*, ed. Rayna R. Reiter (New York: Monthly Review Press, 1975), p. 182.

30. *A Grammar of Motives* (1945: reprint, Berkeley: University of California Press, 1969), pp. 252–62.

31. *The Fragility of Goodness: Luck and Ethics in Greek Tragedy and Philosophy* (Cambridge: Cambridge University Press, 1986), p. 333.

32. *Designs of Carolean Comedy*, pp. 19–20.

33. Ibid., p. 9.

34. "The Scientific Study of Morality," in *Selected Writings*, ed. and trans. Anthony Giddens (Cambridge: Cambridge University Press, 1972), p. 92.

35. *The Political Unconscious: Narrative as Socially Symbolic Act* (Ithaca: Cornell University Press, 1981), p. 95.

36. *Language and Materialism: Developments in Semiology and the Theory of the Subject* (London: Routledge and Kegan Paul, 1977), p. 74.

Chapter 2. Ethical Possibilities

1. For further explanation of this distinction see William K. Frankena's, *Ethics*, 2d ed. (Englewood Cliffs, N.J.: Prentice-Hall, 1973), pp. 12–33. Not everyone uses these terms in this way. For instance, C. B. Macpherson in *The Political Theory of Possessive Individualism: Hobbes to Locke*, (Oxford: Clarendon Press, 1962), says that Hobbes "was able to deduce a moral obligation from the supposed facts, without importing hierarchical and moral values or teleological principles" (17). By teleological here, Macpherson presumably means a moral system based on a perceived purpose and end for man, such as Thomism where man's end, as determined by God, provides the standard by which we make ethical decisions. For my purposes, any time a writer makes moral values contingent on nonmoral values, he is engaged in teleological ethics.

2. *Treatise on Good Works*, reprinted in *A Survey of Christian Ethics*, by Edward Leroy Long, Jr. (New York: Oxford University Press, 1967), p. 132.

3. *After Virtue: A Study in Moral Theory*, 2d ed. (Notre Dame, Ind.: University of Notre Dame Press, 1984), pp. 50–55.

4. Ibid., p. 198.

5. *The Advancement of Learning*, ed. G. W. Kitchin, introd. Arthur Johnston (London: J. M. Dent, 1973), pp. 210, 211, 167. Hiram Haydn argues, however, that Bacon is being disingenuous here, and is merely trying to protect scientific reason from the taint of religious reasoning. See *The Counter-Renaissance* (New York: Grove Press, 1950), pp. 155–56.

6. *Prose Observations*, ed. Hugh De Quehen (Oxford: Clarendon Press, 1979), p. 9.

7. *Enchiridion Ethicum: The English Translation of 1690* (New York: Facsimile Text Society, 1930), p. 17.

8. *Selected Discourses, 1660* (New York: Garland, 1978), p. 286.

9. See Phillip Harth's *Contexts of Dryden's Thought* (Chicago: University of Chicago Press, 1968), pp. 165–66.

10. But it is questionable whether Locke is entitled to argue for deontological ethics granted his empirical epistemology. I agree with Staves who regards Locke as typifying the problem of an inconsistent conception of the relationship between experience and reason: "Like the Platonists, Locke claimed that reason unaided by revelation was able to discover the being and goodness of God, the nature of man, and also the moral obligations of man under natural law. Yet Locke's willingness to admit that many individuals and even entire societies seem oblivious to the principles of natural law coupled with his desire to maintain that the law of nature can be known by reason led him into what seems to me a paradoxical position"; *Players' Scepters: Fictions of Authority in the Restoration* (Lincoln: University of Nebraska Press, 1979), p. 279. The paradox of Locke's position is that he is claiming a role for rationality that his epistemology would tend not to allow. He says in *An Essay concerning Human Understanding* that from the idea of God and the idea of ourselves as rational beings we can demonstrate "the foundations of our duty and rules of action"; *An Essay concerning Human Understanding*, ed. A. S. Pringle-Pattison (Oxford: Clarendon Press, 1924; reprint, 1956), p. 277. He never, however, quite got around to doing so. Locke's skepticism about the possible extent of human

knowledge apparent throughout book 4, chapter 3 of the *Essay*, and his awareness that "Parties of men cram their tenets down all men's throats that they
can get into their power" (280) makes it difficult to see how he ever expected
to demonstrate a subject that a glance at society shows not to be transparent to
experience or intuition. Moreover, Locke recognizes as well that most people
simply do not make ethical decisions based on rational deliberation, but act
from custom and education; see James Tully's, "Governing Conduct," in *Conscience and Casuistry in Early Modern Europe*, ed. Edmund Leites (Cambridge:
Cambridge University Press, 1988), pp. 21–28.

   11. *The Cultural Meaning of the Scientific Revolution* (Philadelphia: Temple
University Press, 1988), p. 112.

   12. Christopher Hill, *The Century of Revolution, 1603–1714*, (London:
Thomas Nelson and Sons, 1961), pp. 242–45. John Redwood points out sen-
sibly that "It is naive in the extreme to take the huge literature aimed against
atheism, and to take it at face value to mean there was an equally sizeable
atheist problem, without questioning the motive behind the writings, and the
causes of the literature itself"; *Reason, Ridicule and Religion: The Age of Enlightenment in England, 1660–1750* (Cambridge: Harvard University Press,
1976), p. 218. But the spirited polemics against atheists are at least evidence
that men recognized the possibility that men might disbelieve in God, and, no
doubt, some did.

   13. *Anthony Ashley Cooper, Third Earl of Shaftesbury, Characteristics of
Men, Manners, Opinions, Times, Etc.*, ed. John M. Robertson (Gloucester, Mass.:
Peter Smith, 1963), 1:264.

   14. See Ernst Cassirer, *The Philosophy of the Enlightenment*, trans. Fritz C.
A. Koelln and James P. Pettegrove (Princeton: Princeton University Press, 1951),
pp. 234–53. The ethical change in the seventeenth century I am arguing for is
summed up by Alasdair MacIntyre: "Intellectually, first deists and then sceptics
question the possibility of miracles, the truth of the historical narratives in
which Christianity is alleged to rest, the traditional proofs of the existence of
God, and the intolerance of ecclesiastical morality. Socially what was a religious morality becomes increasingly a religious form and frame disguising or
merely decorating purely secular ideas and pursuits. As a matter of history, the
culmination of this in the eighteenth century is a victory for the morality whose
ancestors include Hobbes and the sophists"; *A Short History of Ethics* (New
York: Macmillan, 1966), p. 15.

   15. *The Decline of Hell: Seventeenth-Century Discussions of Eternal Torment* (Chicago: University of Chicago Press, 1964), pp. 4–6.

   16. *The Novels of Mrs. Aphra Behn* (London: 1905), pp. 36–37.

   17. *The Works of Thomas Otway*, ed. J. C. Ghosh (Oxford: Clarendon Press,
1932; reprint, 1968), 2:324.

   18. Edward Hyde, Earl of Clarendon, *A Brief View and Survey of the Dangerous and Pernicious Errors to Church and State, in Mr. Hobbes Book, Entitled
Leviathan* (London, 1676), p. 214.

   19. *Leviathan*, ed. C. B. Macpherson (Harmondsworth: Penguin, 1981), p.
120.

   20. *Letters of Sir George Etherege*, ed. Frederick Bracher (Berkeley: University of California Press, 1974), p. 168.

   21. *Oeuvres de Descartes*, 2d ed., ed. Charles Adam and Paul Tannery (Paris:
Librairie Philosophique J. Vrin, 1974), vol. 11, sec. 18. The translation is from
The Philosophical Works of Descartes, trans. Elizabeth Haldane and G. R. T.
Ross (Cambridge: Cambridge University Press, 1911; 1931 corrected ed.; re-

print, 1981), 1:CXXXVIII: "That is why we should make use of experience and reason in order to distinguish good from evil, and to recognize their just value, so that we may not take the one for the other, or rush into anything too violently" (392).

22. *Memoirs of My Life*, ed. Betty Radice (New York: Penguin, 1984), p. 89.

23. In *British Moralists, 1650–1800*, ed. D. D. Raphael (Oxford: Clarendon Press, 1969), 1.105.

24. Popkin points out that Montaigne's skepticism is compatible either with religious sincerity or dissimulation: "Whether Montainge was trying to undermine Christianity or defend it, he could have made the same *non sequitur* that he did, namely, because all is in doubt, therefore one ought to accept Christianity on faith alone. Such a claim was made by Hume and Voltaire, apparently in bad faith, and by Pascal and Kierkegaard, apparently in good faith. The type of Christian Pyrrhonism stated by Montaigne and his disciples was taken by some Church leaders as the best of theology, and by others as rank atheism"; *The History of Scepticism from Erasmus to Spinoza* (Berkeley: University of California Press, 1979), p. 55.

25. In *Rochester: The Critical Heritage*, ed. David Farley-Hills (New York: Barnes and Noble, 1972), p. 60.

26. *Characteristics*, p. 267. As Reginald A. P. Rogers points out, even for Shaftesbury, while "virtue is intrinsically lovable, it is expedient to prove that it agrees entirely with self-interest"; *A Short History of Ethics, Greek and Modern* (London: Macmillan, 1965), p. 154.

27. *Decline of Hell*, p. 169.

28. *Christian Ethics or Divine Morality* (London, 1675), p. 2. For the genesis of Traherne's insistance on felicity in his own poor childhood, see David L. Edwards's *Christian England From the Restoration to the 18th Century*, vol. 2 (Grand Rapids, Mich.: William B. Erdmans, 1983), pp. 373–78; Traherne, 100, 10.

29. *De Legibus Naturae*, in *The British Moralists*, pp. 93–94.

30. *Enchiridion Ethicum*, pp. 21, 242–43. In fact, while More introduces the notion of a hierarchy of good to his ethics, his first *noema* is indistinguishable from Hobbes's definition of good; Vernon J. Bourke, *History of Ethics* (Garden City, N.Y.: Doubleday, 1968), p. 138.

31. *Christian Ethics*, p. 95. Henry Sidgwick examines the differences between Catholic and Protestant casuistry in *Outlines of the History of Ethics* (1886; reprint, Boston: Beacon Press, 1960), pp. 151–56.

32. *Ductor Dubitantium*, in *Jeremy Taylor's Works*, ed. Reverend Alexander Taylor (London, 1864), 10:498.

33. Ibid., 10:499. D. R. M. Wilkinson, in *The Comedy of Habit: An Essay on the Use of Courtesy Literature in a Study of Restoration Comic Drama* (Leiden: Universitaire Pers, 1964), pp. 35–36, discusses cogently the importance of prudence in Francis Osborne's "Advice to a Son." But the chief weakness of Wilkinson's book is his tendency to reduce every ethical element in Restoration comedy into a tired recitation of what he finds in the courtesy literature, without considering the intellectual background of this literature, or examining the extent to which it attempts to deal with ethical issues that were confronting religious writers like Taylor, or philosophers in the period as well. Prudence is important precisely because it provides a clear standard of behavior whose test is the societal consequences of any particular action.

34. *Christian Ethics*, p. 2.

35. "Suggestions toward a Genealogy of 'The Man of Feeling,'" in *The Idea*

of the Humanities and Other Essays Critical and Historical (Chicago: University of Chicago Press, 1967), 1:197–98. Donald Greene argues that Crane's essay has led to a fundamental misunderstanding of the profoundly Augustinian character of the Anglican church in the Restoration; that is, although man may be capable of some degree of innate benevolence and virtuous feeling, he remains reprobate without the direct intervention of Christ, and incapable of salvation without revelation: see "Latitudinarianism and Sensibility: The Genealogy of the 'Man of Feeling' Reconsidered," *MP* 75 (1977): 159–83. Although Greene's article is an important corrective to easy assumptions about the rapidity of the shift toward a more positive view of human nature in the seventeenth-century, I believe it too overstates its case. The examples that Crane cites are crucially different in tone from Saint Augustine, Calvin, or a contemporary Catholic "Augustinian" like Malebranche. Nowhere is this more apparent than in the minority Latitudinarian view that the necessity of revelation does not exclude pagans from salvation: see Harth, *Contexts of Dryden's Thought*, pp. 156–65.

36. See Joyce Oldham Appleby's *Economic Thought and Ideology in Seventeenth-Century England* (Princeton: Princeton University Press, 1978), pp. 52–57.

37. *The Passions and the Interests: Political Arguments for Capitalism before Its Triumph* (Princeton: Princeton University Press, 1981), p. 129.

38. *Leviathan*, p. 120. (Further page references in the text also refer to Macpherson's edition.) In what follows I am arguing that Hobbes can be read as a precursor of what Hirschman regards as the fundamental idea of capitalism: countervailing passions and desires make it to man's interest to act in a restrained manner in society. Hobbes would presumably argue, however, that without a central, all powerful authority that is not enough. C. B. Macpherson's *The Political Theory of Possessive Individualism*, particularly pp. 70–87, provides a powerful argument that Hobbes actually held what I am calling Hobbes's teleological ethics: moral obligation to the social order is derived from the fact of "equality of insecurity" (85), and morality is indistinguishable from prudence.

39. *Epicurus's Morals* (1670; reprint, London, 1926), p. 17. Page references in the text refer to this edition.

40. *The Works of George Savile First Marquess of Halifax*, ed. Walter Raleigh (Oxford: Clarendon Press, 1912), p. 209.

41. *Advice to a Daughter*, in *The Works*, p. 8. Page references in the text refer to this edition.

42. Wayne C. Booth examines the modern tendency to prize sincerity at any cost in *The Company We Keep: An Ethics of Fiction* (Berkeley: University of California Press, 1988), pp. 252–53. His view is, I think, very close to what I have called the ethics of role in Shadwell: "If my character is the totality of all the roles I can play effectively, good and bad, it will be in some sense a product of all the "hypocrisies" I have practiced (good and bad) long enough to perfect them" (253). The key to a good education, then, is to get people to practice playing good roles.

43. See J. G. A. Pocock, *Virtue, Commerce, and History: Essays on Political Thought and History, Chiefly in the Eighteenth Century* (Cambridge: Cambridge University Press, 1985), pp. 103–8.

44. See J. R. Jacob, *Robert Boyle and the English Revolution: A Study in Social and Intellectual Change* (New York: Burt Franklin, 1977), pp. 47–55.

45. Crane Brinton, *A History of Western Morals* (New York: Harcourt, Brace, 1959), p. 281.

46. *Advice of a Father* (London, 1688), pp. 71, 43–44.

47. *The Gentleman's Calling* (London, 1660), p. 11.

48. *Advice to a Son* (London, 1896), pp. 12, 31.

Chapter 3. Religion and Duty

1. *Topics of Restoration Comedy* (New York: St. Martin's Press, 1974), pp. 33, 99.

2. *The Drama of Thomas Shadwell* (Salzburg: Institut für Englische Sprache und Literatur, 1972), p. 386.

3. *Players' Scepters: Fictions of Authority in the Restoration* (Lincoln: University of Nebraska Press, 1979), pp. 310–11.

4. "Restoration Comedy and Its Audiences, 1660–1776," *Yearbook of English Studies* 10 (1980): 57.

5. "Shadwell, the Ladies, and the Change in Comedy," in *Restoration Drama*, ed. John Loftis (New York: Oxford University Press, 1966), p. 247.

6. *The Political Plays of the Restoration* (n.p.: Yale University, 1916), p. 95.

7. "Humane Comedy," *MP* 75 (1977): 35.

8. "The Sentimentality of *The Conscious Lovers* Revisited and Reasserted," *MLS* 9, no. 3 (1979): 48.

9. Ibid., 51.

10. See Donald Greene's critique of R. S. Crane, "Latitudinarianism and Sensibility: The Genealogy of the 'Man of Feeling' Reconsidered," *MP* 75 (1977): 159–83, for an argument that the idea of "self-approving joy" is genuinely original to Shaftesbury (unlike the other tenets of "benevolism" that Crane claimed originated in the Restoration), and is the intellectual property of the anticlerical factions.

11. *The Rewards of Vertue* (London, 1661), p. 37.

12. *A Mirror to Nature: Transformations in Drama and Aesthetics, 1660–1732* (Lexington: University Press of Kentucky, 1986), p. 125.

13. *The Supernatural in Tragedy* (Cambridge: Harvard University Press, 1915), p. 297.

14. *The Theatre of Don Juan* (Lincoln: University of Nebraska Press, 1963), pp. 15–16, 100–105.

15. *An Account of the English Dramatick Poets* (New York: Garland, 1973), p. 448.

16. *The Theatre of Don Juan*, p. 167.

17. "The Myth of the Rake in Restoration Comedy," *Studies in the Literary Imagination*, 10, no. 1 (Spring 1977): 54, rptd. in Robert Hume's *The Rakish Stage*.

18. "Heroic Heads and Comic Tails: Sex, Politics and the Restoration Rake," *ECTI* 24 (1983): 128.

19. *The Collected Works of Samuel Taylor Coleridge*, ed. James Engell and W. Jackson Bate (Princeton: Princeton University Press, 1983), 7:213, 219.

20. "The Limits of Historical Veracity in Neoclassical Drama," in *England in the Restoration and Early Eighteenth Century*, ed. H. T. Swedenberg, Jr. (Berkeley: University of California Press, 1972), p. 39. Robert Markley pairs Don John with Sir Sampson in *Love for Love* and Dorimant as a "caricature"

of the "will to power"; *Two Edg'd Weapons: Style and Ideology in the Comedies of Etherege, Wycherley, and Congreve* (Oxford: Clarendon Press, 1988), p. 223.

21. *Players' Scepters*, p. 310.

22. Albert S. Borgman recounts Nat Thompson's charges against Shadwell in *Thomas Shadwell* (New York: 1928; reprint, New York: Benjamin Blom, 1969), pp. 55–58.

23. As reprinted in Borgman, *Thomas Shadwell* p. 90.

24. *The Development of English Drama in the Late Seventeenth Century* (Oxford: Clarendon Press, 1976), pp. 357, 359.

25. *Sir Barnaby Whigg* (London, 1681). All subsequent page references in the text are to this edition.

26. R. S. Forsythe first pointed out that Sir Barnaby was a caricature of Shadwell in *A Study of the Plays of Thomas D'Urfey* (Cleveland: Western Reserve University Press, 1916).

27. *The Works of John Dryden*, vol. 6, ed. Sir Walter Scott and George Saintsbury, (London: 1883), act 3, 453. All references to *The Spanish Friar* are to this edition by act and page because the California Dryden has not yet released the volume that will contain this play.

28. *The Dramatic Works of John Crowne*, vol. 4 (Edinburgh, 1874; rpt. New York: Benjamin Blom, 1967), 5:116.

29. Allardyce Nicoll discusses *The Lancashire Witches* as one of a number of plays that use religion as a topic of political satire in "Political Plays of the Restoration," *MLR* 16 (1921): 224–42. But Virgil L. Jones points out that religious satire could be distinct from politically motivated satire; thus Crowne in *City Politics* and Behn in *The Roundheads* satirize the Puritans presumably because they were Whigs, but Shadwell satirizes Puritans throughout his career even though he was himself a Whig in "Methods of Satire in the Political Drama of the Restoration," *JEGP* 21 (1922): 667. Neither attempts to account for the fact that over the course of his career Shadwell attacked Catholics, Puritans, and Anglicans.

30. "Shadwell's Use of Hobbes," *SP* 35 (1938): 425.

31. J. C. Ross suggests that Daredevil in *The Atheist* represents Shadwell in "An Attack on Thomas Shadwell in Otway's *The Atheist*," *PQ* 52 (1973): 753–60. On the other hand, Jessica Munns argues that Rochester is a more likely target in "Daredevil in Thomas Otway's *The Atheist*: A New Identification," *Restoration* 11 (Spring 1987): 31–37. It would be nice for my argument if I could agree with Ross, but neither identification is compelling. Ross offers no reason why we should treat *The Atheist* as a dramatic variation on the roman à clef, and Munn's only justification is that Daredevil is a secondary character and it is therefore odd that the play is named after him. Other plays in the Restoration are titled after secondary characters: for example, Crowne's *Sir Courtly Nice*. And thematically, Daredevil is not a secondary character but an important contrast to Beaugard; neither believes in religion, but Beaugard is shown to be a gentleman because he affirms that religion is necessary to prevent social chaos. Most important, neither offers any evidence that anyone in the Restoration recognized Daredevil as a particular satire on anybody, unlike Shadwell's own *The Sullen Lovers* and Otway's *Venice Preserved*, where the caricatures of the Howards and Shaftesbury respectively were recognized immediately.

32. *The Works of Thomas Otway*, ed. J. C. Ghosh, vol. 2 (Oxford: Clarendon Press, 1932), act 1,308. All subsequent references are to this edition by act and page number.

33. *A Short View of the Immorality and Prophaness of the English Stage* (New York: Garland, 1972), p. 97.

34. Ibid., pp. 98–100.

35. Ibid., p. 103.

36. *A Defence of the Short View . . .* (New York: Garland, 1972), p. 70.

37. *A Short View,* p. 136.

38.
> For every Deity must live in Peace,
> In undisturb'd and everlasting ease:
> Not care for us, from Fears and Dangers free,
> Sufficient to his own Felicity.
> Nought here below, Nought in our Power he needs,
> Ne'er smiles at good, ne'er frowns at wicked deeds.

Thomas Creech, *Lucretius His Six Books of Epicurean Philosophy and Manilius His Five Books,* 5th ed. (London, 1700), p. 53. Creech's translation is obviously very loose, but it emphasizes the relevant point of the passage, that God is indifferent to human concerns.

39. *Thomas Shadwell* (New York: Twain Publishers, 1967), p. 68.

40. "Shadwell and the Royal Society: Satire in *The Virtuoso,*" *SEL* 10 (1972): 469–90.

41. When Hooke first saw the play on 2 June 1676 he wrote in his diary, "Damned Doggs. *Vindica me Deus.* People almost pointed"; *The Diary of Robert Hooke,* ed. Henry W. Robinson and Walter Adams (London, 1935). Others thought so too; he writes on 3 June 1676, "At Garaways, Sir J. More, Flamstead, Hill from Play Floutingly smiled."

42. My view is opposed to Don R. Kunz's who says that "no linear progress is made. Numerous cyclical shifts create the illusion of motion, but satyrs and victims end essentially where they began in the fictional world"; *The Drama of Thomas Shadwell,* p. 51. Kunz is right in that Stanford and Emilia recognize that they cannot change society; he is wrong in that they recognize their capacity to control their interaction with it.

43. "Thomas Shadwell and the Jonsonian Comedy of the Restoration," in *From Renaissance to Restoration: Metamorphoses of the Drama,* ed. Robert Markley and Laurie Finke (Cleveland: Bellflower Press, 1984), p. 135.

44. Susan Staves sums up the transition while drawing attention to the gap between theory and practice; see *Players' Scepters,* p. 189.

45. *The Rise of the Egalitarian Family* (New York: Academic Press, 1978), p. 123.

46. *Tradition Counter Tradition: Love and the Form of Fiction* (Chicago: University of Chicago Press, 1987), p. 59.

47. Richard Allestree, *Whole Duty of Man* (London: 1735), p. 300. Subsequent page references in the text are to this edition.

48. *Patriarcha and Other Political Works,* ed. Peter Laslett (Oxford: Basil Blackwell, 1947), p. 57. Subsequent references in the text to Filmer are to this edition.

49. *The Authoritarian Family and Political Attitudes in Seventeenth-Century England* (Brunswick, N.J.: Transation Books, 1988), pp. 180–88. See also James Daly's *Sir Robert Filmer and English Political Thought* (Toronto: University of Toronto Press, 1979), pp. 58–61.

50. 13 July 1684. *Sermons* (London, 1742), 3:421.

51. Richard Allestree, *The Ladies Calling* (Oxford, 1673), p. 160.

52. See *The Second Treatise of Government*, ed. Thomas P. Peardon (Indianapolis: Bobbs-Merrill, 1952), paragraphs 68 and 72.

53. "The Marriage of Convenience and the Moral Code of Restoration Comedy," *Essays in Criticism* 12 (1962): 375.

54. *The Gay Couple in Restoration Comedy* (Cambridge: Harvard University Press, 1948), p. 207; "The Etiquette of the Sentimental Repentance Scene, 1688–1696," *PLL* 14 (1978): 210.

55. "Etiquette," p. 216.

56. *The Country Gentleman*, ed. A. H. Scouten and Robert Hume (Philadelphia: University of Pennsylvania Press, 1976), act 1, p. 66. Subsequent references in the text are to this edition by act and page number. For another example of the benevolent country gentleman, see Thomas Jevon's *The Devil of a Wife* (1686). Jevon may or may not have had help in writing the play from his brother-in-law Shadwell. Alfred E. Richards argues he did on the basis of verbal echoes between this play and *The Squire of Alsatia* and *The Lancashire Witches*, the presence of a dissenting minister who Sir Richard cannot stand, and a short song that occurs in this play, *The Woman Captain* and the *The Squire of Alsatia*; see "A Literary Link between Thomas Shadwell and Christian Felix Weiss," *PMLA* 21 (1906): 803–30.

57. *The Country Gentleman*, p. 35.

Chapter 4. Public Order and Private Attraction

1. *Robert Boyle and the English Revolution* (New York: Burt Franklin, 1977), p. 47.

2. Anne M. Haselkorn, *Prostitution in Elizabethan and Jacobean Comedy* (Troy, N.Y.: Whiston Publishing Company, 1983), pp. 17–20.

3. *A Modest Defense of Publick Stews* (Los Angeles: Augustan Reprint Society, 1973), p. 28.

4. Katharine M. Rogers comments on Shadwell's attacks on learning in women and their subordination as housekeepers in *The Troublesome Helpmate* (Seattle: University of Washington Press, 1966), pp. 181–82.

5. See Stephen D. Cox, "Public Virtue and Private Vitality in Shadwell's Comedies," *Restoration and Eighteenth-Century Theatre Research* 16, no. 1 (1977): 1–22.

6. "Halley's Ode on the *Principia* of Newton and the Epicurean Revival in England," *Journal of the History of Ideas* 39 (1978): 33.

7. *The Gay Couple in Restoration Comedy* (Cambridge: Harvard University Press, 1948), p. 61.

8. "Margery Pinchwife's 'London Disease': Restoration Comedy and the Libertine Offensive of the 1670s," *Studies in the Literary Imagination*, 10, no. 1 (1977): 14–15.

9. David S. Berkeley regards Sir William's reformation in *The Scowrers* as a reversal from Shadwell's attacks on romantic love in his earlier plays; "The Penitent Rake in Restoration Comedy," *MP* 49 (1951): 231. I would argue that Bellamour's recognition of mutual love is just one of many early examples that Shadwell thought throughout his career that love was important to a happy life. In what follows I argue that Shadwell is an example of the changing conception of love in English Literature documented by Jean H. Hagstrum in *Sex and Sensibility: Ideal and Erotic Love from Milton to Mozart* (Chicago: University of Chicago Press, 1980). See also Edward Shorter, *The Making of the Mod-*

ern *Family* (New York: Basic Books, 1975); Lawrence Stone, *Marriage, Sex and the Family: England 1500–1800* (New York: Harper and Row, 1977); Edmund Leites, *The Puritan Conscience and Modern Sexuality* (New Haven: Yale University Press 1986); Randolph Trumbach, *The Rise of the Egalitarian Family* (New York: Academic Press, 1978).

10. *The Plays of Sir George Etherege,* ed. Michael Cordner (Cambridge: Cambridge University Press, 1982), act 1, p. 235, and act 2, p. 239.

11. *The Development of English Drama in the Late Seventeenth-Century* (Oxford: Clarendon Press, 1976), p. 296.

12. Lynch takes Shadwell's documented admiration for *She Wou'd if She Cou'd* to imply an admiration for the rakish heroes: "Throughout a long career, with patient, plodding devotion, Shadwell revived in comedy after comedy the dramatic scheme of *She would if She Could*"; *The Social Mode of Restoration Comedy* (New York: Macmillan, 1926), p. 162. Thus in both *Epsom Wells* and *The Virtuoso* the heroes are typical men of wit and hence attractive; see pp. 163–64 and pp. 176–77. She never, however, attempts to show why an admiration for a play requires an admiration for its heroes, or attempts to refute the potential claim that Shadwell thought that Courtall and Freeman were being satirized.

13. *Thomas Shadwell* (New York: Twain Publishers, 1967), p. 59.

14. "The Significance of Thomas Shadwell," *SP* 71 (1974): 226.

15. *Thomas Shadwell,* pp. 90–93.

16. "Occultism in Restoration Drama: Motives for Revaluation," *MLS* 9, no. 3 (1979): 66.

17. The Common view of Bruce and Longvil is that they are simply admirable rakes. Alssid ventures a brief demurrer in connection with their easy switch from beloved to beloved, but the remark is not developed: "The initial 'blind' pursuit turns into a more meaningful one, but the turnabout shows also an incapacity to see clearly what it is they love"; *Thomas Shadwell,* p. 74. Brian Corman in response to Alssid argues that this is the wrong kind of question to ask about a Shadwell play because the "problems of the lovers in the main plot are of less importance than the follies of the various humours"; "Thomas Shadwell and the Johnsonian Comedy of the Restoration," in *From Renaissance to Restoration: Metamorphoses of the Drama,* ed. Robert Markley and Laura Finke (Cleveland: Bellflower Press, 1984), p. 143. Rose Zimbardo also assumes that Bruce and Longvil are admirable and uncomplex: "In the world of *The Virtuoso* right knowledge is common sense and honor is simple virtue, but very little attention is given to them"; *A Mirror to Nature: Transformations in Drama and Aesthetics, 1660–1732* (Lexington: University Press of Kentucky, 1986), p. 123. But as I have argued throughout this book, what constitutes virtue in the Restoration is anything but "simple." Frances Kavenik and Eric Rothstein come closest to admitting complexity in the presentation of the rakes and I think their view is accurate: "Take Shadwell as sour on rakery and see the gentlemen punished by delay for their flightiness; but take Shadwell as in tune with the Carolean comedy mode in which male libido must be fixed in order to satisfy the woman who must look to the future, and see the marriages delayed in a way that asserts female power": *Designs of Carolean Comedy* (Carbondale: Southern Illinois University Press, 1988), p. 179. As will become clear, I regard the "fixing" of Bruce and Longvil as a function of social and economic imperatives that require "mutual love" as the operant ethical value.

18. Two other uses of this phrase in Restoration drama suggest that "you have reason" is a mark of foolishness: Dryden's *Sir Martin Mar-all* and Wycher-

ley's *The Gentleman Dancing Master* (the *Oxford English Dictionary* lists only the Dryden passage from the Restoration).

The phrase is clearly associated with nonsense and foppishness in Dryden:

> Sir Martin. I shall consider you hereafter Sirrah; but I am sure in all companies I pass for a *Vertuoso*.
> Moody. *Vertuoso!* what's that too? is not *Vertue* enough without *O* so?
> Sir Martin. You have reason, Sir!
> Moody. There he is again too; the Town Phrase, a great Compliment I wiss; you have Reason, Sir; that is, you are no beast, Sir.

The Works of John Dryden, vol. 9, ed. John Loftis and Vinton A. Dearing (Berkeley: University of California Press, 1966), p. 238. While Moody may not be a hero in that his disgust with the mode because it has not "the true English manliness" (237) is exaggerated, his annoyance indicates that the phrase is not an idiomatic English construction and makes sense only if one remembers the French construction. Moreover, Sir Martin is one of the most famous butts of Restoration comedy, which indicates that the use of the phrase is as ridiculous as his claim to be a virtuoso. Despite the appealing linkage of *avez raison* and the ridiculing of the virtuosi, I have no evidence to indicate Shadwell had this passage in mind, but it does show that Dryden used the phrase to indicate folly.

The other use of the phrase is more ambiguous:

> Monsieur. I knew you would be apt to entertain vain hopes from the summons of a lady but, faith, the design was but to make a fool of thee, as you find.
> Gerrard. 'Tis very well.
> Monsieur. But indeed I did not think the jest would have lasted so long and that my cousin would have made a dancing-master of you, ha, ha, ha.
> Gerrard. The fool has reason, I find, and I am the coxcomb while I thought him so.
> (5.1.15–23)

Gerrard clearly is a witty man about town in the play, and he is right when he says this in that Hippolita does manipulate him throughout the play. On the other hand, he is wrong when he says this in that Hippolita's scheme is designed not to take advantage of him but to escape Monsieur and marry Gerrard; in that sense, his use of the French construction indicates his folly in not trusting her. Moreover, the fact that he uses the phrase in the company of Monsieur calls attention to his erroneous doubt, because it is the kind of construction that Monsieur would use in his idiotic aping of the French.

19. Lucretius's attack on love was well known. Molière interpolates it into Eliante's description of love in act 2 of *Le Misanthrope*, and Dryden translated this section as well.

20. David S. Berkeley pairs Shadwell with Congreve and Farquhar as the most persistent satirists of the *précieuse* view of love; "Préciosité and the Restoration Comedy of Manners," *HLQ* 18 (1955): 118.

21. Gellert Spencer Alleman regards Shadwell's use of separate maintenance as historically plausible within the law of the period; *Matrimonial Law and the Materials of Restoration Comedy* (Philadelphia: University of Pennsylvania Press, 1942), pp. 108–10.

22. *The New Woman: Her Emergence in English Drama, 1600–1730* (New York: Twayne Publishers, 1954), p. 150.

23. "Restoration Comedy as Drama of Satire," *SP* 61 (1964), 526.

24. *The Relation of Molière to Restoration Comedy* (New York: Columbia University Press, 1938; reprint, New York: Benjamin Blom, 1964), p. 67.

25. "The Rake's Progress from Court to Comedy," *SEL* 6 (1966): 403.

Chapter 5. The Unwilling, the Unlovable, and the Unimpressed

1. Fredric Jameson, *The Political Unconcious: Narrative as Socially Symbolic Act* (Ithaca: Cornell University Press, 1981), p. 114.

2. "Women as Sign," *M/F* 1 (1978): 56.

3. See Claude Levi-Strauss, *The Elementary Structures of Kinship* (London: Eyre and Spottiswoode, 1969): p. 496.

4. "Wycherley's 'Tendentious Joke': The Discourse of Alterity in *The Country Wife*," *ECTI* 29 (1988): 232.

5. See J. R. Jacob's *Robert Boyle and the English Revolution* (New York: Burt Franklin, 1977): 57–59.

6. "The Significance of Thomas Shadwell," *SP* 71 (1974): 229.

7. "Social Satire in Shadwell's *Timon*," *Studia Neophilologica* 35 (1963): 225.

8. Colley Cibber describes Leigh as an actor whose style pushed the envelope of what was acceptable as "nature": "*Leigh* was of the mercurial kind, and though not so strict an Observer of Nature [as Nokes], yet never so wanton in his Performance, as to be wholly out of her sight. In Humour, he lov'd to take full Career, but was careful enough to stop short, when just upon the Precipe"; *An Apology for the Life of Colley Cibber*, ed. B. R. S. Fone (Ann Arbor: University of Michigan Press, 1968), p. 85. Of course, "nature" is itself a social construct, and a political woman like Lady Addleplot is comic because society has determined that such a role is unnatural for a woman.

9. Ben Ross Schneider, Jr., *Index to the London State, 1660–1800*, (Carbondale: Southern Illinois University Press, 1979), pp. 758–60.

10. Shirley Strum Kenny discusses the remarkable dominance of Congreve, Vanbrugh, Cibber, Farquhar, and Steele over the eighteenth-century stage in "Perennial Favorites: Congreve, Vanbrugh, Cibber, Farquhar, and Steele," *MP* 74, no. 4, p. 2 (1976): S4–S11.

11. "The Rake's Progress from Court to Comedy," *SEL* 6 (1966): 384–85.

12. *The Drama of Thomas Shadwell* (Salzburg: Institut für Englische Sprache und Literatur, 1972), pp. 1–17.

13. *An Account of the English Dramatick Poets*, introd. John Loftis (Los Angeles: Augustan Reprint Society, 1971), 2:447.

14. *The Plays of Richard Steele*, ed. Shirley Strum Kenny (Oxford: Clarendon Press, 1971), p. 176. All subsequent references in the text are to this edition by act, scene, and line numbers.

15. *The Letters of Sir George Etherege*, ed. Frederick Bracher (Berkeley: University of California Press, 1974), pp. 200–201.

16. *The Lives and Characters of the English Dramatick Poets* (London, 1699), p. 124.

17. *The Poetical Register* (London, 1719), p. 223.

18. *The English Dictionarie, (1623)* (Menston, England: Scolar Press, 1968).

19. *Dictionarium Anglo-Britannicum, (1708)* (Menston, England: Scolar Press, 1969).

20. *Dictionary of the English Language* (London, 1755). Thomas Blount's

Glossographia (1656), Edward Phillip's *The New World of English Words* (1658), and Elisha Cole's *An English Dictionary* (1676) do not define "perfect" in any form.

21. *The Tatler,* no. 7, 26 April 1709, ed. George A. Aitken (London, 1898), 1:7.

22. *The Spectator,* no. 141, 11 August 1711, ed. Donald F. Bond (Oxford: Clarendon Press, 1965), 2:58–59.

23. "Art and Integrity: Concepts of Self in Alexander Pope and Edward Young," *MP* 83, no. 4 (May 1986): 367.

24. *The Origins of the English Novel, 1600–1740* (Baltimore: Johns Hopkins University Press, 1987), p. 156.

Bibliography

Drama, Fiction, Poetry

Behn, Aphra. *The Works of Aphra Behn.* Edited by Montague Summers. 6 vols. London, 1915.

———. *Love Letters between a Nobleman and His Sister.* Introduction by Maureen Duffy. New York: Penguin Books/Virago Press, 1987.

———. *The Novels of Mrs. Aphra Behn.* London, 1905.

Crowne, John. *The Dramatic Works of John Crowne.* 4 vols. Edinburgh, 1874. Reprint New York: Benjamin Blom, 1967.

Dryden, John. *The Works of John Dryden.* Edited by Edward Niles Hooker and H. T. Swedenberg, Jr. Berkeley: University of California Press, 1966.

———. *The Spanish Friar.* Vol. 6 of *The Works of John Dryden,* edited by Sir Walter Scott and George Saintsbury. London, 1883.

D'Urfey, Thomas. *Sir Barnaby Whigg.* London, 1681.

Etherege, George. *The Plays of George Etherege.* Edited by Michael Cordner. Cambridge: Cambridge University Press, 1982.

Fountain, John. *The Rewards of Vertue.* London, 1661.

Howard, Sir Robert, and George Villiers, Duke of Buckingham. *The Country Gentleman.* Edited by A. H. Scouten and Robert Hume. Philadelphia: University of Pennsylvania Press, 1976.

Otway, Thomas. *The Works of Thomas Otway.* Edited by J. C. Ghosh. 2 vols. Oxford: Clarendon Press, 1932. Reprint 1968.

Shadwell, Thomas. *The Complete Works of Thomas Shadwell.* Edited by Montague Summers. London: Fortune Press, 1927.

Steele, Richard. *The Plays of Richard Steele.* Edited by Shirley Strum Kenny. Oxford: Clarendon Press, 1971.

Wilmot, John. *The Complete Poems of John Wilmot, Earl of Rochester.* Edited by David M. Vieth. New Haven: Yale University Press, 1968.

Wycherley, William. *The Plays of William Wycherley.* Edited by Peter Holland. Cambridge: Cambridge University Press, 1981.

Secondary Sources

Adams, Percy G. "What Happened in Olivia's Bedroom? or Ambiguity in *The Plain Dealer.*" In *Essays in Honor of Esmond Linsworth Marilla,* edited by Thomas Austin Kirby and William John Olive, pp. 174–87. Baton Rouge: Louisiana State University Press, 1970.

Advice of a Father. London, 1688.

Albury, W. R. "Halley's Ode on the *Principia* of Newton and the Epicurean Revival in England." *Journal of the History of Ideas* 39 (1978): 24–43.

Alleman, Gellert Spencer. *Matrimonial Law and the Materials of Restoration Comedy.* Philadelphia: University of Pennsylvania Press, 1942.

Allestree, Richard. *The Gentleman's Calling.* London, 1660.

———. *The Ladies Calling.* Oxford, 1673.

———. *The Whole Duty of Man.* London, 1735.

Alssid, Michael W. *Thomas Shadwell.* New York: Twain Publishers, 1967.

Appleby, Joyce Oldham. *Economic Thought and Ideology in Seventeenth-Century England.* Princeton: Princeton University Press, 1978.

Armistead, J. M. "Occultism in Restoration Drama: Motives for Revaluation." *MLS* 9, no. 3 (1979): 60–67.

———. *Four Restoration Playwrights: A Reference Guide.* Boston: G. K. Hall, 1984.

Bacon, Francis. *The Advancement of Learning.* Edited by G. W. Kitchin, introduced by Arthur Johnston. London: J. M. Dent, 1973.

Berkeley, David S. "The Penitent Rake in Restoration Comedy." *MP* 49 (1951): 217–41.

———. "Préciosité and the Restoration Comedy of Manners." *HLQ* 18 (1955): 109–28.

Berman, Ronald S. "The Values of Shadwell's *Squire of Alsatia.*" *ELH* 39 (1972): 375–86.

Birdsall, Virginia Ogden. *A Wild Civility: The English Comic Spirit on the Restoration Stage.* Bloomington: Indiana University Press, 1970.

Boone, Joseph Allen. *Tradition Counter Tradition: Love and the Form of Fiction.* Chicago: University of Chicago Press, 1987.

Booth, Wayne C. *The Company We Keep: An Ethics of Fiction.* Berkeley: University of California Press, 1988.

Borgman, Albert S. *Thomas Shadwell.* New York, 1928. Reprint New York: Benjamin Blom, 1969.

Bourke, Vernon J. *History of Ethics.* Garden City, N.Y.: Doubleday, 1968.

Brinton, Crane. *A History of Western Morals.* New York: Harcourt, Brace, 1959.

Brown, Laura. *English Dramatic Form, 1660–1760: An Essay in Generic History.* New Haven: Yale University Press, 1981.

Bruce, Donald. *Topics of Restoration Comedy.* New York: St. Martin's Press, 1974.

Burke, Helen M. "Wycherley's 'Tendentious Joke': The Discourse of Alterity in *The Country Wife.*" *ECTI* 29 (1988): 227–41.

Burke, Kenneth. *A Grammar of Motives.* 1945. Reprint Berkeley: University of California Press, 1969.

Burnet, Gilbert. *Some Passages of the Life and Death of Rochester.* Reprinted in *Rochester: The Critical Heritage*, edited by David Farley-Hills, pp. 47–92. New York: Barnes and Noble, 1972.

Butler, Samuel. *Prose Observations.* Edited by Hugh De Quehen. Oxford: Clarendon Press, 1979.

Calvin, John. *Institutes of the Christian Religion.* Translated by Ford Lewis Battle. Edited by John T. McNeill. Philadelphia: Westminster Press, 1960.

————. *New Testament Commentaries: Corinthians.* Vol. 9. Translated by John W. Frazier. Edited by David W. Torrance and Thomas F. Torrance. Grand Rapids, Mich.: William B. Erdmans, 1960.

Campbell, O. J. *Comicall Satyre and Shakespeare's Troilus and Cressida.* San Marino, Calif.: Huntington Library, Adcraft Press, 1938.

Cassirer, Ernst. *The Philosophy of the Enlightenment.* Translated by Fritz C. A. Koelln and James P. Pettegrove. Princeton: Princeton University Press, 1951.

Charleton, Walter. *Epicurus's Morals.* 1670. Reprint London, 1926.

Cibber, Colley. *An Apology for the Life of Colley Cibber.* Edited by B. R. S. Fone. Ann Arbor: University of Michigan Press, 1968.

Coleridge, Samuel Taylor. *The Collected Work of Samuel Taylor Coleridge.* Edited by James Engell and W. Jackson Bate. Vol. 7. Princeton: Princeton University Press, 1983.

Collier, Jeremy. *A Short View of the Immorality and Prophaness of the English State.* New York: Garland, 1972.

————. *A Defence of the Short View of the Immorality and Prophaness of the English Stage.* New York: Garland, 1972.

Cooper, Anthony Ashley, Third Earl of Shaftesbury. *Characteristics of Men, Manners, Opinions, Times, Etc.* Edited by John M. Robertson. 3 vols. Gloucester, Mass.: Peter Smith, 1963.

Corman, Brian. "Thomas Shadwell and the Jonsonian Comedy of the Restoration." In *From Renaissance to Restoration: Metamorphoses of the Drama,* edited by Robert Markley and Laurie Finke. Cleveland: Bellflower Press, 1984. 127–52.

Coward, Rosalind, and John Ellis. *Language and Materialism: Developments in Semiology and the Theory of the Subject.* London: Routledge and Kegan Paul, 1977.

Cowie, Elizabeth. "Women as Sign." *M/F* 1 (1978): 49–63.

Cox, Stephen D. "Public Virtue and Private Vitality in Shadwell's Comedies." *Restoration and Eighteenth-Century Theatre Research* 16 (1977); 1–22.

The Crafty Whore: or the Mistery and Iniquity of Bawdy Houses. London, 1658.

Crane, R. S. *The Idea of the Humanities and Other Essays Critical and Historical.* 2 vols. Chicago: University of Chicago Press, 1967.

Creech, Thomas. *Lucretius His Six Books of Epicurean Philosophy and Manilius His Five Books.* 5th ed. London, 1700.

Cudworth, Ralph. *A Treatise Concerning Eternal and Immutable Morality.* Reprinted in *British Moralists, 1650–1800,* ed. D. D. Raphael, 1:105–18. Oxford: Clarendon Press, 1969.

Cumberland, Richard. *De Legibus Naturae.* Reprinted in *British Moralists, 1650–1800,* ed. D. D. Raphael, 1: 119–53. Oxford: Clarendon Press, 1969.

Daly, James. *Sir Robert Filmer and English Political Thought.* Toronto: University of Toronto Press, 1979.

Darnton, Robert. *The Great Cat Massacre and Other Episodes in French Cultural History.* New York: Basic Books, 1984.

Descartes, Rene. *Publiees.* Vol. 11 of *Oeuvres de Descartes,* edited by Charles Adams and Paul Tannery. Paris: Librairie Philosophique, J. Vrin, 1974.

————. *Philosophical Works.* Translated by Elizabeth S. Haldane and G. R. T.

Ross. 2 vols. Cambridge: Cambridge University Press, 1911. Corrected edition 1931. Reprint 1981.

Dobree, Bonamy. *Restoration Comedy 1660–1720*. Oxford: Clarendon Press, 1924.

Durkheim, Emile. *Selected Writings*. Edited and translated by Anthony Giddens. Cambridge: Cambridge University Press, 1972.

Edwards, David L. *Christian England from the Restoration to the 18th-Century.* Vol 2. Grand Rapids, Mich.: William B. Erdmans, 1983.

Etherege, George. *The Letters of George Etherege*. Edited by Frederick Bracher. Berkeley: University of California Press, 1974.

Filmer, Sir Robert. *Patriarcha and Other Political Works*. Edited by Peter Laslett. Oxford: Basil Blackwell, 1947.

Fisher, Alan S. "The Significance of Thomas Shadwell." *SP* 71 (1974): 225–46.

Fleischman, Wolfgang Bernard. *Lucretius and English Literature, 1680–1740*. Paris: A. G. Nizet, 1964.

Forsythe, R. S. *A Study of the Plays of Thomas D'Urfey*. Cleveland: Western Reserve University Press, 1916.

Foucault, Michel. *The History of Sexuality*. Vol. 1. Translated by Robert Hurley. New York: Pantheon Books, 1978.

Foxon, David. *Libertine Literature in England, 1660–1745*. New Hyde Park, N.Y.: University Books, 1965.

Frankena, William K. *Ethics*. 2d ed. Englewood Cliffs, N.J.: Prentice-Hall, 1973.

Fujimura, Thomas H. *The Restoration Comedy of Wit*. Princeton: Princeton University Press, 1952.

Gagen, Jean Elisabeth. *The New Woman: Her Emergence in English Drama 1600–1730*. New York: Twayne Publishers, 1954.

Gibbon, Edward. *Memoirs of My Life*. Edited by Betty Radice. New York: Penguin, 1984.

Gilde, Joseph M. "Shadwell and the Royal Society: Satire in *The Virtuoso.*" *SEL* 10 (1972): 469–90.

Gildon, Charles. *The Lives and Characters of the English Dramatic Poets*. London, 1699.

Glanville, Joseph. *Scepsis Scientifica*. In *The Vanity of Dogmatizing: The Three Versions*. Introduction by Stephen Medcalf. Hove, Sussex: Harvester Press, 1970.

Greene, Donald. "Latitudinarianism and Sensibility: The Genealogy of the 'Man of Feeling' Reconsidered." *MP* 75 (1977): 159–83.

Hagstrum, Jean H. *Sex and Sensibility: Ideal and Erotic Love from Milton to Mozart*. Chicago: University of Chicago Press, 1980.

Haller, William, and Malleville Haller. "The Puritan Art of Love." *Huntington Library Quarterly* 5 (1942): 235–72.

Harth, Philip. *Contexts of Dryden's Thought*. Chicago: University of Chicago Press, 1968.

Harwood, John T. *Critics, Values and Restoration Comedy*. Carbondale: Southern Illinois University Press, 1982.

Haselkorn, Anne M. *Prostitution in Elizabethan and Jacobean Comedy*. Troy, N.Y.: Whiston Publishing Company, 1983.

Haydn, Hiram. *The Counter-Renaissance.* New York: Grove Press, 1950.

Hill, Christopher. *The Century of Revolution, 1603–1714.* London: Thomas Nelson and Sons, 1961.

———. *The World Turned Upside Down.* 1972. Harmondsworth: Penguin, 1975. Reprint, 1982.

Hirschman, Albert O. *The Passions and the Interests: Political Arguments for Capitalism before Its Triumph.* Princeton: Princeton University Press, 1981.

Hobbes, Thomas. *Leviathan.* Edited by C. B. Macpherson. Harmondsworth: Penguin, 1981.

Holland, Norman N. *The First Modern Comedies: The Significance of Etherege, Wycherley and Congreve.* Cambridge: Harvard University Press, 1959.

Holland, Peter. *The Ornament of Action: Text and Performance in Restoration Comedy.* Cambridge: Cambridge University Press, 1979.

Hooke, Robert. *The Diary of Robert Hooke.* Edited by Henry W. Robinson and Walter Adams. London, 1935.

Hume, Robert D. *The Development of English Drama in the Late Seventeenth-Century.* Oxford: Clarendon Press, 1976.

———. "William Wycherley: "Text, Life, Interpretation."" *MP* 78 (1981): 399–415.

———. *The Rakish Stage: Studies in English Drama, 1660–1880.* Carbondale: Southern Illinois University Press, 1983.

Hyde, Edward, Earl Of Clarendon. *Animadversion Upon a Book Intituled, Fanaticism Fanatically Imputed to the Catholick Church.* London, 1673.

———. *A Brief View and Survey of the Dangerous and Pernicious Errors to Church and State, in Mr. Hobbes Book, Entitled Leviathan.* London, 1676.

Jacob, Giles. *The Poetical Register; of the Lives and Characters of the English Dramatick Poets.* London, 1719.

Jacob, J. R. *Robert Boyle and the English Revolution: A Study in Social and Intellectual Change.* New York: Burt Franklin, 1977.

Jacob, Margaret C. *The Cultural Meaning of the Scientific Revolution.* Philadelphia: Temple University Press, 1988.

Jameson, Fredric. *The Political Unconscious: Narrative as Socially Symbolic Act.* Ithaca: Cornell University Press, 1981.

Jones, Virgil L. "Methods of Satire in the Political Drama of the Restoration." *JEGP* 21 (1922): 662–69.

Jose, Nicholas. *Ideas of the Restoration in English Literature, 1660–71.* Cambridge: Harvard University Press, 1984.

Kearney, Patrick J. *A History of Erotic Literature.* London: Macmillan, 1982.

Kenney, Shirley Strum. "Perennial Favorites: Congreve, Vanbrugh, Cibber, Farquhar, and Steele." *MP* 74, no. 4, p. 2 (1976): S4–S11.

———. "Humane Comedy." *MP* 75 (1977): 29–43.

Kunz, Don R. *The Drama of Thomas Shadwell.* Salzburg Studies in English Literature, no. 16. Salzburg: Institut für Englische Sprache und Literatur, 1972.

Langbaine, Gerard. *An Account of the English Dramatic Poets.* (New York: Garland, 1973).

————, and [Charles Gildon]. *The Lives and Characters of the English Dramatick Poets*. London, 1699.

Leites, Edmund. *The Puritan Conscience and Modern Sexuality*. New Haven: Yale University Press, 1986.

Levi-Strauss, Claude. *The Elementary Structures of Kinship*. (London: Eyre and Spottiswoode, 1969).

Locke, John. *The Second Treatise of Government*. Edited by Thomas P. Peardon. Indianapolis: Bobbs-Merrill, 1952.

————. *An Essay concerning Human Understanding*. Abridged and edited by A. S. Pringle-Pattison. Oxford: Clarendon Press, 1924. Reprint 1956.

Loftis, John. "The Limits of Historical Veracity in Neoclassical Drama." In *England in the Restoration and Early Eighteenth Century*, edited by H. T. Swedenberg, Jr. Berkeley: University of California Press, 1972. 27–50.

Long, Edward Leroy, Jr. *A Survey of Christian Ethics*. New York: Oxford University Press, 1967.

Love, Harold, ed. *Penguin Book of Restoration Verse*. Harmondsworth: Penguin, 1979.

Lynch, Kathleen M. *The Social Mode of Restoration Comedy*. New York: Macmillan, 1926.

MacCracken, Charles T. *Malebranche and British Philosophy*. Oxford: Clarendon Press, 1983.

McDonald, Charles O. "Restoration Comedy as Drama of Satire." *SP* 61 (1964): 522–44.

MacIntyre, Alasdair. *A Short History of Ethics*. New York: Macmillan, 1966.

————. *After Virtue: A Study in Moral Theory*. 2d ed. Notre Dame, Ind.: University of Notre Dame Press, 1984.

McKeon, Michael. *Politics and Poetry in Restoration England: The Case of Dryden's Annus Mirabilis*. Cambridge: Harvard University Press, 1975.

————. *The Origins of the English Novel, 1600–1740*. Baltimore: Johns Hopkins University Press, 1987.

Macpherson, C. B. *The Political Theory of Possessive Individualism: Hobbes to Locke*. Oxford: Clarendon Press, 1962.

Malebranche, Nicolas. *Oeuvres*. Edited by Genèvieve Rodis-Lewis and Germain Malbreil. Dijon: Editions Gallimard, 1979.

————. *The Search after Truth*. Translated by Thomas M. Lennon and Paul J. Olscamp. Columbus: Ohio State University Press, 1980.

Mandel, Oscar. *The Theatre of Don Juan*. Lincoln: University of Nebraska Press, 1963.

Mandeville, Bernard. *A Modest Defense of Publick Stews*. Los Angeles: Augustan Reprint Society, 1973.

Markley, Robert. *Two Edg'd Weapons: Style and Ideology in the Comedies of Etherege, Wycherley and Congreve*. Oxford: Clarendon Press, 1988.

Mayo, Thomas Franklin. *Epicurus in England, 1660–1725*. Dallas: Southwest Press, 1934.

Milhous, Judith, and Robert D. Hume. *Producible Interpretations: Eight English Plays, 1675–1707*. Carbondale: Southern Illinois University Press, 1985.

Miller, Dwight C. "Benedetto Gennari's Career at the Courts of Charles II and

James II and a Newly Discovered Portrait of James II." *Apollo* 117 (January 1983): 24–29.

Milton, John. *The Complete Prose Works of John Milton.* Edited by Ernest Sirluck. Vol. 2. New Haven: Yale University Press, 1959.

More, Henry. *Enchiridion Ethicum: The English Translation of 1690.* New York: Facsimile Text Society, 1930.

Morgan, Edmund. "The Puritans and Sex." *New England Quarterly* 15 (December 1942): 591–607.

Munns, Jessica. "Daredevil in Thomas Otway's *The Atheist:* A New Identification." *Restoration* 11 (Spring 1987): 31–37.

Nicoll, Allardyce. "Political Plays of the Restoration." *MLR* 16 (1921): 224–42.

Neill, Michael. "Heroic Heads and Humble Tails: Sex, Politics, and the Restoration Rake." *ECTI* 24 (1983): 115–39.

Novak, Maximillian E. "Margery Pinchwife's 'London Disease': Restoration Comedy and the Libertine Offensive of the 1670s." *Studies in the Literary Imagination* 10, no. 1 (1977): 1–23.

———. "The Sentimentality of *The Conscious Lovers* Revisited and Reasserted." *MLS* 9, no. 3 (1979): 48–59.

Nussbaum, Martha. *The Fragility of Goodness: Luck and Ethics in Greek Tragedy and Philosophy.* Cambridge: Cambridge University Press, 1986.

Ober, William B. "Thomas Shadwell: His Exitus Revis'd." *Annals of Internal Medicine* 74 (January, 1971): 126–30.

Osborne, Francis. *Advice to a Son.* London, 1896.

Parnell, Paul E. "The Etiquette of the Sentimental Repentance Scene, 1688–1696." *PLL* 14 (1978): 205–17.

Patey, Douglas Lane. "Art and Integrity: Concepts of Self in Alexander Pope and Edward Young." *MP* 83, no. 4 (1986): 364–78.

Pocock, J. G. A. *Virtue, Commerce, and History: Essays on Political Thought and History, Chiefly in the Eighteenth Century.* Cambridge: Cambridge University Press, 1985.

Popkin, Richard. *The History of Scepticism from Erasmus to Spinoza.* Berkeley: University of California Press, 1979.

Porter, Roy. "Mixed Feelings: The Enlightenment and Sexuality." In *Sexuality in Eighteenth-Century Britain,* edited by Paul-Gabriel Boucé, pp. 1–27. Totowa, N.J.: Barnes and Noble, 1982.

Pourrat, Pierre. *La Spiritualité Chrétienne.* Vol. 3. Paris: Libraire Lecoffre, 1947.

Powell, Jocelyn. *Restoration Theatre Production.* London: Routledge and Kegan Paul, 1984.

Redwood, John. *Reason, Ridicule and Religion: The Age of Enlightenment in England, 1660–1750.* Cambridge: Harvard University Press, 1976.

Richards, Alfred E. "A Literary Link between Thomas Shadwell and Christian Felix Weiss." *PMLA* 21 (1906): 803–30.

Righter, Anne. "William Wycherley." In *Restoration Dramatists,* edited by Earl Miner, pp. 105–22. Englewood Cliffs, N.J.: Prentice-Hall, 1966.

Rogers, Katherine M. "Fatal Inconsistency: Wycherley and the *Plain Dealer.*" *ELH* 28 (1961): 148–62.

————. *The Troublesome Helpmate: A History of Misogyny in Literature.* Seattle: University of Washington Press, 1966.

Rogers, Reginald A. P. *A Short History of Ethics, Greek and Modern.* London: Macmillan, 1965.

Ross, J. C. "An Attack on Thomas Shadwell in Otway's *The Atheist.*" *PQ* 52 (1973): 753–60.

Rothstein, Eric. *Restoration Tragedy: Form and the Process of Change.* Madison: University of Wisconsin Press, 1967.

————, and Frances Kavenik. *The Designs of Carolean Comedy.* Carbondale: Southern Illinois University Press, 1988.

Rubin, Gayle. "The Traffic in Women: Notes on the 'Political Economy' of Sex." In *Toward an Anthropology of Women*, edited by Rayna R. Reiter, pp. 157–210. New York: Monthly Review Press, 1975.

Sacks, Sheldon. *Fiction and the Shape of Belief: A Study of Henry Fielding, with Glances at Swift, Johnston, and Richardson.* Berkeley: University of California Press, 1964.

Savile, George. *The Works of George Savile Marquess of Halifax.* Edited by Walter Raleigh. Oxford: Clarendon Press, 1912.

Schneider, Ben Ross, Jr. *The Ethos of Restoration Comedy.* Urbana: University of Illinois Press, 1971.

————. *Index to the London Stage, 1660–1800.* Carbondale: Southern Illinois University Press, 1979.

Schochet, Gordon J. *The Authoritarian Family and Political Attitudes in Seventeenth-Century England.* New Brunswick, N.J.: Transaction Books, 1988.

Scouten, A. H., and Robert Hume. "Restoration Comedy and Its Audiences, 1660–1776." *Yearbook of English Studies* 10 (1980): 45–69.

Shorter, Edward. *The Making of the Modern Family.* New York: Basic Books, 1975.

Sidgwick, Henry. *Outlines of the History of Ethics.* 1886. Reprint Boston: Beacon Press, 1960.

Smith, J. H. *The Gay Couple in Restoration Comedy.* Cambridge: Harvard University Press, 1948.

————. "Shadwell, the Ladies, and the Change in Comedy." In *Restoration Drama*, edited by John Loftis, pp. 236–52. New York: Oxford University Press, 1966.

Smith, John. *Selected Discourses, 1660.* New York: Garland, 1978.

Staves, Susan. *Players' Scepters: Fictions of Authority in the Restoration.* Lincoln: University of Nebraska Press, 1979.

Steele, Richard. *The Tatler.* Edited by George A. Aitken. Vol. 1. London, 1898.

————, et al. *The Spectator.* Edited by Donald F. Bond. Vol. 2. Oxford: Clarendon Press, 1965.

Stone, Lawrence. *Marriage, Sex and the Family: England 1500–1800.* New York: Harper and Row, 1977.

Stroup, Thomas B. "Shadwell's Use of Hobbes." *SP* 35 (1938): 405–32.

Taylor, Jeremy. *Ductor Dubitantium.* Vols. 9 and 10 of *Jeremy Taylor's Works.* Edited by Rev. Alexander Taylor. London, 1864.

————. "Apples of Sodom: or, the Fruits of Sin." In *The English Sermon, 1650–*

1750, vol. 2, edited by C. H. Sisson. Cheadle Cheshire, England: Carcanet Press, 1976. 20–63.

———. *The Marriage Ring*. London, 1883.

Tillotson, John. "Concerning Family Religion." In *Sermons*, vol. 3. London, 1742.

Traherne, Thomas. *Christian Ethics or Divine Morality*. London, 1675.

Traugott, John. "The Rake's Progress from Court to Comedy." *SEL* 6 (1966): 381–407.

Trumbach, Randolph. *The Rise of the Egalitarian Family*. New York: Academic Press, 1978.

Tully, James. "Governing Conduct." In *Conscience and Casuistry in Early Modern Europe*, edited by Edmund Leites, pp. 12–71. Cambridge: Cambridge University Press, 1988.

Turner, James. *One Flesh: Paradisal Marriage and Sexual Relations in the Age of Milton*. Oxford: Clarendon Press, 1987.

Underwood, Dale. *Etherege and the Seventeenth-Century Comedy of Manners*. New Haven: Yale University Press, 1957.

Vernon, P. F. "The Marriage of Convenience and the Moral Code of Restoration Comedy." *Essays in Criticism* 12 (1962): 370–87.

———. "Social Satire in Shadwell's *Timon*." *Studia Neophilogica* 35 (1963): 221–26.

Walker, D. P. *The Decline of Hell: Seventeenth-Century Discussions of Eternal Torment*. Chicago: University of Chicago Press, 1964.

Weber, Harold. *The Restoration Rake Hero*. Madison: University of Wisconsin Press, 1986.

Whitmore, Charles Edward. *The Supernatural in Tragedy*. Cambridge: Harvard University Press, 1915.

Wilcox, John. *The Relation of Molière to Restoration Comedy*. New York: Columbia University Press, 1938. Reprint. New York: Benjamin Blom, 1964.

Wilkinson, D. R. M. *The Comedy of Habit: An Essay on the Use of Courtesy Literature in a Study of Restoration Comic Drama*. Leiden: Universitaire Pers, 1964.

Williams, Aubrey L. *An Approach to Congreve*. New Haven: Yale University Press, 1979.

Wilson, John Harold. *The Court Wits of the Restoration*. Princeton: Princeton University Press, 1948.

Wright, Rose Abel. *The Political Plays of the Restoration*. N.p.: Yale University, 1916.

Zimbardo, Rose A. *A Mirror to Nature: Transformations in Drama and Aesthetics, 1660–1732*. Lexington: University Press of Kentucky, 1986.

Index